Aldo Ceccato

A Brief History of Conducting

Yesterday, today... and tomorrow?

Preface by Quirino Principe

Pendragon

Aldo Ceccato

A Brief History of Conducting

Yesterday, Today... and Tomorrow?

Translation by Graham Hutton Robertson

INDICE

Preface

by Quirino Principe

For as long as my generation has been around (too many years, perhaps...), a certain number of books on conducting have been published. I won't go into the names of the authors, for whom I have the greatest respect. For all of them... well, nearly all. I think it is interesting, however, to consider the approaches these authors have taken. It seems appropriate to put them into three groups. Some have waxed lyrical in flowery anecdotes around celebrated *maestri* or *Kapellmeister* (or *Dirigenten*). Others have discussed the subject in the form of personal, perfectly respectable opinions of an aesthetic nature. Others again, the least numerous group, have genuinely traced historical and artistic phenomena as they developed. Despite my high regard for the the first two groups (and some of these authors really do deserve the very highest respect), I prefer the third type and this is one of the main reasons I am attracted by this book, written by Aldo Ceccato after years of reflection, study, evaluation and practice, focusing on the need to intervene in the orchestration of great symphonic scores, not to alter their effect, but rather to restore the original effect desired (sometimes dreamed of) by the composer who devised and wrote them.

I won't consider those non-books in which a fledgeling scholar, who styles himself on the cover as a "young musicologist", promptly interviews a dozen or so conductors, making sure they represent various levels of human quality, talent, culture and experience, in order to create, in the eyes of the "critics" (not to be confused with genuine critics) something that is "very democratic". The interviewees taint the atmosphere of these shoddy pages with their expressions of distress and discontent; the distinguished conductors get offended at being mixed up with beginners (this is undeniable, I have evidence galore to back up this statement) and sometimes promising newcomers are furious with the interviewer and writer of the non-book because they have been crushed like a fishing boat against a battleship. The good book is quite a different kettle of fish, fascinating, measured and precise, in which only one conductor is interviewed and he has the leisure and space to express his thoughts coherently in all their complexity. Outstanding exemplars are Lidia Bramani's interview with Abbado and Gastón Fournier-Facio's with Barenboim.

We have to be careful here, however: the subject we are dealing with is undergoing transformation. We started off talking about books describing orchestra conducting that are *not* written by conductors, not even partially in the form of the replies of the interviewees. But now the hypothesis is getting out of hand. Someone might say: "But haven't we forgotten about Walter Abendroth's famous interview with Wilhelm Furtwängler?" Of course, *Gespräche über Musik* is a splendid book, but it does not give a historical overview – it is a philosophical dialogue, rich in sublime writing and stunning definitions. The same is true in at least two other cases: excluding the living, the greatest conductors who have also been high quality writers, that is (in my opinion), Ernest Ansermet, Igor Markevitch and Furtwängler himself, have bequeathed us profound books which are dense with noble culture and pathos, but which do *not* trace the history of conducting. They deal with, to be precise, the philosophy of music. If we think of musicians like Igor Stravinsky, Pierre Boulez, Leonard Bernstein and Hans Werner Henze, and if we consider them not as composers but as conductors, the writings they have left touch only marginally on their jobs as conductors; they explore the poetics of music, the didactics of playing practice, the social dynamic of their art. Other books give guidelines about conducting in performance practice (Hans Swarowski), or are excessively autobiographical (Zubin Mehta).

Aldo Ceccato, born in Milan on Sunday 18 February 1934, and today a towering example of a renowned conductor with widespread international experience, has written this "brief history" of conducting, aimed at professional musicians as much as amateurs, or those who are simply curious. We have books, on one hand, of the "Kapellmeister" type, which make assertions rather than question what the job is, and how it evolved historically and socially, and on the other, the non-"Kapellmeister" type, often by non-musicians who have decided to dabble in historical narrative; this lively and mildly self-mocking work by Ceccato represents a sort of middle way. But it is not all just liveliness and irony. The book is backed up by outstanding professional skills and the conducting experience of a lifetime, unmatched by most of his colleagues. This is, then, a good reason for warmly welcoming and carefully reading this book.

If this reason alone makes it worth reading (by careful and appreciative readers), since it comes from the hand of a living, working leading player who speaks, writes and conducts in the name of a musical civilisation which Italy must (should? still can?) consider as one of its greatest cultural treasures, a second excellent reason derives from a rather negative situation, that is, the collapse of widespread musical culture, dating from the political and legislative unification of Italy in 1861. I have covered this woeful subject hundreds of times in my life (which, chronologically speaking, coincides almost perfectly with that of Aldo Ceccato), and I do not wish to repeat myself.

The result, at a solely cognitive level, is that Italians who are not musical connoisseurs (the vast majority, in fact, almost everyone), more than any other European nation, have no idea what an orchestra is, what instruments make it up or what the job of an orchestra member is. Most Italians cannot recognise a musical instrument or name it. Furthermore, the public who, less dull-witted and attracted by serious music, or at least that worthy of the name of music, attend symphonic concerts and opera houses do not know what "conductor" means when watching *Fidelio* or *Nabucco*, or when the cor anglais or the celesta was introduced into the orchestra.

Ceccato, who has had artistic responsibility for eleven orchestras in the world, "tells it how it is"; he explains principles and theories, certainly, but then he opens up his workshop for us, lets us understand *how*. Against a time-line of historical events, he makes a felicitous selection of conductors who have made a breakthrough in the training methods used in preparing and performing concerts, devoting copious documented description to this.

The pages on Hans von Bülow are splendid and astonishing, especially for anyone who has had a negative impression of this great and often abrasive musician, possibly stemming from hostile sources – they will be moved by his dedication to young musicians at the formative stage.

Among the many pages devoted to Richard Wagner, supported by rare and invaluable quotations, Ceccato cites Felix Weingartner's description of the composer of the *Ring* and *Parsifal* on the podium:

"The old flautist Fürstenau told me in Dresden that when Wagner conducted, the players had no sense of being led. Each believed himself to be following freely his own feeling, yet they all worked together wonderfully". Ceccato is a wordsmith, incisive in his definitions: the dynamics, the "convenient *mezzo forte*", the "elegant" conducting, the problem of tempo...

There is much precision and workmanship in these pages, with concrete examples and illustrations – a real insider's view. One should meditate on, and recall, these pages when one listens to a live opera or concert. One emerges from this book enriched and informed: the author has told us about *being*, not *having*, about a wonderful profession for which the adjective "demiurgic" has been used too often; but here the protagonist does not wish to dominate, but rather to reveal truths that are too often unobserved. The orchestra may appear a collection of heterogeneous instruments and one might tend to think that its symphonic sound is fascinating because of that very heterogeneity. But looking beyond appearance, the orchestra is itself an instrument and it engenders unity and harmony; it is the epitome of the cosmic order. In this sense, the author of this book lets us touch it with our hands – the orchestra modelled by Western history and culture is a touchstone, a benchmark all of us can measure themselves against, with the secret of the art in which various voices create "symphonia" (συμφωνία).

Gustavo Dudamel said: "It's not that people don't like classical music. It's that they don't have the chance to understand and experience it". Aldo Ceccato gives us that chance with his reflections on conducting.

Introduction

by Aldo Ceccato

The arts are all marvellous. Many of them have millennia-old origins and have given up their secrets in terms of technique, style and expression; orchestra direction certainly has to be classified among the youngest. After the Second World War, I was lucky enough to go to La Scala in Milan, feeding my musical curiosity in extraordinary circumstances, since at the time, on that historic stage, there alternated conductors, singers and soloists of the utmost prestige: de Sabata, Furtwängler, Walter, Cantelli and Dobrowen conducted; Tebaldi, Callas, Di Stefano and Del Monaco sang; and the violinists Heifetz e Francescatti played, to mention but a few. There, in September 1952, I had the good fortune to attend a concert by Toscanini, with an all-Wagner programme, just as his final concert, at the Carnegie Hall, New York, on Sunday 4 April 1954 was to be all-Wagner.

My artistic career has also provided me with the great opportunity to meet some of the finest conductors and to enjoy their friendship and professional collaboration: de Sabata, von Karajan, Solti, Maazel, Ormandy, Masur, Mravinsky, Giulini, Gavazzeni and many others. I have experienced the bliss of making music with amazing soloists like Arrau, Serkin, Casadesus, Pollini, Magaloff, Ciccolini, Argerich, Milstein, Kremer, Szeryng, Haendel, Kogan, Perlman and Zukerman as well as singers of the calibre of Kraus, Raimondi, Cappuccilli, Fischer-Diskau, Siepi, Sills, Farrell, Gedda, Panerai, Norman, van Dam, Gruberová, Verrett, Gobbi and Ghiaurov: all artists of great personality and stylistic refinement with whom I have shared unforgettable times and emotions.

After over fifty years on the podium, I thought it might be interesting to put together some historical material combined with

13

personal experiences – avoiding comments on current-day methods – also to point out how difficult and complex it is to conduct an orchestra. But before going into conducting I think we need to remember what an orchestra is: it has long been considered a formation of musicians, who under the guidance of the conductor, produce sounds which, via the "magic" of the player or of the conductor, can become music.

So an orchestra is, by definition, an instrument. An instrument, just as a piano is for a pianist, or a violin is for a violinist, and so on, but multi-faceted and much more complicated, since it pulsates and vibrates in a different way for each conductor.

This happens differently for each individual instrument, since they are gathered in an "unicum", making up a wonderful mosaic, in which the conductor has an immense choice of "sound tiles" to inlay. A conductor can make one instrument emerge more than another, dose the sonority between sections, establish the right tempo to be imposed on a symphonic piece or a whole work, phrase the music and "understand" the composer's intention. As will be mentioned in the section on Felix Weingartner, a conductor cannot improve a composition, if anything, he can only ruin it. At the first reading of an opera or symphony, an orchestra, if it is of good quality, reproduces the notes of a composition with arbitrary sonorities which will be shaped by the conductor, paying also attention to tempos and phrasing.

The orchestra is, first of all, a melting pot of human beings rather than musicians. I have had artistic responsibility for eleven orchestras in the world (in Italy, the USA, Germany, Spain, Norway, the Czech Republic and Slovakia) and directed over a hundred orchestras as guest conductor, from the Berliner Philharmoniker to the New York Philharmonic, from the Chicago Symphony to the London Philharmonic, from the NHK of Tokyo to La Scala of Milan, to name but a few. The experiences I have had with them have been of the most disparate, sometimes even unimaginable. Moreover, one common denominator has characterised these intriguing experiences: women. Up to the 1960s, orchestras were made up primarily of male musicians (in Central/Eastern Europe men even play the harp). But then women infiltrated the orchestral ranks. At the beginning, this created considerable, furious consternation among more conservative musicians – look at the case of Sabine Mayer and the Berlin Philharmoniker, the first woman in the history of this celebrated orchestra.

Soon, however, female instrumentalists gained the respect of their colleagues, however, often proving to be worthier of holding positions of responsibility, as first violin or first flute (as in Mayer's case) or even first trombone. Many orchestras have a first tympanist (as in the case of "La Verdi", Milan, an outstanding player). The tympanist, indeed, is the backbone of the orchestra, the pillar that determines rhythmical stability. But what makes the life and coexistence of many different musicians so curious and exciting, is the presence of women. I say "exciting" not out of any misplaced male chauvinism, but to point out the great number of amorous intrigues I have witnessed: wife-swapping, embarrassing scenes (fortunately not on stage) between love adversaries, abandoned wives who detest sharing the music stand with rivals, refusing to utter a single word to them. We might mention, among the most famous cases in the history of the orchestra, what happened in Chicago between the first flute and the first oboe, who, as is customary, play side by side; the two musicians did not actually speak to each other for ten years. The reason for this hostility remains unknown to this day. Sir Georg Solti, Musical Director at the time, unable to put up with the situation of the two musicians any longer, gave them an ultimatum – they had to make peace or they would have to resign immediately, with resulting scandal and considerable loss of audience and sponsors. In view of this alarming prospect, the two finally made up. And then we find green envy slithering around in the various sections, to say nothing about complaints about salary (often justified, given that in Italy and many other Latin countries orchestra players are inadequately paid). The life of an orchestra performer is hard, sometimes extremely so. In an operatic context orchestra rehearsals can be very exacting: to

15

achieve a satisfactory "whole" (stage and orchestra) it may be necessary to repeat a scene countless times.

Symphonic music practice is less demanding in that, in the best of circumstances, there is normally one daily rehearsal and one concert with one repeat performance. An exception is the Israel Philharmonic, which has over 30,000 season ticket holders in Tel Aviv, plus an intense decentralisation policy, so that a programme may be repeated seven or eight times.

An orchestra, as we have said, is an instrument and accordingly everything has to be tuned. How? Many methods are employed. The most logical and scientific one is reminiscent of the building of a house and begins with the foundations. The double bass section is the base on which the whole tuning of the orchestra hinges – it "carries" the orchestra. It is essential that this section tunes up in absolute silence, separate from the other instruments, since it has to to produce very low sounds that are difficult to control. The instrument that is the point of reference for tuning is the oboe, with its A (La) pitch. This instrument is extremely sensitive to temperature. Moreover, as it is played there is a tendency for the pitch to rise; for this reason the orchestra has to adapt to its instability. The human voice is the most expressive and delicate instrument we have. The violin is considered to be an instrumental emanation of the voice. Many other instruments have fascinating characteristics, for example, the cello, the harp, the flute and the horn.

But when they are merged in an orchestra, an instrument of infinite timbral possibilities is created, with unmatchable sonorous power, an amazing kaleidoscope of sound. And that is why, partly, I abandoned the piano to pick up the baton.

I thank my wife Eliana for her kind help, Quirino Principe for his enlightened advice, Maria Luisa Guizzetti for her invaluable collaboration and Francesco Guttadauro for being such a great source of curious and exotic facts.

A brief history of conducting

The orchestra conductor is essentially a middle man, the indispensable intermediary between the composer and the listener. For the profane among us, his figure is wrapped in a mysterious aura of charisma, esotericism and magic. I might even dare to suggest that his real ancestor is the shaman, a word derived etymologically from the Tungus root *šam*, "intermediary": the shaman is said to have the power to communicate with the divine and the spirit world. Like a modern conductor, he knows all the secrets, rhythms and proto-melodies of extraordinary music to be played during ceremonies and it is always he who guides and coordinates, rhythmically moving, the percussionists and dancers, whipping them into a state of euphoria, hypnosis and ecstasy. This, indeed, is the condition that modern day listeners experience when they attend a musical performance given by a top orchestra conducted by a superlative conductor.

The first evidence we have of proper musical bands is to be found in Mesopotamia: the Bible gives a concise description of the orchestra of King Nebuchadnezzar II and the iconography of the time shows us that music was played on the occasion of religious ceremonies and that dancing was common at banquets and in gardens. Some sources even claim that a wealthy Babylonian landowner could afford a musical band consisting of 150 elements, all women, singers and dancers.

In ancient Egypt a wide range of musical instruments had been created: harps, lyres, flutes, theorbos, crotalums and drums. Hathor, the goddess of dance and music, is always depicted with a sistrum, sacred to her, in her hand. A recent discovery of hieroglyphics dating from the fourth millennium BC, suggests that a rudimentary form of musical notation already existed for indicating rhythm and melody.

Nebuchadnezzar's Orchestra
(Daniel, 3, 1-7)

King Nebuchadnezzar made an image of gold, whose height was sixty cubits and its breadth six cubits. He set it up on the plain of Dura, in the province of Babylon.

Then King Nebuchadnezzar sent to gather the satraps, the prefects, and the governors, the counsellors, the treasurers, the justices, the magistrates, and all the officials of the provinces to come to the dedication of the image that King Nebuchadnezzar had set up

Then the satraps, the prefects, and the governors, the counsellors, the treasurers, the justices, the magistrates, and all the officials of the provinces gathered for the dedication of the image that King Nebuchadnezzar had set up.

And the herald proclaimed aloud, "You are commanded, O peoples, nations, and languages, that when you hear the sound of the horn, pipe, lyre, trigon, harp, zither, bagpipe, and every kind of music, you are to fall down and worship the golden image that King Nebuchadnezzar has set up. And whoever does not fall down and worship shall immediately be cast into a burning fiery furnace".

Therefore, as soon as all the peoples heard the sound of the horn, pipe, lyre, trigon, harp, zither, bagpipe, and every kind of music, all the peoples, nations and languages fell down and worshipped the golden image that King Nebuchadnezzar had set up.

Great religious events or ceremonies in honour of the Pharaoh were accompanied by impressive musical shows in which there stood out a guiding figure whose role was to indicate the rhythmical breaks and development of the melody with hand gestures: a technique that is called cheironomy (from the Greek χείρ, "hand", and νόμος, "law, custom").

The most common cheironomic movements are the thumb touching the index finger, forming a sort of ring and the hand with some fingers outstretched. Scholars maintain that these recurring movements are intended to indicate, in terms of harmony, the fundamental note and the fifth note. The successive notes in the scale are signalled by the angle of the arm in relation to the forearm, thus the more acute the angle, the sharper the pitch of the note will be. This kind of use of gesture, though having lost its original meaning, has been handed down to us today, leaving traces in the gestures and movements of some traditional Middle eastern singers. But we also find cheironomy in the Middle Ages in plainchant, with the figure of the *praecentor* or choirmaster (this is also the case for Gregorian Chant.

The Hellenic World

Music and its theoretical study was also of great importance in the Hellenic world. Bearing witness to this are treatises of the Pythagorean school dating from the sixth century BC, dealing with harmony and the relationships between the registers of musical notes, the identification of "modes", scales and the Music of the Spheres. The seminal role of this art was also stressed by Plato, who considered it a more effective means of expression than the word, a medicine for the soul and body. Aristoxenus, a musical theorist and disciple of Aristotle, in his treatise *Elements of Harmony*, written in 350 BC, emphasised, on the other hand, the importance of the rhythmical aspect. Among the coordinators of tragedies in the classical theatre there featured the "coryphaeus" who, from a raised location, directed the chorus and dancers located in the space in front of the stage, called the "orchestra". The coryphaeus paced up and down to mark the tempo, hence the rhythmical unit (foot) used in classical meter.

But neither in Ancient Greece not Ancient Rome did there exist any kind of musical notation as we know it today. We have to wait for the Middle Ages for the beginning of the use of "neumatic" notation (from the Greek νεύμα, "sign") notation, which involves the use of signs and letters of the alphabet to indicate the development of the musical discourse, a system still employed in Anglo-Saxon countries, Germany and Austria. Neumatic notation allowed an initial transcription of a musical composition to be made – at the time the compositions were mainly choral, like the lyrical melodies of the Byzantines and the Gregorian chants of the *Scholae Cantorum*. These were not, however, completely unambiguous indications, however, since they only signalled the "direction" of the chant, which was characterised by free fluctuation; there was no codification of a proper rhythmic beat and the pitch of the notes was not fixed. Chants therefore continued to be passed down mainly by oral means.

Prayer to St John the Baptist

Only after the year 1000 did the Benedictine monk Guido d'Arezzo devise a simple method for identifying and codifying once and for all the seven musical notes. To make it easier to learn he took inspiration from a prayer to St John the Baptist to create a mnemonic (clearly, three of the notes have subsequently changed their nomenclature):

Ut queant laxis / **Re**sonare fibris / **Mi**ra gestorum /
Famuli tuorum / **Sol**ve polluti / **La**bii reatum /
Sancte **I**ohannes
(*So that your servants can sing with their voice your wonderful feats, clear their lips that are stained with guilt, o Saint John!*)

20

Thus the sol-fa technique was born, a new way of making music, and with it the figure of the composer who could finally convey unambiguously the various voices within a composition. With the subsequent arrival and development of polyphony and *musica mensurata*, which was capable of expressing the relative duration, as well as the pitch, of every note, the need increasingly grew for some kind of guiding figure who could coordinate the singers and keeps them in time with clear gestures. And so the *praecentor* ("he who sings first") came into being; the duties of this prototype of the conductor were described by Jerome of Moravia in his *Tractatus de Musica*, dating from 1274 circa: "The *praecentor* has to know everything about the music being sung, beat time with his hand on the book, correct anyone who sings wrongly"[1].

The First Musical Score

The Renaissance did not bring any particular breakthroughs in conducting techniques. In 1517, the German theorist Andreas Ornithoparchus, in his *Musicae Activae Micrologus*, underscored "the importance of the hand, the movement of which directs the plainchant in relation to the nature of the metrical indications"[2]. Between the mid sixteenth and the seventeenth centuries, the use of the score, that is, the complete setting out of all the played and sung parts placed on various superimposed pentagrams began to spread, also on account of the invention of sheet music printing – leading up to the musical revolution of the seventeenth century which would bring about the birth of the modern orchestra – allowing for the intricate development of polyphonic compositions. In 1577, in Venice, the earliest publication in score or *partitura* notation was issued: *Madrigals* by Cipriano de Rore.

[1] Andreas Ornithoparchus, *Musicae activae micrologus*, Leipzig, 1519.
[2] Hieronymus de Moravia, *Tractatus de musica fratris Jeronimi de Moravia*.

The innovations of this time were highly significant: the idea of the beat was introduced, the steady pulse felt in the rhythm that formalised the concept of upbeat and downbeat. In the pentagram (or stave/staff), the beat is the set of notes contained between the two barlines and may be binary, ternary etc. Though not having any musical value, this facilitates the reading of the piece.

Finally, there began the use of *basso continuo* (or thoroughbass), that part of the *basso harmonico* that runs through the work and is indicated by the chords supporting the melody, which the performer used to improvise on the organ, harpsichord, *chitarrone* (type of large lute) or viola da gamba to accompany monodic and polyphonic compositions.

The Baroque

The constant refinement of both musical instruments and performing techniques – one thinks, for instance, of Arcangelo Corelli (1653-1713), father of the *"concerto grosso"* and the classical school of violin – led to an increase in the production of instrumental music and, as a result, the birth of the first ensembles created with a unified artistic discipline and according to the criterion of the division of the instruments: those essential for the harmony (*basso continuo*) and those needed for the melodic line (violin, flute, oboe).

Les Vingt-quatre Violons du Roi

The custom of possessing one's own orchestra spread among princely courts. One example is an ensemble called *Les Vingt-quatre Violons du Roi* (or *La Grande Bande*), an orchestra made up of string instruments which entertained and accompanied the French Court during official event and ceremonies from 1577 to 1761, the year of its abolition. The band consisted of 24 string instruments, to which were added the *12 Grands Hautbois* of the Grande Ecurie of Versailles and other instruments.

Joining the *Ving-quatre Violons*, and thus enjoying all the advantages that such a position offered was not easy: one had to have an impeccable reputation, be a Catholic and be rich enough to purchase the title whose cost, under the Sun King, was in the region of 1,400 livres. Among the privileges accorded to the players were exemption from taxes and the right to bear a rapier.

Staatskapelle of Dresden

In Dresden, on the other hand, in 1548, Maurice I, Elector of Saxony founded the *Staatskapelle*, one of the oldest and finest orchestras in Europe, whose first conductor was the Lutheran composer Johann Walter. It is no coincidence that in April 2007, the orchestra was awarded the prestigious European Cultural Foundation (ECF) prize for the conservation of the world musical heritage. Directing this extraordinary orchestra for various programmes was one the most exciting experiences in my artistic career; it is with great emotion that I recall the sheer joy I felt when I continued for a while the tradition initiated by Wagner: conducting Beethoven's Ninth Symphony at the Dresden "Semperoper" on the occasion of Easter celebrations.

These early orchestral ensembles were directed by two figures: the *Konzertmeister*, the present-day first violin (concertmaster) or second violin, who coordinated the melodic instruments (violin, flute, oboe etc.) and the *Kapellmeister*, the chapel or choir master, who, with his harpsichord performed the *basso continuo*, kept the rhythm, coordinated the singers and cued the entrances of the various instruments. The co-presence of these two roles is the basis of the so-called technique of "double directing", which found its application in musical theatre. (Kapelle = Orchestra).

Camerata dei Bardi

We are approaching the pivotal century: the seventeenth. Between the end of the sixteenth and the beginning of the seventeenth centuries, in Florence, there was the development of *"recitar cantando"* (acting while singing), the first form of opera, thanks to the efforts of the musicians and theorists of the Camerata de' Bardi (including Vincenzo Galilei, Galileo's father). The aim of the group was to reintroduce the monodic songs of the classical theatre – a rather vague aspiration if if we consider that even today we know little or nothing about music in the Greek theatre – as opposed to the polyphony of madrigals that often made the sung text incomprehensible.

The birth of melodrama

The first fruit of the Camerata, as well as being the first composition to be considered an opera as such, was *Dafne*, 1598, with music by Jacopo Peri (1561-1633) and libretto by Ottavio Rinuccini (1562-1621); while Rinuccini's verses have come down to us, the same cannot be said of Peri's music, which was completely lost. Things went better with *Euridice*, the second collaboration between Peri and Rinuccini, which has survived in its entirety: it was performed at Palazzo Pitti, in Florence, in the autumn of 1600, on the occasion of the marriage of Marie de' Medici with Henry IV of France.

That precise day (6 October 1600) is considered, by convention, to be the date of the birth of melodrama.

The sacred oratorio

In the same year, in the Roman oratory of San Filippo Neri, another new musical form came into being; the composer Emilio de' Cavalieri (1550-1602), also a member of the Camerata de' Bardi, launched the sacred oratorio with his *Rappresentazione di Anima et Corpo* (Representation of the Soul and the Body), a composition of religious inspiration (but not liturgical) with a series of vignettes, presented in narrative form, but not staged. Detractors were at pains to point out that oratorio, which they branded a poor relation of opera, had only been successful because it was Lent – when theatres were closed and real operas could not be performed.

The development of the orchestral ensemble in opera

In the seventeenth century Italian music reached its peak in the figure of Claudio Monteverdi (1567-1643) and his *Orfeo*, a musical fable consisting of a prologue and five acts, with libretto by Alessandro Striggio. The opera was first staged in Mantua in 1607, achieving a resounding success, which continues apace today. For the first time Monteverdi specified clearly how many and which instruments were to be included in the orchestral ensemble: there were about forty, divided into three macro-groups (strings, brass and *basso continuo*).

The need for rehearsals

The complexity of seventeenth century operas and large sacred works made the need for an active coordination of musicians and singers increasingly urgent, hence the importance of the rehearsal phase. It is amazing to think that Monteverdi, in Mantua, allowed himself almost five months for the rehearsals for his *Arianna*, the score for which has unfortunately been lost. In the Baroque theatre, it was the composer who coached the singers during the rehearsal, while after the first performances, he was replaced by the *Kapellmeister*, assisted by the *Konzertmeister*. This custom prevailed up to the nineteenth century: even Verdi, for instance, was obliged to attend the performances of his operas.

25

The first "Conductor"

In Germany the figure of the *Kapellmeister* – who was also the court composer – was well-established; in France, there was that of the *Premier Violon*, while in Italy the two roles tended to overlap. In the eighteenth century, in France, the role of the *Premier Violon* was backed up by that of the *batteur de mesure*, a conductor who beat time by striking the floorboards of the stage with a heavy club (a bit like those used by musical bands today). This habit, subsequently abandoned, was introduced by a brilliant Italian dancer from a Florence family, who attained great success with the Sun King: he was Giovan Battista Lulli (1632-1687), Frenchified into Jean-Baptiste Lully, who, on account of his talent as a musician, dancer, organiser and scheming courtier, came to dominate the musical scene. Having become *surintendant* of the King's Music at the royal court, he created a proper orchestra for his sovereign, the *Petits Violons* (in contrast to the more numerous *Vingt-quatre Violons du Roi*). But, more importantly, Lully may be considered the first real orchestra conductor, famous not just for his sacred (*tragedies en musique*) and profane (*comedies-ballets*) compositions, but he was also victim of a professional mishap. In 1687, in the frenzy of conducting a *Te Deum*, composed by himself to celebrate Louis XIV's recovery from surgery, he struck his foot with his conducting staff, causing a serious infection. Rather than listening to his doctors, who advised the amputation of the gangrenous leg, he allowed himself to be taken in by the treatment of a quack doctor, which proved fatal. But, even on his death bed, he composed a melody: *Il faut mourir, Seigneur, il faut mourir*.

Beating time

As the eighteenth century advanced, it became clear that there was a great number of conducting techniques and tendencies. Some beat time with a baton, others with a *Papierrolle* (a roll of paper used mainly in church), others again with a staff; some clapped their hands or used conventional gestures; then there were others who conducted sitting down or at the harpsichord, tapping their feet on the floor and shaking the head; others beat a rod on the music stand or conducted with the violin, waving the bow. In short, there was no one fixed way of conducting for the theatre, church, concert or dance.

It was not uncommon for the beating of time to be so noisy that it ended up disrupting the performance. This kind of complaint was to continue for a long time: in 1786, in his *Italian Journey*, Goethe describes a concert of choral music he attended in Venice, where he was most upset by the continual racket of the roll of paper being struck against a grating, overpowering and ruining the effect of the music. However, such bad habits gradually disappeared.

The composer conductor

How did the figure of orchestra conductor as we know it today come into being? In the first half of the eighteenth century, most music was still composed on commission and devised to meet the demand of a well-defined audience, whether it be court, church or theatre. Musical pieces were almost exclusively original, unheard previously, which explains the sheer number of compositions being produced at that time: Bach (1685-1750), for example, composed a new cantata for the Church of St Thomas every week; Telemann (1681-1767) produced over 2,000, along with 600 overtures, 400 passions and the same number of operas; Haydn (1732-1809) wrote 400 symphonies and another hundred pieces of quartets and trios. Even so, very few of the works of this kind survived the context of their creation and, given that scores of the time rarely included all the indications required to mark tempo and other dynamics, much room was left for improvisation (especially for opera singers), in line with the tastes of the day. As a matter of fact, the eighteenth-century composer was considered as an artisan rather than an artist; often the creative role was accompanied by that of conductor and performer of their own music, sometimes even that of impresario, as in the case of Vivaldi (1678-1741) in Venice or Handel (1685-1759) in London, and it was seldom that these men had to conduct the music of others.

Court musicians

For the whole of the first half of the century, orchestras, made up of around twenty elements (*basso continuo*, strings and woodwind), were the prerogative of aristocrats who housed them in their palaces. The musician was therefore still considered analogous to a member of the court staff who, as such, was subject to the caprices of the nobleman who had hired him. In these situations there was no such profession as an orchestra member and sometimes it was even the ordinary domestic staff of the nobleman in question who would play in the orchestra: the gardener on the bassoon, the cook on the flute and the butler on the cello. During his employment as *Kapellmeister* with Prince Esterhazy, Haydn wore livery, ate with the other servants and was forced to humour the whims of his rich patron. Due to these very circumstances, wishing to encourage the Prince to leave the summer residence where he had taken the court and its musicians for an extended period, Haydn composed the so-called *Farewell Symphony*, a sort of payback or heavy hint on the part of the orchestra players, who, musician after musician finished their parts, snuffed out the candle, and left the stage

Permanent orchestras

Things changed in the second half of the eighteenth century, with the rise of the first independent, permanent orchestras. Modern orchestral style that envisages the use of dynamics (management of sound intensity) and agogics (slight variations in rhythmical regularity to bring out the full expressiveness of a phrase) was established, as was the habit of paying for tickets for concerts. In 1743, some rich German merchants founded the *Gewandhaus* Orchestra of Leipzig, one of the oldest and most prestigious at international level, which at the time employed sixteen fixed professional musicians. A few years later, in 1781, the growth of the ensemble led to the transfer of the orchestra to a new hall, with 500 seats, built above the textile market, the *Gewandhaus* (literally the "house of the wool-workers and cloth-makers"), hence the name. The first music director was Johann Adam Hiller (1728-1804), considered not just the founder of the great German conducting school, but also the originator of the popular form of music drama known as *Singspiel* and of concerts with season tickets, as well as the founder of the musical magazine *"Wochentliche Nachrichten"* ("Weekly News") containing reviews, essays and information on the latest musical developments.

The classical symphony

Mannheim, again in Germany, was the birthplace of the *Mannheimer Hofkapelle* (Court Orchestra), an excellent ensemble about which Mozart was particularly enthusiastic. When it was set up, it counted 48 members from all over Europe (1745), and 90 in the year in which it was disbanded when the Palatine Court moved to Munich (1778). The Czech composer Johann Stamitz (1717-1757) was not just the founder but also the *Konzertmeister*, a real breakthrough in the history of music. Indeed, with his 76 compositions, he codified the "classical symphony" into four movements, with the dialectical contrast between the first and second theme, the exposition, development and recapitulation (a form that would be perfected by Haydn). Stamitz's son, Carl (1745-1801), was to hold the last position as musical director of the *Mannheimer Hofkapelle*.

Concert Spirituel

Meanwhile in France, the *Concert Spirituel* organisation began to put on public concert series in the Tuileries Palace in 1725, bringing an end to its activities soon after the French Revolution (1789). The concerts started at six in the afternoon and attracted mostly the *haute bourgeoisie*, the minor aristocracy and foreign visitors. The musical director of the concerts was the founder Pierre-Anne Danican Philidor (1681-1728), who, forced to pay an extortionate licence fee to continue his activities (which represented an exception to the monopoly on public performance of music held by the Paris Opera), ended up bankrupt in the space of two years.

The sound of an orchestra changes with the Concertmaster

The progressive increase in orchestra size and the decline of the *basso continuo* occasioned the need for an independent coordinating figure who would not take part in the actual performance – a situation for which a remedy was sought in the introduction of a second harpsichord, not for the concertmaster. In 1752, Joachim Quantz (1697-1773), flautist and favourite author of Frederick II of Prussia, asserted in his celebrated treatise *Versuch einer Anweisung die Flote traversiere zu spielen* (Essay on the method for playing the transverse flute): "The sound of an orchestra changes with the concertmaster; a fine performance depends greatly on who directs it"[3].

Konzertmeister vs Kapellmeister

The rivalry between *Konzertmeister* and *Kapellmeister* continued unabated for the entire century. In 1767, Rousseau wrote in his

---

[3] Letter to Graun, 15/12/1751.

Dictionnaire de musique that the *chef d'orchestre* is the first violin; the task of conducting is thus assigned to the *Konzertmeister* who used his bow like a baton and played his own instrument only in certain solo parts. This practice remained in use in the nineteenth century with Strauss and in the twentieth with Boskovksy and Maazel, on the occasion of the traditional New Year concerts in Vienna.

In Germany, however, the role of the *maestro al cembalo*, the harpsichordist/director prevailed. His job was to emphasise certain expressions of the musical phrase or the dynamics – a very powerful type of direction the Germans call *Affektdirektion*, a far cry from the mechanical regularity suggested today by certain philologists. Telemann held that "music must sparkle like champagne". The composer/conductor was often seated at the harpsichord and could even remain inactive when his instrument was not required by the score (as happened, for instance, with Haydn in London in 1791 during the performance of his final symphonies).

The use of the baton

The orchestra conductor as an autonomous figure did not yet exist. In 1807, Gottfried Weber (1779-1839) stressed in the *Allgemeine Zeitung* "the need for the collective performance to be assigned to one specific musician not engaged in the playing of any instrument, who should devote himself to the direction of the whole by only using the baton". And thus the composer was backed up by a conductor who was completely independent of him; the latter used his baton to intensify his gestures and to be visible to the furthest players. The use of the baton in musical direction appears to have quite ancient origins. The nuns of a the convent of San Vito, in the Ferrara area, are reported to have used it as far back as 1594. The concert mistress would sit at the top of the table with a long, slim, well-polished baton and, when the nuns were ready, she gave the signal to start and continued to mark the tempo required for the singing and playing.

The first use of the baton as a modern tool for orchestra conducting dates from 1820, when it was reported that the renowned German violinist and composer Louis Spohr (1784-1859) availed himself of one to direct his second symphony while on tour in London. But the baton had been in use for some time: as far back as 1776, Johnann Friedrich Reichardt (1752-1814) used one, though the practice failed to catch on. A few years later, in 1810, Daniel Gottlob Turk (1750-1813) brandished his baton

---

Louis-Antoine Julliens, the first celebrity conductor of the nineteenth century

With the proliferation of large orchestras came also the first celebrity conductors like Louis-Antoine Julliens (1812-1860), a true star of the nineteenth century. He had thirty six Christian names since his father, an organist and conductor, not wishing to offend any of the musicians in his orchestra, decided to give his son the names of each of them. Louis-Antoine conducted wearing white gloves and a long ivory baton studded with diamonds, which was handed to him on a silver tray. After every he would collapse exhausted onto a chair that was richly decorated with gold and was placed on the podium specially for him. He organized spectacular concerts with dancing and cannons: his orchestra contained bizarre instruments like a 4.5 meter high double bass, a monster drum, the *clavicorn* and the bombardon [a bass tuba]. In 1846, the London Daily News published an illustration showing one of his *monster concerts* staged in Covent Garden; he had at his disposal his personal orchestra and four military bands, which included at least seven trombones, four at the head of the first section and three in the third row. Yet Julliens was also a fine conductor and he was skilled in popularising classical music; his aim was to extend his audience to include the middle classes and he always featured music by Mozart and Beethoven in his concerts.

with such exuberance that he repeatedly hit a chandelier, causing pieces of glass to cascade onto him. In 1817, in Dresden, Carl Maria von Weber (1786-1826) was subjected to criticism for using a baton and not conducting according to the "Italic custom", namely, using hand gestures while seated at the piano. In Britain, the introduction of the baton was resisted as it was deemed to be a symbol of authority, contrary to the British democratic spirit. Sir Michael Costa (1808-1884), appointed sole conductor of the

To escape his creditors, he had fled France, where he had performed with the orchestra of the *Jardin turc*, but he did not waste any time in becoming the darling of the English, who appreciated particularly his quadrilles. The performance of the *Fireman's Quadrille*, for example, envisaged the outbreak of a fire and the intervention of firefighters, jets of water and sirens blaring, played by a military band which included the oddest instruments.

But his fortune was not to last in England either; in 1852, Julliens found himself in debt up to his eyeballs, having staged at his own expense, in Covent Garden, London, a colossal opera, composed by himself, *Peter the Great*, for which he demanded the the very best singers, costumes and musicians. There ensued a terrible fiasco which forced him to flee to the United States. He returned to France in 1859, but being unable to pay his creditors, he was thrown into prison. His predicament led him to madness and death; he died in in the lunatic asylum of Neuilly-sur-Seine. An anecdote has it that during his confinement he used to repeat that the wind blowing among the trees of the garden was playing Beethoven's *Eroica*.

His fame, however, survived his demise, especially in England. Twenty years after his death, Gilbert e Sullivan, in their operetta *Patience* (1881), defined him as the *"the eminent musico"* (to rhyme with Boucicault!).

London Philharmonic Society in 1846, was much criticised for his habit of conducting with a baton. Even so, there were some conductors who opted to use more than one: Gaspare Spontini (1774-1851), much appreciated by Wagner, had two, one long and one short, the latter being held in the middle rather than the base, a legacy of religious music. Spontini was very meticulous and attached great importance to the role and the expressiveness of the the gaze, so much so that, despite being short-sighted, he conducted without his eyeglasses.

The bow instead of the baton

In nineteenth-century France, however, the violin was still considered to be the conductor's "instrument", as the violinist and composer Edouard Deldevez (1817-1897) confirmed in his treatise *L'art du chef d'orchestre* (1878). Francois Habeneck (1781-1849), the first to introduce rehearsals for separate sections of the orchestra, performed all Beethoven's symphonies with the orchestra of the *Société des Concerts du Conservatoire*, which he himself had founded (managing to impress Wagner, who speaks with enthusiasm of one of his performances, the Ninth Symphony, in his essay on the art of conducting). Habeneck directed from a seated position, in his place as first violin, and marked in red ink on the score where the various instruments were to come in, a widespread practice also in opera houses; every time a musician played a wrong note, Habeneck let the audience know by pointing his bow at the embarrassed culprit.

Berlioz's first large orchestra

After the French Revolution and the emergence of the bourgeoisie, concerts shifted from salons and court *Kapelle* to public concert halls where a charge was made. The arrival of romantic music led to the enlargement of the orchestra: Berlioz (1803-

1869) even envisaged a formation of 465 players. A new dignity was conferred on instruments like the clarinet, which now entered the orchestra fully-fledged, to the extent that Mozart decided to write a second version of Symphony K550 with a clarinet part. After the second decade of the nineteenth century, instruments with valves and pistons like the Boehm flute, Adolphe Sax's saxophone and the Heckel bassoon appeared. Technical virtuosity paved the way for composers like Berlioz, Liszt, Wagner and the development of orchestral ensembles as we know them today, with strings, woodwind, trumpets, horns, tuba, percussion, harps, piano and organ. Scores became increasingly complex, also from the point of view of rhythmical originality. The composer achieved the status of an independent artist and the conducting art was transformed from an occasional experience into a real profession, although the figure of composer/conductor did continue to exist. This was the case with, among others, Berlioz, Mendelssohn, Liszt, Wagner and Strauss, Mahler, Stravinsky, Bernstein, Berio and Boulez, but it does not necessarily follow that a great composer will also be a great conductor: Berlioz' early experiences were, for instance, quite disastrous. During a performance of Beethoven's *Missa Solemnis* in1827, he was overcome by convulsions and had to sit down and let the orchestra rest for a few minutes.

Popularisation of the classical repertoire

The transformation of the role of conductor is also linked to the emergence of a new historical awareness: not only new, previously unheard, music was being played, but masterpieces from the past were being studied and revived, with the consequent broadening of the repertoire to include classic composers alongside contemporary ones. This revival of interest is often credited to Mendelssohn (1809-1847), a rigorous conductor of his own work, who in 1829, directed Bach's *St Matthew Passion*, which had never been played since the death of the composer (1750).

Baton records

A conductor's baton can vary in length from 25 to 50 centimetres, but there are some record breakers. On 14 October 2006, in fact, during the interval at a university football match, Kenton J. Hetrick conducted the *Harvard University Band* in the introduction to *Also Sprach Zarathustra* using a 3-metre long baton. Hetrick's record was smashed, however, by the Dutchman Bas Clabbers, who, on 30 October 2010 conducted at a concert in the town of Heythuysen, the Netherlands, armed with a mega-baton that stretched to 4.25 metres in length.

Those years saw the spread of the classical repertoire and therefore the highest precision, faithfulness to text, professional rigour with musicians, attention to sound quality and the search for expressiveness were all required of the conductor.

The birth of conservatoires and concert societies

The nineteenth century also bore witness to the foundation and development of music conservatoires, both public and private, and concert societies. In France we had the *Société des Concerts du Conservatoire* (1828), Jules Pasdeloup's *Concerts Populaires* (1861), Edouard Colonne's *Concert National* (1873) and Charles Lamoureux's *Nouveaux Concerts* (1881); in England: the London *Royal Philharmonic Society* (1813), *Manchester's Gentleman's Concerts* directed by Sir Charles Halle and the Sir Henry Wood's *Proms* (1895). In the United States, the *New York Philharmonic* (1842) and the *Chicago Symphony Orchestra*, founded by Theodore Thomas in 1891, are still going strong today. Italy, meanwhile, was distinguished particularly by opera conductors, like Giovanni Bottesini (1821-1889), the double bass virtuoso who conducted the first performance of *Aida* in Cairo, but also Angelo Mariani (1821-1873), Franco Faccio (1840-1891), Ettore Pinelli (1843-1915), Luigi Mancinelli (1848-1921), Giuseppe Martucci (1856-1909) and Cleofonte Campanini (1860-1919).

Conducting theory

The art of orchestra conducting began to be subjected to theorising by figures like Berlioz and Wagner. Although neither of them could boast he was an expert in any particular musical instrument – Berlioz played the guitar, while Wagner could barely play the piano – they both became fine conductors, appreciating the importance of their role as moulder of sound. The first real treatise on the subject, entitled *Le chef d'orchestre: theorie de son art*, was published by Berlioz as an appendix to the second edition of his *Traite d'instrumentation et d'orchestration* of 1855. In the essay, the French composer confirmed the abolition of the use of the violin bow in favour of the baton and prescribed the conductor's position, standing (no longer sitting), looking at the players. Moreover, Berlioz stressed the need for a podium that would allow the conductor to dominate the entire ensemble, the compulsory use of musical scores and the importance of eliminating any noise (the habit of tapping one's foot on the floor or striking the music stand was outlawed), considered by him to be a "barbarism"[4]. He also advocated that the study of conducting in conservatoires be quite distinct from the discipline of composition.

---

[4] Hector Berlioz, *Le Chef d'Orchestre*, in *The Orchestral Conductor : Theory of his Art*, New York 1900.

Wagner: the first modern conductor

Wagner was also a great conductor, the first to direct from memory without the use of a score, and he is universally held to be the main theoretician of the art of conducting. In 1869 he published *Uber das Dirigiren* (On Conducting), a treatise that does not deal with procedure or codify theories so much as level harsh criticism against the *Kapellmeister* of his time and, in a rather bigoted way, those of the Mendelssohn school, regarded by him as mere mechanical time-beaters. Wagner insists peremptorily that the conductor must give prominence to the phrasing, breathing and singing: his ultimate aim is to attain what the composer defined *melos* (that which dictates the tempo and character of a melody). If prior to Wagner conducting was seen as a simple procedure of coordinating the producers of sound, with him a new more elastic way of conducting came into being.

In executing a piece, the conductor must know how to choose a tempo that is appropriate to the sense of the work and its comprehension (*Umfassung*); he thus becomes a sacerdotal figure, the medium for the attainment of hypnotic fervour and ecstasy. For this to happen, it is imperative that a true professional steps onto the podium. As Schumann affirmed: "Experience has shown that the composer is not usually the best interpreter of his own work".

Wagner was aware of the importance of placing on the podium a complete artist, a genuine professional who would devote himself exclusively to the realisation of the composer's intention, paying attention to the precision of the phrasing, observation of the dynamic nuances and the blending of the instruments. And for this reason, albeit an excellent conductor himself, he entrusted the first performance of his complex scores to other maestri: Franz Liszt for *Lohengrin* in Weimar in 1850; Hans von Bülow for *Tristan und Isolde* (on the score of which Wagner wrote: "Ideally should be conducted by an Italian") in 1865 and for *Die Meistersinger von Nürnberg* in 1868, in Munich on both occasions; Hans Richter for the first complete performance of the cycle *Der Ring des Nibelungen* in Bayreuth in 1876. Wagner, in spite of his distasteful pamphlet *Judaism in Music* (1850), entrusted the direction of the première of *Parsifal* to Hermann Levi, again in Bayreuth.

Gesamtkunstwerk

Wagner also expounded the *Gesamtkunstwerk* ("total work of art") theory and was inventor – along with the architect Gottfried Semper – of the invisible orchestra, situated in a *mystischer Abgrund*, a "mystical abyss" (the orchestra pit), tried out for the first time at the Bayreuth Festival and resulting in much improved acoustics. With Wagner the figures of the composer and the conductor were definitively separated; the conductor was now the person who, through his interpretation, re-created the work of the composer.

Treatises on conducting

A number of other treatises on conducting were to follow Wagner's: we might mention *Über das Dirigieren* (*On Conducting*) (1895-1896) by Felix Weingartner (1863-1942), *Lehrbuch des Dirigierens* (Conductor's Manual) (1929) by Hermann Scherchen (1891-1966), *Je suis chef d'orchestre* (I am a Conductor) (1954) by Charles Munch (1891-1968) and *Von der Musik und vom Musizieren* (Music and Interpretation) 1957) by Bruno Walter (1876-1962).

Star system

The importance that conducting acquired in the course of the nineteenth century was underscored by the status that was accorded to the most eminent conductors of the time, forerunners to what would amount to nothing less than a "star system" in the twentieth century. In Germany, conductors would all be heirs to Wagnerian theories, and it was there that music took on not just an aesthetic value, but also had political and social implications. Controversially, Hitler exploited the figure of Wagner for his own purposes, with the result that his music is officially banned in the State of Israel.

Conducting from memory

The first conductor entrusted by a composer – in this case, Wagner – with performing his work was Hans von Bülow (1830-1894). Former husband of Wagner's second wife, Cosima, Bülow conducted from memory, often repeating: "Always conduct with the score in your head, not your head in the score"[5]. In 1880, after falling out with Wagner, he became director of the Meiningen Court Orchestra in Saxony, where he shaped an orchestra that set a benchmark for other orchestras of the time. Amazingly, he requested eighty days of rehearsal for the performance of Beethoven's Ninth Symphony. From 1887 to 1892 he led the newly founded *Berliner Philharmoniker*. Bülow considered himself to be a priest, a pedagogue of high music and he launched the fashion of preparing the audience for concerts by giving a detailed explanation of the music to be played before the performance.

In 1876, Hans Richter (1843-1916) was tasked with the first performance of *Der Ring des Nibelungen* at the Bayreuth Festival; the orchestra he conducted had no less than 116 constituents. Richter was inspired by the Wagnerian principle: "let the music sing, not play".

Gustav Mahler (1860-1911) established the figure of the omnipotent director when he was appointed to the prestigious position of *Generalmusikdirektor* at the *Staatsoper* of Vienna from

[5] *Ibid.*

1897 to 1907. Mahler had the final say over everything – from the choice of singers to the stage sets – and he raised the opera house to new heights. He also forbade the entrance of latecomers into the hall.

Felix Weingartner (1863-1942), on the other hand, is considered (somewhat like Sergiu Celibidache) the anti-Mahler. A pupil of Liszt and Wagner, he incurred the hatred of the followers of the latter because, on the death of the, he dared to oppose the artistic choices of Cosima Wagner (daughter of Liszt, first wife of Bülow and second wife of Wagner). In his 1895 essay on conducting, Weingartner introduced for the first time a clear division between the tasks for the right arm, to be engaged in marking the beat, and the left arm, which was to focus on phrasing, expression and the entrances of the instruments.

One of the first itinerant conductors, Arthur Nikisch (1855-1922), directed without a score, often allowing himself great freedom with tempo and rhythm: conducting was a creative art for him. He held the position, for the first time, of conductor-for-life of the *Berliner Philharmoniker*, with whom he made the first gramophone recording of Beethoven's Fifth Symphony.

In the second half of the nineteenth century a number of non-German conductors also distinguished themselves internationally; we might mention Anton Grigorevich Rubinstein (1829-1894) in Russia; Michael Costa, Charles Halle (1819-1895) and Henry Wood (1869-1944) in Great Britain; Willem Mengelberg (1871-1951) in the Netherlands; Giovanni Bottesini, Giuseppe Martucci and Arturo Toscanini (1867-1957) in Italy; Jules Pasdeloup (1819-1887), Charles Lamoureux (1834-1899) and Edouard Colonne (1838-1910) in France.

The evolution of technology

Between the nineteenth and twentieth centuries, technological advances also affected the musical world. In 1877, Thomas Edison conceived of a device for sound recording, subsequently

(1898) developed by Emile Berliner, inventor of the 78 rpm disc and founder of one of the oldest record labels, as well as promoter of the first radio broadcasts. Thanks to these advances, classical music reached the peak of its diffusion in the first half of the twentieth century. This was the century of the superstar "prima-donna" conductor, worshipped by the masses and handsomely paid (sometimes more than the whole orchestra put together), whose name was highlighted more than the composer's on record covers – a sea change if one considers that in 1901, as Bruno Walter recalls in his 1946 autobiography, the programme at the *Wiener Hofoper* listed the names of all the singers, but not the conductor, who often was not even credited with a mention in critical reviews.

The conductor

The ingredients for success for an artist are: talent, hard work, total commitment, perfectionism, generosity of spirit and humility. An aspiring conductor has to be rigorously trained from the point of view of music (study of composition, piano, a string instrument and a wind instrument), culture (interest in the arts and humanistic subjects generally) and languages: Italian is indispensable for understanding musical terms, Latin for the sacred repertoire, English for communication, but German, Spanish and Russian also come in handy).

"In this field empiricism still reigns supreme: no theory, no system"[1], asserted the Ukrainian composer Lazare Saminsky; indeed there are as many ways to conduct and as many possible interpretations of a piece as as there are conductors. A conductor can be hieratic like Herbert von Karajan and Otto Klemperer, demiurgic like Sergiu Celibidache, exuberant like Leonard Bernstein, or else Dionysian like Victor de Sabata e Dimitri Mitropoulos, ascetic like Carlo Maria Giulini, irascible like Arturo Toscanini and George Szell, Mephistophelean like Solti.

However, for all these great masters, the starting point is one and one only: meticulous study of the score, preferably at the piano and in utter silence (reading the score while listening to a record is absolutely taboo). Then, at a later stage, the composition has to be explored more deeply, imagining the sounds of the various instruments, both individually and collectively; before working with the orchestra, the conductor – again in Saminsky's words - "should have already fixed not just the rhythmical

---

[1] Lazare Saminsky, *Essentials of Conducting*. New York 1958.

"plan", but also the sound plan"[2]. But it is not simply a question of analysing and deciphering the score; since the conductor is the intermediary between the composer and the audience, he has to interpret it and to be able to convey his own interpretative vision to the players clearly and unequivocally, respecting the spirit of the music to be performed. I talk about deciphering, since in music not everything can be written down and the conductor has to be capable of going beyond the pure and simple indications to penetrate to the real intention of the composer: reading a score means discovering allusions hidden in its depths, being able to see what a note behind or above itself covers, being able to decipher a score in all its individual significances while managing at the same time to maintain a unified musical discourse.

In this respect, Wagner was the first to stress the importance of *melos* in the art of conducting: through singing. it is possible to determine the exact movement and the most correct phrasing and accent, and to manage confidently the singers' breathing and the wind instruments. In his *On Conducting*, the German composer relates how the singing of the soprano Wilhelmine Schröder-Devrient alone, heard in 1839, was responsible for giving him a true understanding of Beethoven's music, which had been so mistreated and misunderstood at the time. Accompanying Frau Schröder-Devrient there was the Orchestra of the Paris Conservatoire, conducted by François-Antoine Habeneck. Thanks to the influence of Italian music, for French musicians playing a melody well and singing it perfectly coincide: and it is to this, and to the the long rehearsals the conductor the conductor subjects his performers to, that Wagner attributes the success of execution. "With this indication", he wrote in his treatise, "I only wish to point out [...] what new force a conductor would have at his disposal for perfecting his musical education from the point of view of performance, if he understood

[2] *Ibid.*

44

well his duties in the theatre to which he owes his position and reputation"[3].

Indeed, the duties expected of an opera conductor are not the same as those of the concert conductor. In the theatre sphere, the conductor is only one of many people who contribute to the event and his activity is thus less independent as compared with that of the concert conductor, who has the principal role. Opera directing requires, besides a finely-honed musical sensibility, a certain predisposition towards dramatic art: Wagner criticises mercilessly the ambition of those conductors who completely lack any spontaneous impulse or passion, who wish they could compose and direct a successful opera, but, unable to do so, disguise their shortcomings by attributing to melodrama a lesser value than a pure musical performance. This impossibility of having access to opera houses and understanding opera fully also indirectly hinders their work in the concert hall since, not being able to avail themselves of singing, they have difficulty in probing the real significance of the music they are playing. In more recent times, conductors have tended to venture into both spheres, rarely adhering exclusively to one as opposed to the other. The fact that there are now conductors that can be equally outstanding in both fields has meant that the orchestra has returned to the situation of being in the forefront in opera too, where previously the voice had long been considered the absolute main priority. In this way, symphonic and operatic interpretative techniques mutually influence each other.

The execution of a symphony is a blend of elements that need to be interpreted and evaluated in all their individual aspects, in line with a double reading, from the general to the particular, and again from the particular to the general; paying attention to the individual parts and understanding what links them allows the central thread (the *melos*) of the piece to emerge. Sometimes,

---

[3] Richard Wagner, *Wagner on Conducting*, New York 1989 (originally published in German in 1869).

even in the scores of the greatest compositions in history the *melos* is not immediately recognisable. It is for this reason that some conductors, strengthened by their meticulous preparation and certain to have captured the true intention of the composer in question, allow themselves to intervene in their music.

Weingartner, for example, claimed that the means at Beethoven's disposal were insufficient (in terms of both the instrumentation and his physical condition), practically asserting

Long-lived conductors: Arturo Toscanini

In his treatise on orchestra conducting, Charles Munch asserts that being a conductor is not a profession, but a real vocation, a priesthood, even an illness that only death can cure.

But is conducting a dangerous job, a physically demanding job or an elixir of long life? Is the gymnastic aspect of conducting harmful or beneficial for the health? The conductor is like a bullfighter – he knows how to get on to the podium, not how to get off. If we consider a number of (plus) octogenarians and some who have died of a heart attack on the podium, it would be more accurate to say – banally – that every man has his destiny.

Among the conductors who have lived longest , let us take the case of Arturo Toscanini (1867-1957), judged by many of his contemporaries (critics, musicians and general public) to be the greatest conductor of his time, capable of fusing the Dionysian aspects of Wagner's opera and the Apollonian features of Mendelssohn.

Toscanini became so celebrated not just for his famous outbursts of fury, but also for his brilliance, unstinting perfectionism, phenomenal ear for sound and photographic memory (developed to compensate for his myopia, which would require the use of spectacles) which enabled him to correct errors that none of his colleagues had ever noticed.

that if the maestro had been able to compose in ideal conditions, he himself would have revised his score[4]. On the subject of Beethoven's timbre, Saminsky had something similar to say: "In any Beethoven symphony, in order for the notes held by the woodwind or their solo playing to be heard through the mass of strings that abound today, the tone-colour indications marked on the score have to be modified".[5]

To test Toscanini's memory during a concert in New York, a cellist decided to eliminate a bar of secondary importance. When it came to the omission, Toscanini stopped the orchestra and shouted at the musician; "You've missed a bar!". "No, maestro", the other replied, "I played everything that was written". To which Toscanini responded: "Well, there must be a mistake in the score".

He was also the first conductor to achieve the status of radio star: in 1937, NBC broadcast his concerts leading the *NBC Symphony Orchestra*, a radio orchestra, specially set up for him.

When you are at the opera and you cry out for an encore of a famous aria and the request is denied, remember Toscanini: it was he who abolished this custom and for this very reason, in 1903, he terminated his contract with La Scala of Milan (or perhaps, as the gossip-mongers had it, it was a love affair with a singer that forced him to resign). At the end of the day, though, it must be said that his outbursts of rage were actually far fewer than legend would have it.

---

[4] Cfr. Aldo Ceccato, *Beethoven Duemila*, Pendragon, Bologna 2010.
[5] Lazare Saminsky, *Essentials of Conducting*.

The choice of tempos

Only singing allows *melos* to emerge and only a clear awareness of the *melos* to be emphasised lets the conductor identify the correct pace. And once again it was Wagner who stressed the variations in the Italian terms used by composers to denote movement: Mozart's *allegro* does not coincide with Beethoven's *allegro*; Bach – who, according to Wagner, was so convinced that anyone able to understand his music would have no difficulty in establishing the right tempo[6] – decided to give no tempo markings, so it had long been impossible to determine whether *andantino* is faster or slower than *andante*. Things get even more complicated when tempo markings other than the Italian ones are used (music, it is well-known, speaks Italian), as in the case of Wagner , who opted for German. In order to decipher and understand composers' instructions well, one needs to be very well-versed in their music, habits and the age they lived in. The work of one given composer represents a single moment in a much wider ranging production, which in turn has to be viewed in a precise historical/cultural context – all of which the conductor has to know intimately.

The cultural Zeitgeist in which Mozart operated is not the same as that of Beethoven, not forgetting also that the science and techniques of the musical art evolve; it only takes a few years for the instrumentation at a composer's disposal to change drastically, making possible what was impossible before. A good conductor is able to recognise these considerations and calibrate them perfectly to exploit to the full the score he intends to perform.

---

[6] Weingartner is not of the same opinion; in his *On Conducting* he claims that Bach limited his markings because he never imagined anyone else playing his music in his place.

The metronome

Among technical devices that appeared, one is definitely worth mentioning: the metronome, invented and patented by Johann Nepomuk Malzel in 1816, arousing the curiosity and interest of Beethoven who, the following year, he subjected all his symphonies to "metronomisation". Beethoven, in the entire sequence of his symphonies, adopted metronome markings that were not always playable or even stood in contrast with his own statement for the tempo and character of the movement. For example, in the second movement of his First Symphony, Beethoven's metronome reads SYMBOL = 120: no great player would respect that metronome, in that it is maddeningly fast. The *presto* of the first movement of the Ninth is marked SYMBOL = 96: Beethoven must have distractedly inverted the original number of 69 = SYMBOL, which is, instead, a logical tempo.

Let us look at some examples from great conductors, who are often closer to each other that the tempos noted by Beethoven.

FIRST SYMPHONY
First movement
Introduction (*Adagio molto*)   (*Allegro con brio*)

Beethoven (rev. 1817) ♪ = 88	Beethoven (rev. 1817) ♩ = 112
Furtwaengler ♪ = 76-66	Toscanini ♩ = 100 fino 108
Toscanini ♪ = 84-80	Furtwaengler ♩ = 88 fino 96
Walter ♪ = 80-76	Walter ♩ = 104
Mengelberg ♪ = 80	Mengelberg ♩ = 108-112
Klemperer ♪ = 80-84	Klemperer ♩ = 92
Szell ♪ = 84	Szell ♩ = 96
Schuricht ♪ = 92	Schuricht ♩ = 104
Karajan ♪ = 69	Karajan ♩ = 104
Abbado ♪ = 84	Abbado ♩ = 108
Ceccato ♪ = 72-76	Ceccato ♩ = 112

Second movement

Beethoven (rev. 1817) ♪ = 120
Toscanini ♪ = 93
Furtwaengler ♪ = 84
Walter ♪ = 84
Mengelberg ♪ = 104-108
Klemperer ♪ = 84
Szell ♪ = 84
Schuricht ♪ = 96
Karajan ♪ = 108-104
Weingartner ♪ = 104
Abbado ♪ = 104
Ceccato ♪ = 96

Mengelberg ♩. = 108
Klemperer ♩. = 88
Szell ♩. = 96
Schuricht ♩. = 108
Karajan ♩. = 96
Weingartner ♩. = 108
Abbado ♩. = 104
Ceccato ♩. = 108

Third movement

Beethoven (rev. 1817) ♩. = 108
Toscanini ♩. = 104
Furtwaengler ♩. = 100
Walter ♩. = 104

(*Trio*)

Toscanini ♩. = 96
Furtwaengler ♩. = 86
Walter ♩. = 100
Mengelberg ♩. = 104-108
Klemperer ♩. = 86
Schuricht ♩. = 100
Karajan ♩. = 86
Weingartner ♩. = 100
Abbado ♩. = 100
Ceccato ♩. = 100

Along with the metronome timings I myself produced, I thought it might be interesting to show those of some of my historical predecessors.

The accuracy of the metronome used by the genius of Bonn is debatable, given that this was the first exemplar and was still far from perfect. Moreover, Beethoven was frequently subject to fits of rage and often this new device was flung not just at the walls of his house, but also at his hapless biographer/secretary, Schindler. Beethoven said of the metronome:

"It is superfluous for anyone who possesses a true musical mind; and equally, it is of no use whatsoever to anyone without one".

The role of the conductor

The role of the conductor is thus seminal: as intermediary between the composer and the public, he has to be interpreter of the wishes of the composer and ensure the music is played in the best way possible. In his treatise of conducting, Berlioz stresses the importance of having a conductor who is able to let himself be guided by the "vague terms used to indicate tempo"[7], by his own instinct and by his knowledge of the composer's style: but without a real professional, these elements are not sufficient to assure the proper execution of a score. In a letter to the *Generalmusikdirektor* of Leipzig, Weber compares the tempo of a composition to a man's heartbeat and recommends eschewing any stark categorisation: "There is no slow time in which there are not passages that require more rapid playing to avoid the impression of dragging [...] Conversely, there is no *presto* that does not need a quiet delivery by many places, so as not to throw away the chance of expressiveness by hurrying"[8]. One can only Put oneself in the hands of the conductors, since unambiguous instructions do not exist: "These are found only in the heart of the man who *feels*"[9], asserts Weber, and no artifice can compensate for for the lack of true sensitivity.

---

[7] Hector Berlioz, *Grand Traité d'Instrumentation et d'Orchestration Modernes*, Paris 1844

[8] Carl Maria von Weber, *Letter to Generalmusikdirektor Praeger Felix Weingartner*.

[9] *Ibid.*

The problem of tempo

Wagner devotes considerable attention to the problem of tempo in his *On Conducting*, stressing how a choice of wrong tempo may often lead to the complete misreading of a given score and he never fails to condemn those conductors who rush a movement simply to disguise defects in the playing, a habit he attributed to Mendelssohn. A habit that was elevated to the level of dogma by his followers.

Colour

Moving to the area of sound intensity, Wagner's judgement is no less harsh. The German composer bewails the terrible habits of conductors who do not pay due attention to tone-colour; incompetence that is also reflected in their orchestras, apparently unable (because they are disaccustomed) to play a continuous, uniform *forte* or a *piano sostenuto*, with disastrous results: "The *dolce* sound [...] and the *forte sostenuto* sound [...] are the two poles of the whole orchestral dynamic amidst which the playing flows. What happens when one does not bother about one or the other? If the extreme limits of the dynamism remain indistinct, what can the degrees of variety in this performance be?"[10].

Convenient mezzoforte

The orchestras of his time, according to Wagner, all played *mezzoforte*, a convenience that reduced dynamic differentiation to a minimum and greatly weakened the musical texture of any piece. For this reason the conductor should insist on extreme dynamics, in particular with the *pianissimos*. Around twenty years

---

[10] Richard Wagner, *Wagner on Conducting*.

after Wagner, Gounod also stressed "how much respect of colour is indispensable for anyone who wishes to render the expression of a musical phrase faithfully and to what extent the arbitrary whim of the conductor can alter the sense and character to the point of sometimes making it unrecognisable"[11] and, even today, evidently things have not changed so much if, during a concert he attended in the audience, Sergiu Celibidache was to define a conductor from beyond the Alps as a "mezzofortist"!".

Dynamics

Also as far as dynamics are concerned, it should not be forgotten that the markings may change meaning according to the composer being played, hence one of Haydn's *fortissimo* will not coincide with one of Stravinsky's *fortissimo*. Each composer and, accordingly, each piece have different characters and styles. Also here the conductor has to know how to decipher the instructions referring to dynamics on the basis of the score being studied, of the composer's entire production and the cultural context in which the work was born, in order to bring out nuances and accents and to maintain the purity of sound. As Berlioz said: "Often, a conductor, out of overzealousness or lacking delicacy of musical sensibility, forces his players to exaggerate the timbres. This means that he does not understand either the character or the style of the piece. The colours thus become stains and the accents shout. The intentions of the poor composer are completely disfigured and betrayed".[12]

Sometimes, as Wagner emphasised, to obtain the desired effect it is necessary to rebalance the sections of the orchestra and

---

[11] Charles Gounod, *Interpretation of the Music of Mozart*.
[12] Hector Berlioz, *Grand Traité d'Instrumentation et d'Orchestration Modernes*, Paris 1844.

arrange them in such as a way as to ensure that no one sound is swamped by the others (brass and percussion, for instance, tend to drown out the sound of the strings) and that all the instrumental sections are clearly perceptible in the name of orchestral "democracy". Indeed, with regard to instrumentation, Charles Halle maintained that an effective conductor should be able to play as many instruments as possible (even though some of the great conductors of the nineteenth century could barely manage two – de Sabata could play them all); at any rate he should be well aware of the nature of each instrument and know their scope and limits, in order to be able to give helpful and precise instructions to the musicians.

An amateur conductor: Gilbert Kaplan

There are some incredible cases, like that of Gilbert Kaplan (1941-2016), a successful American tycoon and publisher, who sold his company for 72 million dollars in 1984 and set up the Kaplan Foundation, dedicated to the music of Gustav Mahler. Although he never studied music and could consider himself at best a fledgeling conductor, Kaplan hyper-specialised in his beloved Mahler's Second Symphony (the so-called *Resurrection Symphony*), the only complete work ever conducted by him in his career. In 1982, Kaplan made his debut – at his own expense – at the Avery Fisher Hall in New York, and then went on to repeat the feat with at least fifty orchestras, some among the most prestigious in the world.
Apart from his live performances, Kaplan recorded his version of the symphony twice: the first time in 1987 with the *London Symphony Orchestra* (hailed by the New York Times as one of the best classical music discs of the year in 1988) and the sec-

Collaboration between conductor and performers

Collaboration between musicians and the conductor must be *total*. In order for this to happen, the conductor's technical skills will not be sufficient unless accompanied by attention to two requirements: on one hand, training that allows him to maintain the best physical and mental conditions so that he can face the psychophysical demands that are constantly placed on him; on the other, the ability to collaborate with the orchestra.
The psychophysical aspect is essential. Strauss the elder, principal horn player with the Munich Court Orchestra recounted: "As soon as [the conductor] stepped onto the podium and opened

ond time in 2002 with the *Wiener Philharmoniker*.
In the course of his rather improbable career, Kaplan received much critical acclaim, but also (and mostly) fierce criticism. In 2008, a journalist of the New York Times defined one of his concerts as a "woefully sad farce" and said that he was only allowed to conduct because he had paid out huge sums of money. The words of David Finlayson, trombonist of the *New York Philharmonic*, are no more magnanimous:
"My initial impression was that Mr Kaplan displays an arrogance and self-delusion that is off-putting. As a conductor, he can best be described as a very poor beater of time who far too often is unable to keep the ensembles together and allows most tempo transitions to fall where they may. His direction lacks few indications of dynamic control or balance and there is absolutely no attempt to give phrases any requisite shape. In rehearsal, he admitted to our orchestra that he is not capable of keeping a steady tempo and that he would have to depend on us for any stability in that department".

the score, even before he picked up his baton, we knew immediately if it would be he or the orchestra that would be taking command". The way the conductor behaves in his relations with the massed orchestra, the singers and the soloists is of paramount importance. He has to be able to emanate charisma, the sense of leadership, a perfect mastery of himself and the score, as well as a superb organisational awareness. On the podium – an indispensable asset, so that he can be seen by all the musicians – the conductor must have a positive attitude, instil calm

Orchestras without a conductor

The twentieth century also saw experiments with modern conductorless orchestras. The most famous of these was undoubtedly the *Persimfans* (from the Russian *Perviy Simfonicheskiy Ansambl' bez Dirizhyora*, that is, First Conductorless Symphony Ensemble), founded in Moscow in1922 and active until 1932. Inspired by Communist principles, Lev Zetlin, violinist and creator of the ensemble, wanted all orchestra members to have the same freedom and the same responsibility: everyone had to be equal, on a par. The musicians were arranged in a semicircle so as to be opposite each other and, following some prescribed signals, exchanged the directions necessary for the performance. Within the ensemble a small group of musicians was appointed, whose task was to decide on the volume, dynamics, tempo and style for each piece. At the rehearsals one of the orchestra members sat in the place of the audience to monitor and report on the effect obtained.

In 1927, Prokofiev played his Third Piano Concerto with *Persimfans*. And the German conductor Otto Klemperer led the Russian orchestra on at least one occasion, although he laid down his baton half way through the concert and let the musicians finish by themselves.

and tranquillity in his players, ensure that courtesy and firmness go hand in hand. It is true that the figure of the conductor-tyrant who dominates overbearingly belongs to the past – a past in which orchestras were much less skilled than they are today – but even today, the conductor must be a demiurge and prove himself to be consummate master of the situation and the score, know what he wants from his musicians and to be capable of conveying his interpretative vision in the clearest possible way.

Albeit made up of the best players of the time, the experiment soon ran out of steam because the number of rehearsals needed to fine-tune each performance were often excessive (up to a hundred) and because the performances – though perfect – were criticised for being too mechanical, lacking that certain something, the improvisation that only a conductor can pull off during a concert.

When Stalin came to power, the obvious contradiction between the totalitarianism of his dictatorship and the idealistic democracy of *Persimfans* made continuing the orchestra untenable: in 1932 the orchestra was disbanded and its musicians sent to the Gulag.

Among conductorless orchestras still active today we find the *Orpheus Chamber Orchestra* of New York, made up of 28 elements and founded in 1972 by the cellist Julius Fifer who, apart from organising tours, holds lessons on the decision-making process that underlies his ensemble's raison d'etre. This method, christened the *Orpheus Process*, has even entered the hallowed halls of the University of Harvard. Irrespective of the bravura of the individual players, there still remains the technical problem of the tempos to be set at the rehearsals: sometimes even a month, as compared with the two or three days required for an orchestra led by a conductor.

Rehearsals

Unlike the instrumentalist, who can fine-tune his perform-ance at any time, the conductor passes to the practical stage of his art only at the moment of the rehearsals, the number of which has to be established on the basis of the programme to be played. This is a stage that is delicate and extremely impor-tant for the solving of all issues and difficulties: the conductor must be able to detect these and point them out to the players, who will then be placed in a position to correct themselves where necessary. To save precious time, it is advisable that the conductor has already sent the score for the string quintets with their associated bow-strokes and all necessary instructions to the orchestra archive. In the event of an error, the conductor should always interrupt the orchestra (a rule which is also valid for the dress rehearsal with the public present), noting the mis-take in simple, precise language. If he is unsure whether he can provide a valid solution to a problem, it is better to say nothing. This is a sort of reciprocal adaptation stage for conductor and orchestra; if the players prove unable, due to technical limita-tion, to do full justice to the conductor's interpretation, it is bet-ter to indulge them. Generally speaking, a conductor cannot de-mand either more or less than what an orchestra is actually ca-pable of. However, it is his duty to put the utmost effort into boosting the various sections.

If he is tackling an opera, it is advisable for the conductor to practise on the piano with with the soloist and choir before re-hearsing with the orchestra. During the performance of a sym-phonic programme or opera, the conductor must not under any circumstances sing the musical script or libretto, but should lis-ten attentively to each element of the ensemble: the orchestra, choir and soloists.

Gesture

The preparation stage concerns not just every aspect of the musical piece to be played, but also the conducting gesture. During the performance, the musician will be used to concentrating on his own part and, at the same time, paying attention to conductor's movements, which must follow the music religiously and be crystal clear and immediately comprehensible. In certain respects, it is the score itself that suggests the appropriate gesture: the conductor has to be able to choose the gestural mode on the basis of the music to be played, finding a way to give directions that will bring it out the best in it.

In communicating with the orchestra by means of gesture, the conductor has to realise which section requires greater attention and where it is necessary to intervene with the support of a specific gesture.

This also serves to correct, check and prevent any weaknesses and, in adapting to external factors that are not immediately predictable, he has to be able to intervene swiftly to ensure that the initial thread is faithfully resumed.

After seeing one of my concerts for the first time, my children (aged respectively four and six at the time) commented: "But Daddy, everyone's playing an instrument but you're not!"; the gesture is the conductor's instrument and he has to be able to master it just as a virtuoso does with his violin. Direction by a conductor with unclear gesture is no help for the players, rather, it is an added difficulty. Also the gaze plays an extremely important role; for this reason the use of reading glasses is not recommended – this creates a real barrier between the conductor and the orchestra.

On this subject, at the turn of the eighteenth century, Gaspare Spontini said to a young Wagner:

> My left eye is the first violin, my right the second violin; to be effective with one's glance one must therefore not wear spectacles (only bad conductors wear them) [...] I can

scarcely see one step in front of me, and yet with my eyes I make certain that everything goes according to my wishes".[17]

Child prodigies
Even in the world of conducting there is no lack of child prodigies

Willy Ferrero (1906-1954), Italian but born in Portland, Maine, began to conduct at the tender age of six at the Teatro Costanzi, Rome. It was not long before his fame spread, so much so that Tsar Nicholas II invited him to Moscow; in addition to giving him a valuable gold watch with a dedication, the Russian sovereign arranged for a troika pulled by three white horses to be waiting for him outside the theatre to take him on a ride through the city by night. In 1917, when he was eleven, Ferrero conducted for the first time at La Scala and at the end of that year he left to study in Vienna where, without interrupting his conducting career, he graduated in conducting in 1924. News of his talent and bravura spread throughout the world, to the extent that Arturo Toscanini invited him to direct *La Scala Symphony Orchestra* several times. Ferrero was only 48 years old when he died, struck down by heart disease.
Roberto Benzi was born in Marseilles of Italian parents in 1937. At just nine, he took the podium and at seventeen he had already directed his first opera. His career lasted more than fifty years and saw him leading the most famous orchestras in the world.
The French director Georges Lacombe made two musical films

[13] Dennis Albert Libby, *Gaspare Spontini and his French and German Operas*, PhD dissertation, Princeton University, 1969.

based on his story, in which Benzi himself acted: *Prelude a la gloire*, 1950 and *L'Appel du destin*, 1953.

Pierino Gamba (1936) from Rome, achieved fame in the 1950s. He directed his first concert when only eight, appearing on the podium with shorts and knee-length socks – an outfit he would continue to sport in the years to come.

Lorin Maazel (1930-2014) was only eight when he directed the Pittsburgh University Orchestra. In 1939 he made his debut in New York leading the *Interlochen Orchestra* and he would go on to direct the *Los Angeles Philharmonic*. In 1941, at the age of eleven, he was invited by Arturo Toscanini the *NBC Symphony Orchestra*, commenting on his performance with a "God bless you" that has gone down in history. The following year he was already on tour, leading some of the most prestigious orchestras in the USA. A curious fact: "mazel", in Yiddish, means "fortune". *Nomen omen*…as they say.

Giannella De Marco (1943-2010) debuted at the age of five at the Teatro Massimo of Pescara. The following year, in 1949, he directed the *Orchestra Nazionale dell'Accademia di Santa Cecilia* at Teatro Adriano in Roma. In 1953 he took up his baton for the *London Philharmonic*: it was his 123rd concert! Very active in Spain and South American countries, De Marco retired from conducting to devote himself to teaching, up to his death in 2010.

Clarity of gesture and perfect mastery of the use of the baton are thus fundamental. In his *Le chef d'orchestre*, Berlioz produced the first specific instructions on the use of the baton, with illustrations to show the basic movements. But, as with everything related to musical science, baton technique has also had to move with the times and adapt to particularly fragmentary and complex compositions. The conductor's gesture has always to balance out any possible difficulties in deciphering a score and for this reason, attention must be paid to posture and physical presence. Scherchen recommends "standing in a natural position, without any affectation and with the feet together"[14] and to reduce movements on the podium to a minimum, to prevent the orchestra losing cohesion. Saminsky, on the other hand, says to guard against "symmetric movement of the arms, since in doing this the gesture does not gain anything in terms of clarity or expressive effectiveness"[15]. If the right hand has the job of indicating the tempo, the left deals with phrasing and cues; it is preferable to phrase with the left arm rather than give non-indispensable cues. The main thing is that the two hands should move independently of each other. Claude Debussy described the movements of Hans Richter as he directed the Ring cycle at Bayreuth in 1876:

> If Richter looks like a prophet, when he is conducting he is Almighty God… and you may be sure that God himself would have asked Richter for some hints before embarking on such an adventure.
>
> While his right hand armed with a small unpretentious baton, secures precision of rhythm, his left hand, multiplied a hundredfold, directs the performance of each individual. The left hand is undulating and diverse, its suppleness un-

---

[14] Hermann Scherchen, *Handbook of Conducting*, Oxford 1935.
[15] Lazare Saminsky, *Essentials of Conducting*, New York 1958.

believable! Then, when it seems there is really no possibility of obtaining a greater wealth of sound, up go his two arms, and the orchestra leaps through the music with so furious an onset as to sweep the most stubborn indifference before it like a straw. Yet all this pantomime is unobtrusive and never distracts the attention unpleasantly or comes between the music and the audience.[16]

A robot on the podium

On 13 May 2008, the anthropomorphic robot ASIMO (*Advanced Step in Innovative MObility*), created by Honda engineers at the beginning of the new millennium, directed the *Detroit Symphony Orchestra* during a performance of *The Impossible Dream*, a piece taken from the musical *Man of La Mancha*, inspired by Don Quixote. But ASIMO has its limits: although it was programmed to imitate perfectly the gestures and movements of Charles Burke, conducting teacher with the Detroit orchestra, it cannot interact with the musicians. If any mistakes were to occur, ASIMO would be unable to intervene as a flesh-and-blood conductor would do. More recently a TV concert was shown in which the famous tenor Andrea Bocelli was accompanied by an orchestra directed by a robot.

---

[16] Claude Debussy, *Monsieur Croche the Dilettante Hater*, New York 1928.

Composure

A conductor should be composed and avoid walking on the podium; he should remain stiff and immobile like a statue: the best posture is not with legs wide open or feet together, a position that could compromise balance. According to Weingartner, the conductor "[must] not make any movements other than those necessary"[17] and Richard Strauss also warned against the dangers of excessively theatrical or histrionic gestures. He replied to a friend who encouraged him to move around more on the podium: "No, I don't like distracting or disturbing the audience with too much movement. The public want to listen above all else". Strauss was convinced that with an opera the orchestra should be in a secondary position in relation to the stage performance going on, and this was the principle he applied rigorously throughout his career, directing the great masters, but also with his own compositions, like the tone poem *Ein Heldenleben* (A Hero's Life), completed in 1898 and characterised by a particularly complicated score. The performance was executed with enormous concentration, passionately, but without going over the top. Strauss interpreted himself and did it by exploiting a virtuosity that was anything but self-referential, enabling him to widen the spiritual scope of his poem– not a tragedy but an intimate drama; many have considered it to be autobiographical.

Igor Stravinsky, one of the most brilliant composers of the twentieth century, also conducted with clear, simple gestures. His whole oeuvre is orientated towards limpidity and brightness: "Too much mystery has been made about art for too. We have to finally strip music away from mystery, as we have to do with painting, literature, nature itself. Mystery is what we don't know. We seek to not be unaware of anything and especially to not hide anything".[18] Whether composing or conducting, Stravinsky

---

[17] Felix Weingartner, *On Conducting*, London 1906.
[18] According to Italian composer and conductor, Adriano Lualdi.

makes balance and form his most important principles, and he favours the heightening of the *melos* also by means of some adjustments to the score. What counts is allowing the work to be understood and conveying its true spirit.

Bad conductors

"Bad orchestras do not exist", asserted Bülow, "only bad conductors". According to an anecdote, when asked by a lady about what he would play during an upcoming concert, a musician of the *Wiener Philharmoniker* allegedly replied: "What the maestro is going to direct we don't know. *We* are playing Beethoven's Seventh Symphony!"[19]. In general, the conviction that an orchestra plays better on its own than with a rotten conductor is never questioned.

This is because the conductor is the ideal bridge between the composer and the public, interpreting the former to convey it to the latter, channelled via the orchestra. Understanding the great masters does not mean simply knowing how to play the scores, but also having a deep insight into the spirit, the historical context, the whole output of the composer: only lengthy and in-depth study will allow the conductor to acquire the essential, intimate familiarity required. This is proved especially when a conductor has the dual role of house conductor/artistic director for a fixed period, tasked with deciding on the programme on the basis of the type of target audience and the cultural aims he set himself at the outset. It is not simply a question of selecting some musical pieces, but a veritable cultural quest that takes account of various historical epochs, allowing the rediscovery of less well-known music by the great masters or a first encounter with contemporary composers. In this sense his role is social, educative and managerial.

[19] In *Dictionary of Music and Musicians*, edited by Eric Blom, London 1954.

Conducting schools

Due to the lack of schools and courses teaching the art of conducting, conductors of the past had no other choice but to develop their own personal technique, not just by trusting their instincts and musical talent, but also, above all, by attending rehearsals and getting on-the-job practice. A young conductor can learn a great deal by drawing on the practical experiences of an orchestra, particularly at the beginning. One had to wait for the twentieth century for the advent of specialist schools: conducting classes were set up by, for example, the Italian Franco Ferrara (1911-1985), the Austrian Hans Swarowsky, the Finnish Jorma Juhani Panula (1930) and the Romanian Sergiu Celibidache: his method is to be considered the most scientific, since it stresses the logic of the relationship between music and the conducting gesture and the study of musical phenomenology.

The conductor turns something virtual into a concrete performance, taking on, indeed, the dignity of being co-author of the work. To fulfil this duty, he has to be inspired by a *heroic passivity* (the sixth and last ingredient for artistic success: humility) that allows him to place himself at the service of the composer, rather than presumptuously and counter-productively imposing his own personality. The conductor handles the interpretation and models the expression, the latter responsibility mainly being entrusted to the strings section. According to Hermann Scherchen, "conducting means establishing a spiritual contact among a plurality of men. The more sensitive and focused the activity aiming for this is, the more intelligible the outcome will be, generating more pleasure and deeper emotional intensity to the musicians of the orchestra". And it is this spiritual contact that shows to what extent the art of conducting is still impossible to define, let alone express in words. When the conductor succeeds in putting across his vision, his intentions, mysterious, magnetic, perhaps even magical, mechanisms come into play – and it is in this shadow zone that the fascination of the conductor continues to be felt.

Orchestral singing

The sound – the Melos

> *What is sound for a conductor? Sound is a ve-*
> *hicle for conveying a certain substance, about*
> *which we can say nothing, because it is intellec-*
> *tual in nature. Music is not sound, sound can*
> *become music.*
>
> Sergiu Celibidache

Among the fundamental principles of the conducting art,
Richard Wagner singled out one extremely important one in his
treatise *On Conducting*: the idea of *melos*. The method chosen by
Wagner was the assessment of the quality of singing.

> The best guide – he wrote – from the point of view of the
> tempo and proper execution of Beethoven's music, I found
> one day in the soulful singing of Schroeder-Devrient... But I
> was quite tranquil after I listened to, in 1839, the Ninth Sym-
> phony, which I'd had so many misgivings about, played by
> the Paris Conservatoire Orchestra. The scales fell from my
> eyes; I came to understand the value of correct execution and
> the secret of a good performance. The orchestra had learnt
> to look for Beethoven's melody in every bar – that melody
> which the worthy Leipzig musician had failed to discover;
> and the orchestra *sang* that melody.
> The influence exerted by the French musician of the Ital-
> ian school is good in this sense: music only becomes acces-
> sible through singing; playing an instrument well is, for him,
> singing. And this excellent Parisian orchestra snag this sym-

phony well. But to sing it well, it was necessary to find the true tempo; and this is the second point that impressed me at the time. Old Habeneck was not the medium of any abstract-aesthetical inspiration. He was devoid of genius – but he found the right tempo whilst particularly fixing the attention of his orchestra upon the *melos* of the symphony.

The right comprehension of the *melos* is the sole guide to the right tempo; these two things are inseparable; the one implies and qualifies the other. As a proof of my assertion that the majority of performances of instrumental music with us are faulty it is sufficient to point out that our conductors so frequently fail to find the true tempo because they are ignorant of singing. Singing is thus the only way that leads to precise comprehension, to the the accurate interpretation of any music, even apparently less singable music.

Not only the "discovery" of the exact tempo is to be found in the concept and the practice of singing; there is also phrasing, the right accent, punctuation, pausing and breathing. This was the only method, which Wagner acknowledged as having been borrowed by the French from the Italians, and which was followed instinctively not just by all Italian nineteenth-century conductors, but also by all Italian composers. And this is one of the cornerstones (among various traditional and special features) of Italian opera.

Start with singing: this is what has always been done in Italy in the vocality of opera, from Jacopo Peri to Puccini. Out of Italy it has always been followed by all composers who wrote dynamic operas: Wagner in his most powerful, dramatic works, the Moussorgsky of *Boris Godunov*, the Debussy of *Pelléas and Mélisande*, Bloch's *Macbeth*. *Start with singing*: this is what was in the mind of all composers, from Giovan Battista Lulli to Verdi; and composers, once, were also conductors.

"Specializing" in conducting only came later, prompting the decadence of the art. *Start with singing*: this is what has always been done by the greatest conductors, from Mariani to

Mancinelli to Toscanini to Victor de Sabata, and what is still being done today. No method can match *singing* a phrase for effectiveness, to convey the model to be imitated, the character, the tempo, the accent, the breathing, intimate feeling – all that makes up the *indefinable* in music.

I heartily recommend that young conductors attend singing schools and sing at the top of their voices the scores they have to learn by heart. For example, Verdi's *Falstaff*, accompanying themselves on the piano. Singing means being able to follow sung music; getting a feel for the phrasing, penetrating the secret of that spontaneous elasticity of the tempo that only this way will fully harmonise with the sense of the phrase quadrature. *Start with singing*: not just solo singers, but also choral or orchestral ensembles. Arturo Toscanini also stressed this: "Many times I have felt that the choir and the orchestra need to sing, and so, without them noticing, I gradually abandon them to their sound instincts and enthusiasm; and it's me who's following them".

Wagner, speaking about a *cantabile* passage of the Prelude to *Die Meistersinger*, was of the same opinion; he wrote: "It is enough to follow the spontaneous sentiment of the players to obtain the warmth required".

To clarify the concept of *melos* as expounded by Wagner – which underpins every symphonic performance – it should be specified that the art of orchestral singing, the search for *melos*, lies in isolating each part of the whole, the concatenation of which makes up the interrupted line of the melodic idea, the central thread. This thread may also be a rhythmical design or a fragment of symphonic dialogue; a particular orchestral colour can be "isolated" when all the parts making it up are highlighted and brought to the right degree of intensity of sound and expression. It sometimes happens that the tone-colours indicated in relation to the totality of the parts are insufficient to ensure (spontaneously with the execution) that the central thread is asserted strongly. In such cases the conductor has to emphasise the internal part which, remaining in in the shadows, might compromise the *melos*.

Claude Debussy often used the expression *en dehors* in his scores, thus putting the emphasis on the melodic idea. It is essential to recognise and highlight the *melos* of every musical work. Wagner, in some cases, did not hesitate to lay his hands even on Beethoven's works (as I noted in my book *Beethoven 2000*, Pendragon, Bologna 2007).

But Felix Weingartner also observed, drew attention to, and found to be fully justified what for years was called *"arbitrio"*, or free will, a sort of manipulation of the score. He intervened dramatically in Beethoven's compositions in which the instrumentation did not reflect the intentions of the author, due to the limitations of the instruments of the time and because the increasing deafness of the composer altered the balance of the various instruments.

Lazare Saminsky was of the opinion too that some scores required "touching up": "For the woodwind's notes or their solos to be perceived through the mass of strings, in any Beethoven symphony, the instructions for the timbres in the score have to be subjected to some modification. In the canon of the *allegretto* of the Seventh Symphony, the group of strings, if following the notation, would stifle the clarinet solo, if we examine Beethoven's colours...". The clarinet solo, a fragment of *melos*, takes absolute priority. Emphasis on the *melos*, the overarching thread of the musical discourse, is the primary element that has to be observed by the the conductor to achieve clarity of performance.

Even in executions by renowned conductors (not Antonio Guarnieri, who is among the most sensitive directors of this work by Debussy, or the French (including the outstanding Albert Wolf), I have happened to notice several times, in these pages of *L'Apres midi d'un faune*, that the cellos' two semiquaver triplets (after the 3 horn and the violas have stopped at Re) disappear, despite the hairpin of *crescendo*; and that the extremely important entrance of the cor anglais and the two clarinets on the second bar, a crucial element of the *melos*, is barely audible and not stressed sufficiently.

Claude Debussy, *Prelude a l'Après midi d'un faune*

This usually happens because the conductor does not understand the value and the musical delicacy of the cello passage and hence cannot convey this to the musicians; and because, in the second case, he allows the *forte* of the horns, oboe, second violins and violas to be overwhelming, heavy and flat, while he fails to let the music breathe freely or let the poetic life force emerge.

We have on this page of *La notte di Platon [The Night of Plato]* by Victor de Sabata, an example of *melos* fragmented and split between various classes of instruments; it has to be recomposed in a particular way and kept extremely prominent above the subsidiary parts. The lines that should be most emphasised are those of the oboes, cor anglais and bassoons, to which the vigorous responses of the three trumpets are at once a conclusion and an impulse towards further developments. The orchestra has to be well aware of this woodwind-trumpet dialogue; it is therefore necessary to practise it separately.

Victor de Sabata, *La notte di Platon*, Ricordi

Movement

Another basic issue to which Wagner frequently returns in his essay is that of Tempos and Indications. According to J.S. Bach one should set the tempo by starting with singing. But Bach tended to measure everything by the yardstick of genius, and this may not be appropriate for every rhythm and every form. Moreover, we must consider that the meaning of "fixed" words to denote tempo changed considerably, not just from one century to another, but also among composers of the same epoch, leading to various interpretations. It would be impossible to cite here even a tiny fraction of the cases in which totally different meanings are applied to the words *allegro,* or *adagio* or *andante* in terms of pace in a written text. Wagner's observation should be noted: "In Haydn and Mozart the indication of tempo was often generic. *Andante,* a mean between *allegro* and *adagio,* included all that they deemed necessary in a few simple expressions and gradations". In J.S. Bach, indication of tempo is almost wholly absent and this is, from a musical point of view, for the best. Bach wrote: "For he who does not understand my theme and who does not feel its character or expression, what good can this indication of tempo in Italian do?".

Wagner continued: "The character of the the older classical, or as I call it naïve, *allegro* differs greatly from the new emotional, sentimental *allegro* peculiar to Beethoven".

And elsewhere, apropos of Beethoven's *allegro*: "On careful examination of the principal motifs of the *allegro,* it will be found that the melody (Gesang) derived from the *adagio* predominates". And of the *adagio*: "None of our conductors is courageous enough to take an *adagio* in the correct manner; they always begin by looking for some bit of figuration and arrange their tempo to match".

One only has to reflect on the different meanings of the word *andante,* to realise how difficult it is to establish absolute fixed rules. "*Andante*", one of the oldest musical markings, means at a moderately slow tempo. *Più andante, un poco andante,* mean faster, not slower. *Meno andante* means a little slower. Apart from countless cases, however, where *andante* can mean at a moderate pace, indeed rather *mosso* (fast, animated).

We have substantial evidence of conductors, even among the most authoritative, of the last century, who considered *andante*, especially when applied to eighteenth-century music, as being closer to *lento* than *mosso*. There was a notorious dispute between Vincent d'Indy and the Opera Comique di Parigi, after a performance of *Iphigénie en Aulide* by Gluck and Camille Saint-Saens's tirade: "Avec cette lenteur que l'on croit devoir infliger aux oeuvres de Gluck, alors que, dans les oeuvres modernes, on semble ne pouvoir jamais courir assez vite, comment peut-on que ces oeuvres anciennes ne paraissent pas ennuyeuses?". In many of Maelzel's metronomes the *andante* goes from about 120 to 152, approaching tempos that can lie within some *allegro* gradations: there is a wide difference of opinions regarding the meaning of certain derivations from this principal tempo; Hugo Riemann asserts that the diminutive form *andantino* more often than not refers to a short extension of the piece or to the brevity of its subdivisions (cfr. *Adagietto*).

But the vast majority of authors, and current praxis, attribute to the word *andantino* a meaning of movement; just that some claim it means slower than *andante*, and others, more *vivo* (brisk, lively) than *andante*.

Curiously, in the *Encyclopedie des gens du monde*, under the entry for "*Andantino*", we read: "*plus vif qu'andante*"; and under the entry for *mouvement* we find: "*Andantino, plus lent qu'andante*".

Undoubtedly, *andantino* is faster than *andante*.

Hector Berlioz, who was usually very confident in his own opinions, also felt uncomfortable in this regard. Let us take a look at his words from his wonderful *Appendix* to *Treatise on Instrumentation: on Conducting*:

If the conductor has neither the instructions of the composer nor traditional metronomic indications – as is frequently the case with works written before the invention of the metronome – he had no other guide than the customary, very vague tempo markings; for the rest he must rely on his own instinct and feeling for the composer's style. To be sure, it cannot be denied that these guides are frequently insufficient or misleading.

This is proved by the manner in which older operas are given in towns where the tradition for these works has been lost. I once heard a chorus from *Ifigenia in Tauride* performed in a German theatre. Instead of an *allegro non troppo* in 4-4 time, it was played *allegro assai* in 2-2 time, i.e. twice as fast.

I could quote an immense number of similar mistakes caused either by the ignorance and negligence of the conductor, or by the fact that sometimes it is really very difficult for even the most talented and careful man to discover the exact meaning of the Italian tempo marks.

Still on the subject of tempo, Berlioz complains about another fault that is still very common today:

> There are men in the prime of their life, but with a sluggish temperament, whose blood seems to circulate *moderato*. If they have to conduct an *allegro assai*, they gradually let it become a *moderato*. If, on the contrary, it is *largo* or *andante sostenuto* of some length, they will have speeded it up to a *moderato* long before the end has been reached. *Moderato* is their natural pace and they will return to it as infallibly as a pendulum whose oscillations have been accelerated or retarded for a moment. These people are born enemies of all characteristic music and the greatest destroyers of style.

Carl Maria von Weber, who was also a conductor, indeed among the finest of his time, had greater trust in the players' instincts and feelings. In a letter to to *Generalmusikdirektor* Praeger, of Leipzig, which Weingartner reproduced almost in its entirety, he says, among other things, on the subject of movement: " The beat must not be a tyranically impeding or driving hammer, but rather should be to a piece of music what the pulse-beat is to the life of man. There is no slow tempo in which there aren't passages that demand a quicker motion, in order to prevent a feeling of dragging. Consequently, there is no *presto* that does not need at some points a quieter delivery, so as not to preclude, through rushing, the means of expressiveness".

"For all of this" concluded Weber, "we have in music no means of notation. These lie solely in the feelings of men's heart: and if they cannot be found there, then neither the metronome, which can only prevent the crudest of blunders, will help nor will such at beat incomplete indications as I might be prepared to incorporate to enrich my material, were I not warned against this by many experiences as a result of which I am forced to consider this already as superfluous and useless, and fear them as being misrepresentative".

Felix Weingartner also contrasts, aphoristically, the two extreme tempos: "No tempo *lento* should be so slow that the melody is no longer recognisable; no tempo *allegro* should be so fast that the melody comes out no longer recognisable".

If the *accuracy* of the tempo is therefore necessary for establishing the character of the work of art (Wagner says of his *Tannhauser* overture: 12 minutes in a performance directed by him; 20 minutes in a performance directed by one of his beloved Kapellmeister; a small error of principle, in the Movement), elasticity of tempo is necessary for making it sing, making it vibrate with life. Or at least, for not annihilating it.

Is enormous effort required to achieve this, which is another fundamental element in the art of conducting? Also in this case, education and enthusiasm count to some extent. What is essential above all, however, is an artist's soul, talent and temperament.

Dynamics – "colour"

Dynamics relates to the the importance of the musical phenomenon as far as balance and the possibilities of the various instruments is concerned

Sergiu Celibidache

"For example, the orchestra played nothing but *mezzo forte*, it never reached real *fortes*, nor descended to real *pianos*".

This oft repeated observation by Richard Wagner might be reiterated today with regard to the majority of orchestras. Of curse, it depends very much on the undemanding conductor. The sense of *melos*, the right tempo, clarity, the expressiveness of the baton, sense of pitch, colour and dynamics, combined with rhythm, are the essential qualities that distinguish a conductor. Sound artistic discipline in an orchestra can only be attained by spending a long time playing together, with constant guidance. A conductor must be conscientious and passionate, capable of instilling in his orchestral ensemble a mental habit, a sense of musical culture and professional ethic. Here is a noteworthy example of artistic discipline:

Johannes Brahms, *Variations on at Theme by Haydn*

In this magnificent page of J. Brahms' Variations on at Theme by Haydn, at bars 5 and 6 of letter G, it is of paramount importance to play the ties between the wind and string instruments clearly and vigorously. Starting with the *piano e leggero* (soft and light) that follows the first *sforzato* (strained) chroma of the first bar, the effect should be, in these 5th and 6th bars, like a sudden crackling eruption of a fire of passion. To achieve maximum effectiveness in executing both the ties and the accent, it is advisable to practise separately with the wind and string instruments, also to ensure that, at the 5th bar, the orchestra does not immediately fling itself into the *forte*, but observes the hairpin.

Recalling what Wagner said about orchestras always playing *mezzo-forte* (a common occurrence): "This sonority, which one might define "of convenience", does not cost the orchestra any effort. Reaching *piano* or *forte*, let alone, *pianissimo* or *fortissimo*, requires enormous effort. It is the conductor's duty to demand the greatest dynamic differentiation". Allowing an orchestra to always play *mezzo-forte* is, for the conductor, cultivating one of the worst forms of indifference towards the art. It is a mark of insensitivity that the conductor brands on himself. It is like removing light, shadow and colour from a painting. A fundamental rule regarding dynamics was set out by Wagner: "The *piano sostenuto* sound and the *forte sostenuto* sound are the two poles of the entire orchestral dynamic". He went further: " Our orchestras nowadays hardly know what is meant by equally sustained tone".

As for the opening of his Symphony in C minor, Beethoven suggests this beginning: "Hold firm my *fermata* firmly, terribly!".

How many times, while listening to this symphony, have I heard that robust E flat in the opening motif dissolve from *fortissimo* into *mezzoforte*, and lose all its dramatic quality.

Hans von Bülow loved to repeat a fundamental principle of orchestral dynamics, recalled by Weingartner: "The beginning of a *diminuendo* means *forte* and the beginning of a *crescendo* means *piano*":

Crescendo: *PIANISSIMO; PIANO; MEZZO-PIANO*
        MEZZO-FORTE; FORTE; FORTISSIMO.
        (The opposite for *diminuendo*)

Another common mistake made by novice conductors, and even the odd mature, expert one, is that of not judging the proportions of the extreme poles of orchestral sonority, from *pianissimo* to *fortissimo*. It is obvious that the *fortissimo* of one of Haydn's symphonies could not, nor should not, have the same volume as the *fortissimo* of a Brahms' symphony, nor the same weight as the *fortissimo* of a symphonic poem by Strauss or a symphonic piece by Stravinsky.

On account of the different instrumental components that the compositions in a programme demand, it is essential to adapt the various sonorities to suit the style and character of each piece. One might notice that a conductor forces the sonority inappropriately, demanding an excessive *forte* in classical compositions, while he neglects to call for a *fortissimo* in contemporary composers, who often rely on these provocative, exasperating sounds to lend their work its special character.

Another error should be pointed out: not making the *accents*, the *sforzando*, the *forcelle* (hairpins) of *crescendo* and *diminuendo* proportionate to the fundamental colour, to the sound environment. It is obvious that in a *piano*, a *sforzando* or an *accent* touch either *fortissimo* or *forte*; they should, at most, reach the *mezzo piano*. This should also hold for the *forcelle*; and for the sudden *piano* or *smorzando* (dying away) effects in a *forte* or *fortissimo*.

Berlioz is right when he says: "Often a conductor demands from his musicians a certain exaggeration of the nuances indicated by the composer, either from a lack of delicate musical feeling or from a desire to give emphatic proof of his zeal. He does not understand the character and style of the work. The nuances become distortions, the accents turn into outcries. The intentions of the poor composer are completely disfigured". The conductor/artist must pay great attention to the nuances and accents.

There may sometimes be the need to correct certain deficiencies in the instrumentation, by modifying the balance of the instrumental groups or lessening the equilibrium of the timbres. I have been able to gain much invaluable experience by watching numerous rehearsals led by Sergiu Celibidache, Herbert von Karajan and Georg Solti. I might summarise this experience as follows:

1) The conductor must take particular care with the quality, sound balance and purity of sound of the orchestra, as well as totally respecting the dynamics. The *forte* should never be too boisterous or coarse; and, conversely, the *piano* should never be lacking in vibration and spirit. Nothing is more common, more

banal, in string instruments than, to obtain *pianissimo*, barely brushing the strings.

One should avoid brass instruments overrunning, woodwinds hardening sounds to the point of sounding unpleasant, strings "scraping" to obtain a *fortissimo*. Quality, beauty of sound and a tastefulness should be the conductor/artist's watchwords in his work.

2) To dose the *forte* and the *fortissimo* in the style of the composition, it is advisable to balance the various instrumental groups in such a way as to hear the particular sonority with clarity. A *fortissimo* of Mozart in which the two trumpets and the horns smother all the rest of the orchestra is an aesthetic and stylistic error. Therefore, it is essential to arrange the orchestral components according to the style and character of the programme to be executed.

The conductor should interpret the composer's intentions, without imposing his own construction on it, and keep a check on the apocalyptic sonorities of the brass section and the excessively delicate sounds of the strings, in order to attain the right balance and audibility of all the instrumental groups. Giving prominence to solo instruments can be achieved through the active collaboration of the orchestra: all players must constantly listen to themselves, and diminish their sound appropriately to allow the soloist to stand out. This principle of individual control on the part of the players was summed up perfectly, in terms of dynamics, by Arturo Toscanini: "I don't know who taught me this, but I always repeat this axiom: in the *pianissimos* each player should get to the point where he no longer hears his own instrument; in the *fortissimos* he should hear *his* instrument among all of them".

The baton and technique

Cheironomy

Hector Berlioz, in his treatise *On Conducting*, discussing the conductor's baton, complains that many conductors are unable to accompany the "allures capricieuses du recitatif" with the orchestra. "Nathan Bloc [conductor of Berlioz' song *La mort d'Orphée*] était dans ce cas; ... Or, quand vint, après le premier air d'Orphée, un récitatif entremelé de dessins d'orchestre concertants, il ne put jamais venir à bout d'assurer certaines entrées instrumentales".

If Bloc had arranged *La mort d'Orphée* on the piano at the time, Hector Berlioz would surely have withheld his harsh criticism.

To successfully execute recitatives and accompaniments of the solo, vocal or instrumental parts, it is essential for the conductor to firstly hold a piano rehearsal. It is through this invaluable preparation that the conductor fixes the general and particular aspects of his interpretation. Moreover, all the appropriate "conventions" for a successful and expressive execution of the recitatives and declamations are in this way fine-tuned. The rehearsal should be run with great patience and thoroughness, with the aim of removing any uncertainties among the players about their live performance, so that "going on stage" will be considered by them to be arriving at their destination. For a novice conductor, rehearsals are the best testing ground to perfect his gestures so that they are in line with the music. Many little problems regarding gesture can be cleared up in practice with a piano.

We have already mentioned the active collaboration of the orchestra. Before coming on to conducting gestures, however, we might consider the situation of a young conductor finding himself in front of a massed orchestra. If he does not succeed in instilling interest and attention in the orchestra, he will be waving his arms around for nothing; he will never obtain the collaboration that is vital for delivering a fine performance. What does interest mean? It means being totally familiar with the score, having a very clear plan of interpretation, never wasting time and never stopping the orchestra without good reason. As the rehearsals proceed, the conductor should gradually demand more and more of the players; the orchestra should be stopped to clear up any misconceptions, even the slightest nuances, and a "breather" may be taken – the conductor should not speak until there is total silence.

It is imperative that the orchestra should not be made to repeat a page without first having had it explained to them in crystal clear terms what mistakes have been made, what colours need to be touched up. Conductors who stop the ensemble and say simply "Take it from the top", without any explanation will have a disastrous effect on the orchestra from the psychological point of view. They should never lose their temper or erupt into fits of anger. Histrionic gestures are now out of fashion. They were common among conductors of previous centuries, who tried to outdo each other in rudeness towards the players. This is no longer the case; orchestras have attained an extremely high level of quality as compared with the past.

Anyone who loses his temper only shows that he is weak. What he should do is isolate the erring instrument or row of instruments. The passage should be repeated as often as necessary until perfect performance is achieved. Meanwhile the orchestra is silent and listens, realising that the conductor knows exactly what he wants. This serious way of working is often hampered for young conductors by shyness and the best medicine for overcoming this is time. Age, experience and the confidence deriving from one's past achievements work wonders. There are only two ways of improving: self-control and unending study. Watching many rehearsals is very helpful for the novice, who can thus take on board how the conductor instructs the various instrumentalists (phrasing, agogics, dynamics) and the effect the his directions produce, the global reaction. One must be completely sure of the rhythmical structure of a piece, of the development of the various movements.

Advising one to practise one's conducting gestures in front of the mirror is unnecessary – I do not see any point in this method. The gesture has to come from within, it has to be measured and relevant to the music being played, so that someone who is conducting has only one concern: listening to the orchestra. A sense of humour is a great advantage – psychophysically, after at least an hour of intense practising, some witty banter can do much ease the tension.

Berlioz explained the fundamentals for the use of the baton and he added schematic illustrations of figures to the theoretical data: that the baton should trace in the air in accordance with the binary, ternary or polyrhythmic beat patterns and their associated subdivisions. Of all the nineteenth-century essays on the subject, Berlioz' was the most accurate, and was subsequently perfected in practical terms by Wagner.

New technical issues in conducting arose as a result of compositions that were fragmentary and characterised by polyrthythmic parts: the first was Igor Stravinsky, con *Petrushka*, and particularly *Sacre du Printemps* (1913). Now the new technique no longer had to hinge on the division of the beat, but on a synthesis of various different rhythmical structures: and this is simply absurd and amateurish. The conductor, supported by clear scientific technique, has to respect the polyrhythm, without disguising the original scansion intended by the composer.

The form, the architectural proportions of the work and the balance of the great rhythmic cycles and their phrasing are the constant concerns of Stravinsky. Even in the pages that at first sight look more complicated and demanding in their rhythmic structure, it does not take long for the sense of order and equilibrium typical of the artist to reveal themselves to the scholar and the performer and to offer simple solution to the technical problems of the baton, even the ones that are apparently most

Igor Stravinsky, *Sacre du Printemps*

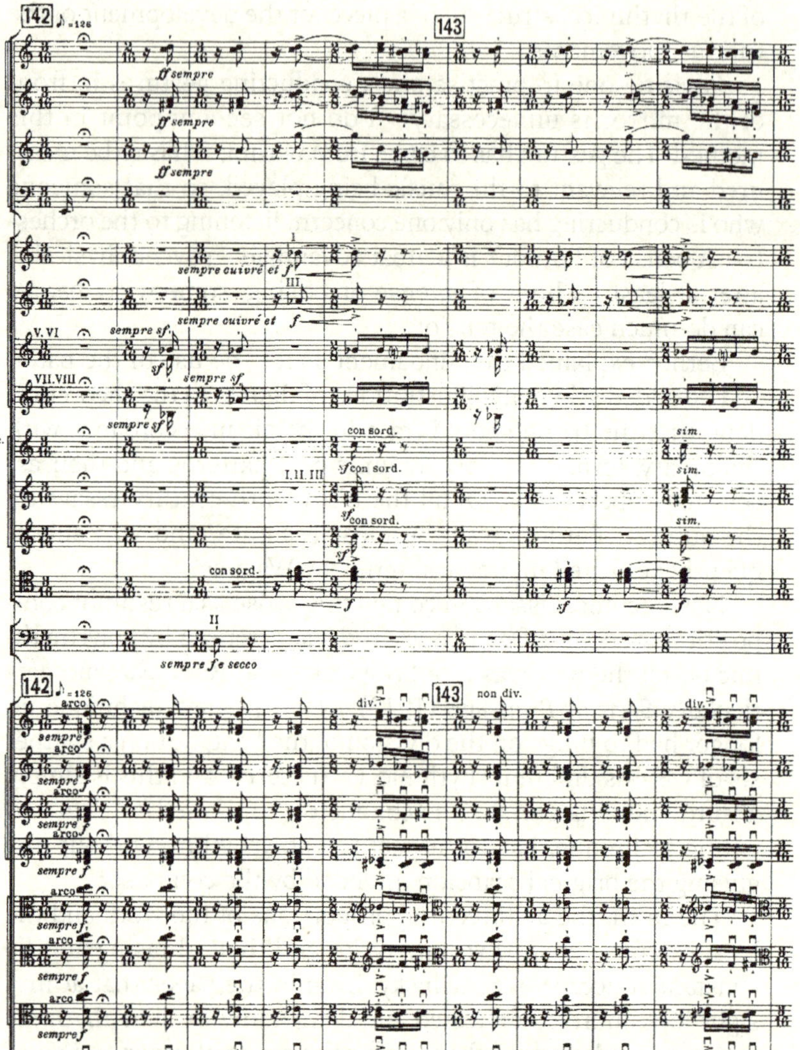

abstruse. Looking at this page one can see how the rhythmic phrasing of bars 3 and 4 are easily identifiable and naturally suggests what the strategy regarding the baton should be.

Hermann Scherchen stressed: "Even where the musicians' scores lack directions on the timbres of execution, the degree of dynamic, the speed, the tone-colour and the strength of expression with which a phrase should be played, they should be able to understand everything immediately and clearly via the gesture. Conducting means establishing a spiritual contact between a multiplicity of men; the more sensitive and focused this bond is, the more intelligible the result will be, giving greater pleasure and deeper emotional intensity to the musicians of the orchestra".

His method prescribes that the young conductor must only step onto the podium after he has learnt the score by heart – extremely helpful and important advice. Then whether he conducts with or without the score when on the pedestal is relatively unimportant.

Weingartner asserted that a good execution directed with a score has value, while a bad execution conducted from memory is worthless. The public goes to concert halls to listen to good performances, not to see a conductor show off how wonderful his memory is. Anyone who takes the art of conducting seriously has to realise that it is virtually impossible to take the podium and exploit the hours of rehearsal, be respected by the orchestra and achieve a sense of cohesion, not just in terms of discipline, but also of bonding, collaboration, and spiritual communication, if one has not memorised the score.

Nevertheless, the art is not a simple one. It is an arduous task for the conductor, but the orchestra will immediately be aware that on the podium there is a conductor who, as Hans von Bülow said, keeps the score in his head and not his head in the score.

Other two pieces of advice from Hermann Scherchen that should be noted: "On the podium stand in a natural position, without affectation, with feet almost together". Young conductors tend to stand with their legs wide apart like the Colossus of Rhodes or go for a stroll on the podium. So no walking or dancing... Apart from aesthetic considerations, there are also practical ones. With continual waggling of legs, arm and baton, how is an orchestra supposed to play as a compact, closely-knit unit? The only point of reference should be the baton.

"Maximum adherence of the gesture to the music"

Saminsky made an acute observation about the wrong way to conduct, that is, using symmetrical movements of the arms: indeed, the gesture gains nothing in terms of clarity or expressive effectiveness by this. In conducting, the left hand should not know what the right hand is doing. If the role of the right hand is rhythmical, that of the left is "multi-purpose". Increasing or reducing sonority, marking the accents, controlling the syncopation, ensuring the correct entries of instrument groups or soloists, removing a *fermata*, supporting instruments that have to hold a long note – these are just some of the duties of the left hand.

It is interesting to note how Claude Debussy described the conducting gestures of Hans Richter, the renowned Hungarian master, who was chosen by Richard Wagner in 1876 in Bayreuth:

> If Richter seems like a prophet, when he conducts he seems like Almighty God...

And here we have in Richter, "the right hand not knowing what the left hand is doing"; like all great conductors, he had an innate gift for gesturing with the arms, hands and eyes (eyeglasses not recommended). He recalled Weingartner, on the subject of *tempo rubato* (tempo marking that instructs the performer to freely, expressively speed up or slow down at certain passages) conductors "who fail to make obscure passages simpler and go looking for insignificant details".

Cheironomy (the art of gesture): a little aside to outline the history of this old word and the art it generated. Cheironomy means the totality of gestures that can be seen in Egyptian sculptures and paintings dating from as far back as 4000 BC, where a leader used hand signals to direct a group of singers; and thus, by extension, the method of directing choral performances, whose origins can be traced back to antiquity, which consisted of indicating with movements of the hand the tempo, as well as how high or low the notes that the voice had to sing were, going to make up the choral melopoeia. Indeed, so interlinked with the idea of singing was cheironomy that for "sing" in the ancient Egyptian language, one said: *hsjt m drt*, "make music with the hand".

The Hindus had a treatise, *Manduki s'iksha* in which a series of hand movements is presented schematically in tables. The Greeks frequently used the word *cheironomia* (χειρονομία) to describe the direction of musical performances, and it is mentioned in the writings of Quintilian and Xenophon. It appears that cheironomy was passed on to the Christians through the Coptic Church; it is certain, however, that in some miniatures of medieval liturgical codices we can see choir leaders with their hands raised, but not in the gesture of indicating the beats. And it is from hand gestures that the seeds of the medieval neumatic notational system derived, that is, the graphic symbols of *arsis* (*tempo forte*, acute accent, from bottom up and from left to right – upbeat) and *thesis* (*tempo debole* [weak, faint], from top down and from left to right – downbeat).

From these drawings it is easy to infer the origins of the neumatic notational marks that have come down to us via Gregorian chant. Evidence shows that the use of cheironomy was a normal practice in the Middle Ages. Rhythm and melody were "painted" or "incited" by movements of the hand: *"meditari manu, manum ad modulos sequentiae pingendos levare, incitare manu"*. In his work *Über das Dirigieren mittelalterlicher Gesangschöre*, the Benedictine Gregorian authority Ambrosius Kienle wrote: "the hand, stretched up to express a passionate *crescendo* in the melody, is lowered slowly and solemnly in the performance of more languid music and gently denotes an emotional tone; then the hand is raised again slowly and solemnly, then suddenly is lifted rapidly for a moment, like a column reaching skyward". Indeed, the cheironomic system is so closely linked to Gregorian chant that cheironomic directions is still in use today and is considered necessary for achieving an effective, expressive choral performance of Gregorian monophonic chant.

Even when not directing plainchant, choirmasters rarely use a baton, but follow the cheironomic system which is universally judged to be the most efficacious for choral singing.

Interpretation – expression

The performer cannot enhance the value of a
work; if anything, he can only reduce it
Felix Weingartner

In order to achieve an excellent performance, it is necessary to pay careful attention to sound quality; consequently, a conductor must have an excellent knowledge of the techniques employed by each instrument. Sir Charles Halle said that that a good conductor should be able to play as many instruments as possible, and that he should also have "psychological" powers to inculcate in the orchestra members a desire to play "above and beyond"; he must demand, involve, arouse enthusiasm.

He must constantly impose the strictest technical-artistic discipline: uniformity and intensity of *cavata*, equivalence of vibrato, total unity in bow-strokes, in particular with the various types of *staccato* and *legato*.

The conductor should possess charisma, authoritativeness and technical competence, since modern orchestras are highly professional ensembles that can even play without a conductor; he has to be a psychologist and know how to motivate a massive group of people, where esprit de corps and camaraderie have been known to create unpleasant situations.

He has to gain the esteem and trust of the musicians, who will know the repertoire inside out.

Franz Strauss, father of the composer Richard, and first horn of the Munich Court Orchestra, asserted in his autobiography that he could gauge the quality of a conductor as soon as he came on stage: "as soon as he stepped onto the podium, before even picking up the baton, we immediately knew whether it would be he or the orchestra that was in command"

Hans Von Bülow was wont to repeat that "bad orchestras don't exist, just bad conductors".

A New York critic wrote in the 1920s that "A good orchestra plays better without any conductor at all than with a bad conductor!" (R. Simon in a review of a concert by a newly-founded conductorless orchestra). The hardest and most strenuous task for the conductor is undoubtedly interpretation. It is only possible to attain total faithfulness to the works of the greatest composers in history if one manges to "come out of oneself" and devote the fullest attention and energy to understanding the piece to be performed. "Heroic passivity": passive, since the need for the sacrifice is implied, imposing a constraint on any free initiative; and heroic, since this mythical quality emerges in the performance: interpreting Mozart or Beethoven means "experiencing" the anxieties and dramas of their lives.

These kinds of ideas elevate the figure of the musical performer to an extremely high status – in his sphere he is seen as a genius, a co-author. A dignified status, not to be confused with the foolish presumption of thinking one can superimpose one's personality on the brilliance or taste of Bach or Wagner, of Monteverdi or Verdi, who warn: "What we have composed, respect it!".

The agonising aim of the performer as he approaches a work of art can only be one: reproducing the spirit of the work of art, to the letter.

Interpretation is, in our musical world, above all "expression". But if in the wind section, expression may be suggested to each individual soloist by the conductor, as far as the strings are concerned, they must be coordinated and moulded only by the conductor. Heinrich Heine stressed this too: the string ensemble is the basis of the expression for an orchestra.

Instructions should be given concisely and precisely – excessively dramatic and frenzied direction, apart from confusing the players, arouses in them a sort of goliardic exuberance and spirit of transgression, thus compromising the authority and credibility of the maestro and distracting the audience.

In 1835, Schumann said that "affectation and frenetic gesticulation are buffoonery if displayed in public, although they may be acceptable at rehearsal stage". Weingartner, in his treatise, emphasised that the conductor "should not make any movement that is not strictly necessary".

Our forerunners had no conducting schools to rely on, so they were forced to devise their own technique, supported by unfailing instinct and a brilliant sense of musicality. In the past conductors could afford to have a substantial number of rehearsals to prepare their programme. Today, due to the high costs involved in running an orchestra, this luxury is no longer possible.

Equally, it is advisable to avoid gestures that are too restrained or "laid back". Conducting technique, as we have seen, is a crucial factor, a starting point for every maestro on the podium; for anyone who has not painstakingly acquired it, conducting becomes impossible. It often happens in London that the *Sacre du Printemps* is put on after only one rehearsal. Charisma cannot be taught, technique can. For this reason, in the twentieth century, schools devoted to perfecting conducting technique sprung up: among these we might mention that of the unforgettable Franco Ferrara – thirty years of mentoring hundreds of now acclaimed conductors, the Accademia Chigiana in Siena, Jorma Panula's academy in Finland and my numerous Masterclasses in many European countries. But the most rigorous, "scientific" school remains Sergiu Celibidache's.

The young aspiring conductor can also learn many important things from Richard Strauss. Strauss recalled that in Vichy, after a performance of *Salome*, directed on the occasion of a music festival, he rejoined his friends, fresh as a daisy, not the least fatigued, without a drop of sweat on his brow, not even having had to change his shirt. Often one of his acqaintances would urge him before he took to the podium: "Come on, move around a bit, do something, that's what the audience wants to see". But he, during performances of *Salome*, did not move at all and the orchestra remained well in the background in relation to the

stage; in this way the opera was revealed in all its real significance and expressive force; it was no longer the usual symphonic
poem with its scenic pantomime. After *Salome*, Richard Strauss
would smile good-naturedly and say: "No, I don't like distracting
or disturbing the audience with too much movement; the public
wants to listen above all else".

Also in a symphonic concert in Rome, Richard Strauss remained loyal to his conducting style and if anyone had tried to
get him to "move around a bit, do something", he would have
been wasting his time and breath. He directed not only Rossini
and Haydn, but also his own *Ein Heldenleben*, that supreme expression of German baroque music, with its heroic struggle to
assert individuality and and ideal: this monumental, passionate
page of autobiography, in which the spirit of an unquestionably
magnificent art is abandoned to the most colourful and enthralling excesses, with the imperturbable detachment of an integral classic. In every moment of the score, with its rhythmic
and polyphonic complexity and richness, Strauss displayed total
clarity and impeccable technical precision. The incident of the
fight, after the fanfare of the trumpets, led to an extremely powerful climax. Richard Strauss was able to instil so much spirituality and profundity into the whole execution!

The contained gesture, absolutely devoid of any theatrics, but
lit by a fierce internal flame, during the performance of *Ein
Heldenleben*, directed by himself, restored the poem to its true,
original expression, which is that of an intimate drama, not a
tragedy.

Indeed, through his magisterial auto-interpretation, Strauss'
music gained much in spirituality, depth and poetic significance,
as well as in harmony and proportion in relation to the whole.
He shunned the ostentation of virtuosity, which he regarded as
a means of expression and not an end in itself; and he brought
to the fore the spiritual quintessence of the work. Less fire-
works, more music. This is the lesson that Richard Strauss imparted, without, however, appearing to do so.

One cannot, of course, forget to mention the conducting art

of one of the most brilliant figures of the twentieth century: Igor Stravinsky. In Naples, for a concert at the Conservatoire San Pietro a Majella, he had read the whole of Tchaikovsky's Third Symphony, never previously performed in Italy, and wisely suggested: "It is necessary for the orchestra to know the whole work and form an idea of its architecture before beginning the practice". He employed confident, clear-cut gestures and simple strategies; on the podium he showed the profound musicality and spontaneous sensitivity that distinguish truly great composer-conductors. As the creator, he could read between the lines and convey the spirit of the composition to the orchestra masterfully. One has to have seen his rehearsals to realise just how many points of contact exist between the composing art and the conducting art. The primitive force in him was possessed of its own light and impetus, revealing starkly what is opaque.

He demonstrated such knowledge and irony as to make one think of *Praise of Folly* by Erasmus of Rotterdam, and so much craftsmanship as to make one meditate. His surprising leaps, from *Petrushka* to *Sacre du Printemps*, from *Feu d'artifice* to *Rossignol*, from *Oedipus Rex* to *Jeu de cartes*, showed his constant wish to renew himself, to relish his sense of freedom.

One day Stravinsky was speaking with Diaghilev and Michel Georges about education: "Yes, I've shown my son how babies are made by taking him to a field to see the animals running free, why make a mystery of the most natural thing in the world?". "But mystery – came the reply – enriches love". "It's a mistake, a beautiful naked body will always be more attractive than a beautiful clothed body. We've had mystery in art for far too long. We have to at long last strip music of its mystery, like painting, like literature, like nature itself. Mystery is what we don't know. We don't want to "not know" anything, or, especially, to hide anything. Mystery is still a sort of impressionism".

In Stravinsky's music there is so much sun, and everything is so blatantly illuminated and precise, that there is no room for mystery. Polyrhythm, the brilliance of the orchestration, the harshness of the clashes of certain cords and timbres, the ironic mischievousness, the cynical cruelty of some of his jests these are all phenomena associated with the sun. His conducting art, whatever the piece that was being played, was underpinned perfectly by clarity of exposition, balance of the masses of sound and the prominence of *melos*. Sometimes, on the entrance of a soloist, he would replace the part marked *piano* in the score with a *mezzo piano* or even a *mezzo forte*, to assure a "democracy of sound" to the sections responsible for creating the *melos*. His rhythm is precise, his movements impeccably "right", his interpretative sense is that of a true great artist. What Stravinsky said and did when he conducted an orchestra was always clear, essential and strictly musical. Cherubini's *Anacreonte*, Tchaikovsky's Third Symphony and his own *Petrushka* and *Sacre du Printemps* were all treated in the same masterful way by him, as he conveyed to the orchestra the character and spirit of the compositions. He often said he was a believer; and, as such, an anti-materialist. He showed this even when on the podium, searching for ideal values in the music and placing great importance on the phrasing.

Now, however, we are entering the realm of the absolute in music; we find ourselves at the limit beyond which words are insufficient. So after our long journey together, it is time to close one's eyes and listen. And may the reader's life be *dolce* and *amabile*, lived *con brio*, and their path be *andante cantabile*...

Antologia

Introduction to the essays

The first critical and theoretical writings on orchestra conducting date from the nineteenth century and are dominated by three great figures: Hector Berlioz, Franz Liszt and Richard Wagner. Since no definitive single conducting technique exists, I thought it appropriate to add, in the second part of this book, some of the most significant commentaries produced with regard to conducting: a letter written by Franz Liszt in 1853, in which he takes issue with those who branded him as a terrible conductor, followed by a preface intended for future performers of his Symphonic Poems (1856); an extract from *L'Art du chef d'orchestre: théorie de son art* by Berlioz, published in 1855 as an appendix to his *Traité d'instrumentation et d'orchestration*; a condensed version of *On Conducting* by Richard Wagner, published in 1869, to which Felix Weingartner's work of the same title acts as a counterpoint (the integral text of the fourth edition (1913) of the work which originally appeared in 1895); a short article by Charles Gounod published as an appendix to his commentary on Mozart's Don Giovanni (1890); some notes by Lazare Saminsky which appeared for the first time in 1932 and were subsequently collected in the manual *Essentials of Conducting* (1958); a passage from *The Conductor* (*Ai giovani che intendono dedicarsi all'arte direttoriale*) by Tullio Serafin (1940); concluding with a conversation between Adriano Lualdi and Victor de Sabata regarding a concert held in Salzburg in 1953.

In future, I intend to have the extraordinary lectures of the unforgettable Sergiu Celibidache republished – he was one of the most effective conductors in scientifically addressing modern conducting techniques.

FRANZ LISZT

A letter on conducting – 1853

With his profound sensitivity, Franz Liszt (1811-1886) was the first to transform the role of conductor according to the principles of romanticism: no longer a mechanical time-beater whose only duty was to read the score, but a fully-fledged performer following the score to the letter and attentive to the aesthetic and spiritual character of every work. Wagner, his great friend and continuer of his ideas described thus the emotion of seeing him conduct his music:

> *I watched Liszt as he conducted the rehearsals for my Tannhäuser and I was astonished to see in him a second version of myself. What I heard as I composed it, I heard as he directed it: he was able to reproduce the feelings I wished to express as I wrote it, translating them into sound. Strange as it may sound, through my bond with this true friend, at a time when I was forlorn, I found that sympathy that up to then I had desired and sought in others, always in vain.*

During the years spent in Weimar as Kapellmeister, *the Hungarian composer took part in the organisation of the Karlsruhe Festival, one of the first to be held in Germany after the uprisings of 1848. The festival programme contained not just the great classics, but also the ill-treated Beethoven and some contemporary composers, including Berlioz. The selection of music to be performed and, especially, Liszt's new conducting methods provoked outrage among music lovers who preferred a more traditional repertoire and who criticised him harshly, despite the enormous success of the concerts directed by him at the festival. Liszt hit back at his detractors in this letter, dated 5 November 1853.*

With all due respect for my kind critics, I shall
continue to follow my deepest convictions,
which will never allow me to descend to the
level of mere time-beater.

F. Liszt

In various accounts that I have read of the Festival at Karlsruhe, there is one point on which people seem pretty much agreed — namely, the insufficiency of my conducting. Without here examining what degree of foregone judgement there may be in this opinion, without even seeking to know how much it has been influenced by the simple fact of the choice of myself as conductor, apart from the towns of Karlsruhe, Darmstadt, and Mannheim, it certainly would not be for me to raise pretensions quite contrary to the assertion which it is sought to establish if this assertion were based on facts or on justice. But this is precisely what I cannot help contesting in a very positive manner.

As a fact one cannot deny that the ensemble of the Karlsruhe programme was very remarkably performed, that the proportion and sonority of the instruments, combined with a view to the locale chosen, were satisfactory and even excellent. This is rather naively acknowledged in the remark that it is really surprising that things should have gone so well "in spite of" the insufficiency of my conducting. I am far from wishing to deck myself in the peacock's feathers of the Karlsruhe, Mannheim, and Darmstadt orchestras, and am assuredly more disposed than anyone to render full justice to the talents — some of them very distinguished — of the members of these three orchestras; but, to come to the point, whatever may be said to the contrary, it is acknowledged, even by the testimony of my adversaries, that the execution was at times astonishing, and altogether better than there had been reason to expect, considering that I was conductor.

This fact placed beyond discussion, it remains to be seen whether I am so completely a stranger there as they try to make out, and what reasons there can be for thus crying down a conductor when the execution was satisfactory, especially if, as is just, one bears in mind the novelty of the works on the programme for almost the entire audience. For, as everyone knew at Karlsruhe, the Ninth Symphony, as well as the works of Wagner, Berlioz, Schumann, etc., were not well known by anyone but myself, seeing that they had never been given before in these parts (with the exception of the Berlioz piece, which a portion only of the Karlsruhe orchestra had played under the direction of the composer). Now as regards the question of right — to know whether in good conscience and with knowledge of the matter one can justly accuse me of being an insufficient conductor, inexperienced, uncertain, etc.

***

Without endeavouring to exculpate myself (for which I do not think there is any need amongst those who understand me), may I be permitted to make an observation bearing on the basis of the question? The works for which I openly confess my admiration and predilection are for the most part amongst those which conductors more or less renowned (especially the so-called "qualified Kapellmeister") have honoured but little, or not at all, with their personal sympathies, so much so that it has rarely happened that they have performed them. These works, reckoning from those which are commonly described nowadays as belonging to Beethoven's last style (and which were, not long ago, with lack of reverence, explained by Beethoven's deafness and mental derangement !)— these works, to my thinking, exact from executants and orchestras a progress which is being accomplished at this moment — but which is far from being realised in all places — in accentuation, in rhythm, in the manner of phrasing and declaiming certain passages, and of distributing light and shade — in a word, progress in the style of the execution itself. They establish, between the musicians of the desks and the musician chief who directs them, a link of a nature other than that which is cemented by an imperturbable beating of the time. In many cases even the rough, literal maintenance of the time and of each continuous bar | 1, 2, 3, 4, | 1, 2, 3, 4, | clashes with the sense and expression.

There, as elsewhere, the letter kills the spirit, a thing to which I will never subscribe, however specious in their hypocritical impartiality may be the attacks to which I am exposed. For the works of Beethoven, Berlioz, Wagner, etc., I see less than elsewhere what advantage there could be (which by-the-bye I shall contest pretty knowingly elsewhere) in a conductor trying to go through his work like a sort of windmill, and to get into a great perspiration in order to give warmth to the others. Especially where it is a question of understanding and feeling, of impressing oneself with intelligence, of kindling hearts with a sort of communion of the beautiful, the grand, and the true in Art and Poetry, the sufficiency and the old routine of usual conductors no longer suffice, and are even contrary to the dignity and the sublime liberty of the art.

Thus, with all due deference to my complaisant critics, I shall hold myself on every occasion ulterior to my "insufficiency" on principle and by conviction, for I will never accommodate myself to the role of a beater of time, for which my twenty-five years of experience, study, and sincere passion for Art would not at all fit me.

Whatever esteem therefore I may profess for many of my colleagues, and however gladly I may recognise the good services they have rendered and continue to render to Art, I do not think myself on that account obliged to follow their example in every particular.

***

These pages written by the great Liszt also reach the conclusion shared by Count Keyserling, which is applicable to all genres and all times: "A score is nothing but a promise of music".

In our chaotic times, continued Liszt, young people should not miss out on the most valuable form of teaching: watching orchestra rehearsals; and he deplores the fact that directors choose not the music which would give most pleasure to the audience, but those that most allow the "brio" of the performer to be shine through and be admired.

He concluded his introduction with a phrase of Berlioz who, cited by a professional of the baton, comes out with an even more biting comment: being a conductor is, *"le plus redoutable des intermédiaires entre la musique e le public"*.

After the first publication in the volume *The Music Festival of Karlsruhe* (Richard Pohl) in 1853, and after the outrage occasioned by Liszt's ideas, firstly applied in his conducting practice and later confirmed and supported in this controversial letter, there was a radical shift in the way of looking at the art of conducting.

Not only were the ideas espoused by Franz Liszt accepted and, but they soon found, in Richard Wagner and then Hans von Bülow, two staunch, authoritative supporters, and ended up being asserted triumphantly. This letter bears witness to another of Franz Liszt's great innovations in the art of modern conducting.

An introductory note by Lina Ramann, who edited the complete five volumes of the literary and artistic writings of Liszt (as well as some minor works: *Franz Liszt als Psalmensanger, Liszt Christus, Liszt Pädagogium*) relates that this *Letter on Conducting* appeared immediately at the Karlsruhe Music Festival, where Liszt was orchestra conductor.

To grasp the significance of the letter better, it should be borne in mind that this Festival was among the first to be organised in the "New Germany" and that, at the behest of Liszt, artistic director, it was cast in a somewhat unusual mould, aimed at promoting two new trends.

The first of these original features was the performance of (alongside well-established works by famous composers) Beethoven's Ninth Symphony, not so well-known at the time and still regarded with a measure of wariness by critics and the public (one of the reasons can be found in what Wagner noted in his performance of it at the time) and Berlioz' choral symphony with soloists, *Roméo et Juliette*, composed in 1839, as well as some pieces taken from Wagner's operas.

The second new feature was Liszt's use of the conducting baton: now, flying in the face of tradition, the role of the conductor was transformed from being a sort of human metronome, who divides each bar precisely and inflexibly, to the much more important function of giving appropriate prominence to musical periods and phrases, thus raising the phrasing, accent, tonecolour, balance, articulation and mood to the highest level of dramatic expression. The immediate effect of Liszt's innovations in conducting practice provoked a storm of violent attacks in the press against his iconoclastic shattering of so many old, stronglyrooted habits.

Franz Liszt responded to these attacks with his *Letter on Conducting*.

In the same year in which Berlioz published his *Le chef d'orchestre*, Liszt was in Rome, and his visits to various monuments and artworks inspired a letter to Berlioz. Indeed this letter is sort of self-portrait.

"*Raphael et Michel-Ange me font mieux comprendre Mozart et Beethoven. Jeano de Pise, Fra Beato, Francia, m'expliquent Allegri, Marcello, Palestrina; Titien et Rossini m'apparaissent comme deux astres de rayons semblables. Le Colisée et le Campo Santo ne sont pas si étrangers qu'on pense à le Symphonie Héroique et au Requiem. Dante a trouvé son expression pittoresque dans Orcagna et Michel-Ange; peut-etre un jour son expression musicale dans le Beethoven de l'avenir*".

His Roman wanderings, accompanied by the artist Ingres, made him feel, deep down inside, "*tout un mystère de poésie s'ac-*

complit". To what extent the restless Hector could share his friend's impressions is unclear, given that a few years previously he had been unable to find escape and salvation from the intolerable boredom of Roman life, except in adventurous explorations of the mountains of Abruzzo. However, this very resistance to the special charms that Rome works on the spirit is also part of his self-portrait.

Let us compare the two brief confessions: we shall find confirmation of a distinct difference in spirit in the two texts on our subject, the one dating from 1839 and the other from 1833.

When Liszt wrote his *Letter on Conducting*, he had already been Kapellmeister for six years at the Weimar Court. In 1847, a year that found him so elated and delighted about the meeting with Princess Carolyne zu Sayn-Wittgenstein and his appointment to the Chair of Weimar, Liszt, basking in the charmed life he lived in Worodice as guest of Carolyne, found the time, or perhaps was driven by his feelings of euphoria, to consider the current state of music; and he saw, with the exception of the great classical composers like, Bach, Gluck, Haydn, Mozart and Beethoven, and two newcomers, Berlioz and Schumann, the art of music as languishing in an impoverished state, lacking in ideas and identity, boding nothing but ill for the future. At that time, enjoying the trappings of his position as Kapellmeister at the Ducal Court, he began to devote himself to his mission and he sensed the projects to be carried out surfacing in his mind in embryonic form.

After a few months, in 1848, his mission as reorganiser and reformer of the musical life of Weimar was already well underway. Liszt concentrated his efforts on achieving a more intelligent and appreciative attitude towards the maestri of the past, a more conscientious and less superficial study of their works, greater attention not just to the technical demands, but also the spiritual and aesthetic characteristics of the works to be performed, whether ancient or modern, as well as a greater sense of human understanding, of support and investment in young artists and artists as yet unknown

Wagner, Berlioz, Schumann, Raff and Hans von Bülow were the first to benefit from his policies.

As far as his principles regarding performance are concerned, these were put into practice with a vengeance in Weimar from 1844 on. He had to face a professional environment characterised by mediocrity, unable to accept that a great pianist could also be a fine conductor. The musical bien pensants awaited the entry of this inexperienced upstart into the concert hall with benevolent diffidence. And when they saw him mount the podium with neither baton nor score, sniggers were heard. But not for long. It soon had to be agreed that this diabolical Hungarian showman knew the score and the entries of all the instruments by heart: his ear was magnificent in picking up errors and, above all, he managed to instil in the orchestra a spirituality, an intangible, transcendent sound and a warmth of expression never previously heard – things nobody would ever have believed that the Weimar Court Orchestra capable of. In his first contact with the orchestra, Franz Liszt revealed the revolutionary principles of the performing art of the conductor that he had nurtured and developed in his mind and sensibility in his nine years at the Karlsruhe Festival – principles that he was to expound so fierily in his controversial letter of 1833. That is to say, a more careful attention to accent, rhythm, phrasing and management of proportion and distribution in the interplay of light and shade in the scores; he stressed the urgent need for advances to be made in performance style, an area in which the orchestras of the time were seriously lagging behind.

All requirements of a spiritual, an aesthetic, nature, which went far beyond mere conducting gestures and the letter printed above (basically a written note). All the conducting techniques and mechanics which Hector Berlioz had covered in an essay fifteen years before were now considered to be taken for granted and in the public domain, paving the way and setting the stage for the experiments and profound analyses of Richard Wagner – which were to form the substance and soul of his own treatise fifteen years later.

The extremely close friendship between Wagner and Liszt represents a highly significant link in historical terms. In 1849, Wagner visited Weimar, where Liszt was opera director. Enormous mutual respect and esteem grew between the two artists and Liszt became one Wagner's staunchest supporters in the difficult years in which his music was not widely accepted.

Franz Liszt referred to three Beethoven styles as "the Child, the Man, God".

Preface to the Symphonic Poems – 1856

In a brief preamble to the first edition of his Symphonic Poems of 1856, Liszt addresses future performers of his music, emphasising particularly the importance of separate rehearsals, the proper use of the baton and the need for a meticulous reading of the score.

In order to attain a result that respects the intentions of my orchestral works and to give them colour, rhythm, accent and the vibrancy they require, it is advisable to precede the general rehearsal with separate practices for the strings, woodwinds, brass and percussion instruments. By dividing up the work, time will be saved and the performers grasp the work more easily. Allow me to ask, therefore, that the conductors who wish to execute one of my symphonic poems ensure they strictly follow this order in their rehearsals.

I would also like to stress that in works of this kind the baton should be handled with greater delicacy, flexibility and awareness of the tone-colours, rhythm and expression, an approach not yet in use with most orchestras. It is not enough for a performance to be directed by the book, more or less correctly but mechanically, to keep the composer happy about the dissemination of his work and appreciative of a faithful interpretation of his thought. The lifeblood of a good symphonic execution lies above all in the understanding – which the conductor must have and be able to convey – of the work, done in such a way as to divide and accentuate the passages and highlight the contrasts by managing the transitions, to be careful to both balance and integrate the various instruments, singly or in groups, since at times it is opportune to simply to bring the notes into tune and mark the notes, while at other moments it is a question of phrasing, singing or even declaiming. It is the conductor's duty to indicate to each component of the orchestra the significance of the role he has to play.

I have been at pains to expound my principles regarding nuances, acceleration or suspension of tempos etc – almost imperceptible shifts that can be effected thanks to a careful following of modern musical notation. Nevertheless, the belief that what contributes to the beauty and character of the piece can be put down on paper is nothing but an illusion. Success is assured only by the aptitude and inspiration of the artists – conductors and players – who are in on the secret and know how to give their very best in performing my works.

Franz Liszt, a great admirer of Berlioz' principles, with his extraordinary sensitivity, was to effect a romantic transformation of orchestra.

The art of the pianoforte and of conducting

Advice to young musicians

The cultivation of the Ear is of the greatest importance. Endeavour early to distinguish each several tone and key. Find out the exact notes sounded by the bell, the glass, the cuckoo, etc.

Practise frequently the scale and other finger exercises; but this alone is not sufficient. There are many people who think to obtain grand results in this way, and who up to a mature age spend many hours daily in mechanical labour. That is about the same, as if we tried every day to pronounce the alphabet with greater volubility! You can employ your time more usefully.

There are such things as mute pianoforte-keyboards; try them for a while, and you will discover that they are useless. Dumb people cannot teach us to speak.

Play strictly in time! The playing of many a virtuoso resembles the walk of an intoxicated person. Do not take such as your model.

Learn betimes the fundamental principles of Harmony. Do not be afraid of the words Theory, Thoroughbass, Counterpoint, etc.; you will understand their full meaning in due time.

Never jingle! Play always with energy and do not leave a piece unfinished.

You may play too slow or too fast; both are faults.

Endeavour to play easy pieces well and with elegance; that is better than to play difficult pieces badly.

Take care always to have your instrument well tuned.

It is not only necessary that you should be able to play your pieces on the instrument, but you should also be able to hum the air without the piano. Strengthen your imagination so, that you may not only retain the melody of a composition, but even the harmony which belongs to it.

Endeavour, even with a poor voice, to sing at first sight without the aid of the instrument; by these means your ear for music will constantly improve. In case you are endowed with a good voice, do not hesitate a moment to cultivate it; considering it at the same time as the most valuable gift which heaven has granted you!

You must be able to understand a piece of music upon paper.

When you play, never mind who listens to you. Play always as if in the presence of a master.

If anyone should place before you a composition to play at sight, read it over before you play it.

When you have done your musical day's work and feel tired, do not exert yourself further. It is better to rest than to work without pleasure and vigour.

In maturer years play no fashionable trifles. Time is precious. We should need to live a hundred lives, only to become acquainted with all the good works that exist.

With sweetmeats, pastry and confectionery we cannot bring up children in sound health. The mental food must be as simple and nourishing as the bodily. Great composers have sufficiently provided for the former; keep to their works.

All bravura-music soon grows antiquated. Rapid execution is valuable only when used to perfect the performance of real music.

Never help to circulate bad compositions; on the contrary, help to suppress them with earnestness. You should neither play bad compositions, nor, unless compelled, listen to them.

Do not think velocity, or passage-playing, your highest aim. Try to produce such an impression with a piece of music as was intended by the composer; all further exertions are caricatures.

Think it a vile habit to alter works of good composers, to omit parts of them, or to insert new-fashioned ornaments. This is the greatest insult you can offer to Art.

As to choice in the study of your pieces, ask the advice of more experienced persons than yourself; by so doing, you will save much time.

You must become acquainted by degrees with all the principal works of the more celebrated masters.

Do not be elated by the applause of the multitude; that of artists is of greater value.

All that is merely modish will soon go out of fashion, and if you practise it in age, you will appear a fop whom nobody esteems.

Much playing in society is more injurious than useful. Suit the taste and capacity of your audience; but never play anything which you know is trashy and worthless.

Do not miss an opportunity of practising music in company with others; as for example in Duets, Trios, etc.; this gives you a flowing and elevated style of playing, and self-possession. Frequently accompany singers.

If all would play first violin, we could not obtain an orchestra. Therefore esteem every musician in his place.

Love your peculiar instrument, but be not vain enough to consider it the greatest and only one. Remember that there are others as fine as yours. Remember also that singers exist, and that numbers, both in Chorus and Orchestra, produce the most sublime music; therefore do not overrate any Solo.

As you grow up, become more intimate with scores (or partitions) than with virtuosi.

Frequently play the fugues of good masters, above all, those by J. S. Bach. Let his "Well-tempered Clavier" be your daily bread. By these means you will certainly become a proficient.

Let your intimate friends be chosen from such as are better informed than yourself.

Relieve the severity of your musical studies by reading poetry. Take many a walk in the fields and woods!

From vocalists you may learn much, but do not believe all that they say.

Remember, there are more people in the world than yourself. Be modest! You have not yet invented nor thought anything which others have not thought or invented before. And should you really have done so, consider it a gift of heaven which you are to share with others.

You will be most readily cured of vanity or presumption by studying the history of music, and by hearing the masterpieces which have been produced at different periods.

A very valuable book you will find is: *On Purity in Music*, by Thibaut, a German Professor. Read it often, when you have come to years of greater maturity.

If you pass a church and hear an organ, go in and listen. If allowed to sit on the organ bench, try your inexperienced fingers and marvel at the supreme power of music.

Do not miss an opportunity of practising on the organ; for there is no instrument that can so effectually correct errors or impurity of style and touch as that.

Frequently sing in choruses, especially the middle parts, this will help to make you a real musician.

What is it to be musical? You will not be so, if your eyes are fixed on the notes with anxiety and you play your piece laboriously through; you will not be so, if (supposing that somebody should turn over two pages at once) you stop short and cannot proceed. But you will be so if you can almost foresee in a new piece what is to follow, or remember it in an old one,—in a word, if you have not only music in your fingers, but also in your head and heart.

But how do we become musical? This, my young friend, is a gift from above; it consists chiefly of a fine ear and quick conception. And these gifts may be cultivated and enhanced. You will not become musical by confining yourself to your room and to mere mechanical studies, but by an extensive intercourse with the musical world, especially with the Chorus and the Orchestra.

Become in early years well informed as to the extent of the human voice in its four modifications. Attend to it especially in the Chorus, examine in what tones its highest power lies, in what others it can be employed to affect the soft and tender passions.

Pay attention to national airs and songs of the people; they contain a vast assemblage of the finest melodies, and open to you a glimpse of the character of the different nations.

Fail not to practise the reading of old clefs, otherwise many treasures of past times will remain a closed fountain to you.

Attend early to the tone and character of the various instruments; try to impress their peculiar sound on your ear.

Do not neglect to attend good Operas.

Highly esteem the Old, but take also a warm interest in the New. Be not prejudiced against names unknown to you.

From a pound of iron, that costs little, a thousand watch-springs can be made, whose value becomes prodigious. The pound you have received from the Lord,—use it faithfully.

The object of art is not to produce riches. Become a great artist, and all other desirable accessories will fall to your lot.

The Spirit will not become clear to you, before you understand the Forms of composition.

Perhaps genius alone understands genius fully.

It has been thought that a perfect musician must be able to see, in his mind's eye, any new, and even complicated, piece of orchestral music as if in full score lying before him! This is in-

deed the greatest triumph of musical intellect that can be imagined.

There is no end of learning.

Ten Commandments for the score reader

Attributed to Robert Schumann

1 – The study of the score is not an activity to be done in the company of others. The more one studies the score on one's own, the more easily it will give up its secrets.

2 – If you have to listen to a musical piece for the first time, leave the score at home – it might only put you off.

3 – If you play an instrument, try to perfect your playing as much as time allows. A "musician without an instrument" is the most hostile condition to the art of the modern era.

4 – Once you have overcome the greatest technical difficulties of the piano, try also to play the orchestra score. This will give you amazing encouragement and pleasure.

5 – The most important skill that has to be developed in you by reading scores is mentally reproducing the sound (inner ear). Try to represent a sound with the greatest intensity possible and verify the accuracy of your sound image by listening with the score in your hands.

6 – If, when you are following a musical performance and you lose the place and cannot find it again immediately, do not flick through the score but rather close it and listen.

7 – Flicking through the score aggressively is not allowed. It is better to conduct from memory, at least for the repertoire of the great composers.

8 – Conducting exercises practised at home are an innocent and useful pastime; but beating the time at a concert with the head,

foot or other part of the body is as useless as it is inappropriate, as is humming along the melody being listened to. The listener who is genuinely moved by a piece is silent and does not move.

9 – Have respect for every Maestro and every masterpiece. Detecting errors is not art, but myopia and pedantry.

10 – Listening to music is like a rite. If you are not prepared for it, it is better to stay at home.

HECTOR BERLIOZ

The Conductor and his art – 1885

In 1855, the French composer Hector Berlioz (1803-1869) published
L'Art du chef d'orchestre: théorie de son art *as an appendix to the*
second edition of his Traité d'instrumentation et d'orchestration.
This was the first theoretical essay entirely devoted to orchestral conduct-
ing and technique. In his study, of which we include an extract, Berlioz
emphasises the importance of the role of conductor (in good and bad as-
pects), stresses the need for separate rehearsals for each section of the or-
chestra and demonstrates the problems of phonic equilibrium and of the
ensemble.

Music appears to be the most exacting of all the Arts, the cultivation of which presents the greatest difficulties, for a consummate interpretation of a musical work so as to permit an appreciation of its real value, a clear view of its physiognomy, or dis-
cernment of its real meaning and true character, is only achieved
in relatively few cases. Of creative artists, the composer is almost
the only one who is dependent upon a multitude of intermediate
agents between the public and himself; intermediate agents, either intelligent or stupid, devoted or hostile, active or inert, capable—from first to last—of contributing to the brilliancy of his
work, or of disfiguring it, misrepresenting it, and even destroying it completely. Singers have often been accused of forming
the most dangerous of these intermediate agents; but in my
opinion, without justice. The most formidable, to my thinking,
is the conductor of the orchestra.

A bad singer can spoil only his own part; while an incapable
or malevolent conductor ruins all. Happy indeed may the composer esteem himself when the conductor into whose hands he

has fallen is not at once incapable and inimical; for nothing can resist the pernicious influence of this person. The most admirable orchestra is then paralysed, the most excellent singers are perplexed and rendered dull; there is no longer any vigour or unity; under such direction the noblest daring of the author appears extravagant, enthusiasm beholds its soaring flight checked, inspiration is violently brought down to earth, the angel's wings are broken, the man of genius passes for a madman or an idiot, the divine statue is precipitated from its pedestal, and dragged in the mud. And what is worse, the public, and even auditors endowed with the highest musical intelligence, are reduced to the impossibility (if a new work is rendered, and they are hearing it for the first time) of recognizing the ravages perpetrated by the orchestral conductor—of discovering the follies, faults, and crimes he commits.

If they clearly perceive certain defects of execution, not he, but his victims, are in such cases made responsible. If he has caused the chorus-singers to fail in taking up a point in a finale, if he has allowed a discordant wavering to take place between the choir and the orchestra, or between the extreme sides of the instrumental body, if he has absurdly hurried a movement, or allowed it to linger unduly, if he has interrupted a singer before the end of a phrase, they exclaim: "The singers are detestable! The orchestra has no firmness".

Except in listening to great works already known and esteemed, intelligent hearers can hardly distinguish the true culprit, and allot to him his due share of blame; but the number of these is still so limited that their judgement has little weight; and the hostile conductor—in presence of the public who would pitilessly hiss a *vocal accident* of a good singer—reigns, with all the calm of a bad conscience, in his baseness and inefficiency.

The malevolent orchestral conductor—whether capable or not—is very rare. The orchestral conductor full of goodwill, but incapable, is on the contrary very common. Without speaking of innumerable mediocrities, directing artists who frequently are much their superiors, an author for example, can scarcely be accused of conspiring against his own works. Yet how many are there who, fancying they are able to conduct, innocently injure their best scores!

Beethoven, it is said, more than once ruined the performance of his symphonies; which he would conduct, even at the time when his deafness had become almost complete. The musicians, in order to keep together, agreed at length to follow the slight indications of time which the Konzertmeister (first violin-player) gave them; and not to attend to Beethoven's conducting-stick. Moreover, it should be observed, that conducting a symphony, an overture, or any other composition whose movements remain continual, vary little, and contain few nice gradations, is child's play in comparison with conducting an opera, or like work, where there are recitatives, airs, and numerous orchestral designs preceded by pauses of irregular length. The example of Beethoven, which I have just cited, leads me at once to say that if the direction of an orchestra appears to be very difficult for a blind man, it is indisputably impossible for a deaf one, whatever may have been his technical talent before losing his sense of hearing.

The orchestral conductor should *see* and *hear*; he should be *active* and *vigorous*, should know the *composition* and the *nature* and *compass* of the instruments, should be able to *read* the score, and possess—besides the especial talent of which we shall presently endeavour to explain the constituent qualities—other indefinable gifts, without which an invisible link cannot establish itself between him and those he directs; otherwise the faculty of transmitting to them his feeling is denied him, and power, empire, and guiding influence completely fail him. The performers should feel that he feels, comprehends, and is moved; then his emotion communicates itself to those whom he directs, his inward fire warms them, his electric glow animates them, his force of impulse excites them; he throws around him the vital irradiations of musical art. If he is inert and frozen, on the contrary, he paralyses all about him. His task is a complicated one. He has not only to conduct, in the spirit of the author's intentions, a work with which the performers have already become acquainted, but he must also introduce new compositions and help the performers to master them.

He has to criticise the errors and defects of each during the rehearsals, and to organize the resources at his disposal in such a way as to make the best use he can of them with the utmost promptitude; for, in the majority of European cities nowadays [especially Italy], musical artisanship is so ill distributed, performers so ill paid and the necessity of study so little understood, that *economy of time* should be reckoned among the most imperative requisites of the orchestral conductor's art.

The conductor is, above all, bound to possess a clear idea of the principal points and character of the work of which he is about to superintend the performance or study; in order that he may, without hesitation or mistake, at once determine the time of each movement desired by the composer. If he has not had the opportunity of receiving his instructions directly from the composer, or if the *times* have not been transmitted to him by tradition, he must have recourse to the indications of the metronome.

I do not mean to say by this that it is necessary to imitate the mathematical regularity of the metronome, all music so performed would become of freezing stiffness, and I even doubt whether it would be possible to observe so flat a uniformity during a certain number of bars. But the metronome is none the less excellent to consult in order to know the original time, and its chief alterations. If the conductor possess neither the author's instructions, tradition, nor metronome indications,—which frequently happens in the ancient masterpieces, written at a period when the metronome was not invented,—he has no other guide than the vague terms employed to designate the time to be taken, and his own instinct, his feeling—more or less distinguishing, more or less just—of the author's style. We are compelled to admit that these guides are too often insufficient and delusive.

I once heard a chorus of *Iphigenia in Tauride* performed in a

German theatre *allegro assai, two in the bar,* instead of *allegro non troppo, four in the bar;* that is to say, exactly twice too fast. Examples might be multiplied of such disasters, occasioned either by the ignorance or the carelessness of conductors of orchestras; or else by the real difficulty which exists for even the best-gifted and most careful men to discover the precise meaning of the Italian terms used as indications of the time to be taken.

Of course, no one can be at a loss to distinguish a *largo* from a *presto.* If the *presto* be two in a bar, a tolerably sagacious conductor, from inspection of the passages and melodic designs contained in the piece, will be able to discern the degree of quickness intended by the author. But if the *largo* be four in a bar, of simple melodic structure, and containing but few notes in each bar, what means has the hapless conductor of discovering the true time? And in how many ways might he not be deceived? The different degrees of slowness that might be assigned to the performance of such a *largo* are very numerous; the individual feeling of the orchestral conductor must then become the sole authority; and, after all, it is the author's feeling, not his, which is in question. Composers therefore ought not to neglect placing metronome indications in their works; and orchestral conductors are bound to study them closely. The neglect of this study on the part of the latter, is an act of dishonesty. The tempos marked by the metronome are relative: the acoustics of the hall or theatre, the ability if the orchestra, the room and the mood of the performer are all factors that determine the tempo to be set.

It is essential that the orchestra and choir have a conductor who is familiar with tempos, is well-versed in the art of singing and is capable of making technical and critical observations.

I conclude by expressing sincere regret at beholding choral and orchestral studies still so badly organized. Everywhere, for grand choral and instrumental compositions, the system of rehearsals in the mass is maintained. A faithful, well-coloured, clever interpretation of a modern work, even when confided to artists of a higher order, can only be obtained, I firmly believe, by partial rehearsals. Each part of a chorus should be studied singly until it is thoroughly known, before combining it with the others. The same step should be taken with regard to the orchestra, for a symphony at all complicated. The violins should first be practised alone; the violas and basses by themselves; the wooden wind instruments (with a small band of stringed instruments, to fill in the rests, and accustom the wind instruments to the points of re-entrance) and the brass instruments the same; and very often it is necessary to practise the instruments of percussion alone; and lastly, the harps, if they be numerous.

The studies in combination are then far more profitable, and more rapid; and there is then good hope of attaining fidelity of interpretation, now, alas, but too rare.

A daguerreotype of the Germany of 1869

Along with Felix Mendelssohn and Franz. Liszt, Wagner was the creator of the modern figure of the conductor as star.

"All things considered, what we have is honest nonentities who become dishonest just out of rage": thus spoke Richard Wagner of conductors in 1869: he was fifty six years old at the time, not a novice given to excesses, but a mature artist who produced the volume *On Conducting*, which was to be of fundamental importance in the development of his ideas.

The writing is somewhat prolix, replete with digressions and parentheses that sometimes make the reader lose track of the central argument. And Wagner was only capable of expressing his creative ideas, as well as their manifestations in music, poetry and prose, in his ponderous, monumental style. So that for an observation for which ten lines would be sufficient, he devotes three or four pages. Despite the abundance of digressions, however, this essay provides a solid framework and is grounded in his perfect knowledge of the art and of those who practise it, the trends and tastes, nastinesses and the overarching imbecilities that all go to make up the atmosphere of the musical scene of the time. Of the hundreds of pages, many are devoted to personal issues, rebutting offences suffered, denouncing ignoble plots against him and mocking the hypocrisy and insignificance of certain individuals.

But do we wish to blame Wagner if in these pages the convictions of the artist are dictated with a tone of indignation? After all, when he wrote *On Conducting*, we was already well-established as a conductor and he had put on in German theatres *Lohengrin* (1850), *Tannhäuser* (1853), *Tristan und Isolde* (1865) and *Die Meistersinger* (1868) as well as, in the same year (1869) Das *Rheingold*, the first of the four music dramas that *Der Ring des Nibelungen*.

Just one of these works would be sufficient in any normal context to for one to qualify as a great, multifaceted, dynamic artist, such as Wagner was.

But five of these scores, and his works in the guise of writer and conductor, restorer and defender of national spirit and taste, proved insufficient for the various Germanic musical cabals. Take Joseph Joachim, fine violinist and close friend of, and collaborator with, Brahms (he made numerous modifications of the orchestration of many of the Hamburg composer's works), Director of the Royal Music Academy of Berlin, who was still awaiting in that year, 1869, a "new Messiah" in German music; and German musical circles echoed his sentiments, totally unaware of the towering figure in their midst, Richard Wagner.

Wagner had adopted an extremely contemptuous, judgemental attitude towards the German conductors of the time. "In their case, unfortunately, reputation, talent, culture, even faith, love and hope, are artificial. Each of them was, and is, so busy with his personal affairs, and the difficulty of maintaining his artificial position, that he cannot occupy himself with measures of general import—measures which might bring about a connected and consistent new order of things". But where did all this repugnance in Richard Wagner come from? Not just from his personal affairs, from his lengthy suffering, from struggling against so many of his colleagues who were deaf to his art – it came above all from his profound understanding of his people. The "general issues" he addresses and discusses so energetically in his essay focused on what was actually going on at the time. Many pages are devoted to the criticism Wagner levelled against the contemporary way of conducting and on whimsical interpretations and distortions.

From a practical point of view, novice conductors should pay great attention to these observations, since they contain precious teachings. From each of the cases described by Wagner stem the general concepts that go to make up the modern conductor's art. The noble Wagner rails against the theories and techniques he deems mistaken, with undying passion and polemical, sometimes irate, tones, putting forward the notions and technical suggestions that he himself had discovered and perfected. Indeed, we have the outpourings of the temperament of a great artist, of an outstanding genius – a benchmark for those who wish to embark on this arduous career. Profound passion, the courage in one's convictions and the strength to steadfastly adhere to these: all those who aspire to the highest goals should imitate his example. This art, never easy, has become more difficult than ever today. It demands not just genuine talents and cultivated minds, but people who are serious and resistant to opportunism and compromise, prepared to struggle with the utmost determination. It is, then, heart-felt advice to young musicians, to those who rely on patronage or outside help.

Felix Weingartener also stressed: "Without temperament, one can't do anything brilliant. It's something that doesn't come from education, from zeal or even from patronage. It is a natural gift, it is innate".

Anyone who, on reading these pages of Wagner or of other great artists does not feel spurred on by passion and fighting spirit should take up some other pastime. This art is definitely not for fearful or shallow spirits.

RICHARD WAGNER

On conducting – 1869

Wagner's On Conducting *was published in 1869, when the author was already a mature artist. Unlike Berlioz, who addressed the conducting art from a technical viewpoint, Wagner's starting point is quite another: he inveighs against the conductors of his age, accusing them of being incompetent, if not dishonest; he criticises mercilessly other aspects of the German musicals scene, branded as inept and corrupt, all backed up by his wide-ranging personal experience. Wagner's disillusion and disappointment, his feelings of not being appreciated as much as he should have been and the sight of colleagues he considers vastly inferior triumphing fire the polemical vein of his essay throughout. The advice the great German composer dispenses in* On Conducting, *of which we offer a selection, is precious and it delineated for the first time a real philosophy of orchestra conducting.*

Composers cannot afford to be indifferent to the manner in which their works are presented to the public; and the public, naturally, cannot be expected to decide whether the performance of a piece of music is correct or faulty, since there are no data beyond the actual effect of the performance to judge by. [...]

The demands upon the orchestras have increased greatly of late, their task has become more difficult and more complicated; yet the directors of our art-institutions, display increasing negligence in their choice of conductors. In the days when Mozart's scores afforded the highest tasks that could be set before an orchestra, the typical German Kapellmeister was a formidable personage, who knew how to make himself respected at his post—sure of his business, strict, despotic, and by no means polite [...]

The attitude of these men towards modern music was certainly "old fashioned". The older conductors of this stamp if they happened to be less gifted than those mentioned, found it difficult to cope with the complications of modern orchestral music—mainly because of their fixed notions concerning the proper constitution of an orchestra.

I am not aware that the number of permanent members of an orchestra, has, in any German town, been rectified according to the requirements of modern instrumentation. Nowadays, as of old, the principal parts in each group of instruments, are allotted to the players according to the rules of seniority —thus men take first positions when their powers are on the wane, whilst younger and stronger men are relegated to the subordinate parts—a practice, the evil effects of which are particularly noticeable with regard to the wind instruments.

Latterly, by discriminating exertions, and particularly, by the good sense of the instrumentalists concerned, these evils have diminished; another traditional habit, however, regarding the choice of players of stringed instruments, has led to deleterious consequences. Without the slightest compunction, the second violin parts, and especially the viola parts, have been sacrificed. The viola is commonly (with rare exceptions indeed) played by infirm violinists, or by decrepit players of wind instruments who happen to have been acquainted with a stringed instrument once upon a time.

At best a competent viola player sits at the first music stand, so that he may play the occasional solo for that instrument; but, I have even seen this function performed by the leader of the first violins [...] Such a state of things may be excusable from a humane point of view; it arose from the older methods of instrumentation, where the role of the viola consisted for the most part in filling up the accompaniments; and it has since found some sort of justification in the meagre method of instrumentation adopted by the composers of Italian operas, whose works constitute an important element in the repertoire of the German opera theatres.

At the various court theatres, Italian operas have always found favour with the Directors. From this it follows as a matter of course, that works which are not in the good grace of those gentlemen stand a poor chance, unless it should so happen that the conductor is a man of weight and influence who knows the real requirements of a modern orchestra. But our older Kapellmeister rarely knew as much—they did not choose to recognize the need of a large increase in the number of stringed instruments to balance the augmented number of wind instruments and the complicated uses the latter are now put to. In this respect the attempts at reform were always insufficient; and our celebrated German orchestras remained far behind those of France in the power and capacity of the violins, and particularly of the violoncellos.

Now, had the conductors of a later generation been men of authority like their predecessors, they might easily have mended matters; but the Directors of court theatres took good care to engage none but demure and subservient persons. It is well worth while to note how the conductors, who are now at the head of German music, arrived at the honourable positions they hold. Perhaps those who have been thus advanced to posts of honour, are themselves cognizant of how they got there—to an unpractised observer it is rather difficult to discern their particular merits.

The so-called "good berths" are reached step by step: men move on and push upwards. Now and then, however, things come to pass in a more erratic manner; grand personages, hitherto unknown, suddenly begin to flourish under the protection of the lady-in-waiting to some princess, etc. etc.—It is impossible to estimate the harm done to our leading orchestras and opera theatres by such nonentities.

Recently, the post of chief conductor has here and there been filled by a man of practical experience, especially engaged with a view to stimulating the slumbering energy of his colleagues. Such "chiefs" are famed for their skill in "bringing out" a new opera in a fortnight; for their clever "cuts"; for the effective "closes" they write to please singers, and for their interpolations in other men's scores.

Now and again the managers look out for "a conductor of reputation". Generally none such are to be had at the theatres; but, according to the feuilletons of the political newspapers, the singing societies and concert establishments furnish a steady supply of the article. These are the "music-brokers", as it were, of the present day, who came forth from the school of Mendelssohn, and flourished under his protection and recommendation. They differ widely from the helpless epigones of our old conductors: they are not musicians brought up in the orchestra or at the theatre, but respectable pupils of the new-fangled conservatoires; composers of Psalms and Oratorios, and devout listeners at rehearsals for the subscription concerts. They have received lessons in conducting too, and are possessed of an elegant "culture" hitherto unknown in the realms of music. [...] I believe the influence of these people upon German orchestras has been good in many respects, and has brought about beneficial results: certainly much that was raw and awkward has disappeared; and, from a musical point of view, many details of refined phrasing and expression are now more carefully attended to. [...]

One thing however is wanting to these gentlemen, without which they cannot be expected to achieve the needful reconstruction of the orchestras, nor to enforce the needful reforms in the institutions connected with them, viz., energy, self-confidence, and personal power. In their case, unfortunately, reputation, talent, culture, even faith, love and hope, are artificial. Each of them was, and is, so busy with his personal affairs, and the difficulty of maintaining his artificial position, that he cannot occupy himself with measures of general import—measures which might bring about a connected and consistent new order of things. As a matter of fact, such an order of things cannot, and does not concern the fraternity at all. [...]

It is clear from this account of the survivals of the earlier and of the latest species of Kapellmeister and Musikdirektor, that neither of them are likely to do much towards the reorganization of our orchestras. On the other hand the initiative has been taken by the orchestral performers themselves; and the signs of progress are evidently owing to the increasing development of their technical attainments. Virtuosi upon the different orchestral instruments have done excellent service, and they might have done much more in the circumstances had the conductors been competent. Exceptionally gifted and accomplished players easily got the upper hand of the decrepit Kapellmeisters of the old sort, and of their successors, the parvenus without authority—pianoforte pedagogues patronized by ladies in waiting, etc.

Virtuosi soon came to play a role in the orchestra akin to that of the prima donna on the stage. The elegant conductors of the day chose to associate and ally themselves with the virtuosi, and this arrangement might have acted very satisfactorily if the conductors had really understood the true spirit of German music.

It is important to point out in this connection that conductors are indebted to the theatres for their posts, and even for the existence of their orchestra. The greater part of their professional work consists in rehearsing and conducting operas. They ought, therefore, to have made it their business to understand the theatre—the opera—and to make themselves masters of the proper application of music to dramatic art, in something like the manner in which an astronomer applies mathematics to astronomy. Had they understood dramatic singing and dramatic expression they might have applied such knowledge to the execution of modern instrumental music. A long time ago I derived much instruction as to the tempo and the proper execution of Beethoven's music from the clearly accentuated and expressive singing of that great artist, Frau Schröder-Devrient. [...] and from the touching emotional impressions I got [...] I gained a new point of view, from which the entire movement appeared in a clearer and warmer light.

I am content to point out that a conductor might exercise great influence upon the higher musical culture with regard to execution, if he properly understood his position in relation to dramatic art, to which, in fact, he is indebted for his post and his dignity.

But our conductors are accustomed to look upon the opera as an irksome daily task (for which, on the other hand, the deplorable condition of that genre of art at German theatres furnishes reason enough).

Now to estimate the value of a quondam conductor of concerts and of choral societies at a theatre, it is advisable to pay him a visit at home, i.e., in the concert-room, from which he derives his reputation as a "solid" German musician. Let us observe him as a conductor of orchestral concerts. Looking back upon my earliest youth I remember to have had unpleasant impressions from performances of classical orchestral music. At the piano or whilst reading a score, certain things appeared animated and expressive, whereas, at a performance, they could hardly be recognised, and failed to attract attention.

I was puzzled by the apparent flabbiness of Mozartian Melody (*Cantilena*) which I had been taught to regard as so delicately expressive.

Assuredly, the reasons lie in the want of a proper Conservatorium of German music—a Conservatory, in the strictest sense of the word, in which the traditions of the classical master's own style of execution are preserved in practice—which, of course, would imply that the masters should, once at least, have had a chance personally to supervise performances of their works in such a place. Unfortunately German culture has missed all such opportunities; and if we now wish to become acquainted with the spirit of a classical composer's music, we must rely on this or that conductor, and upon his notion of what may, or may not, be the proper tempo and style of execution.

In the days of my youth, orchestral pieces at the celebrated Leipzig *Gewandhaus* Concerts were not conducted at all; they were simply played through under the leadership of the Conzertmeister [...]. At least there was no "disturbing individuality," in the shape of a conductor! The principal classical pieces which presented no particular technical difficulties were regularly given every winter; the execution was smooth and precise; and the members of the orchestra evidently enjoyed the annual recurrence of their familiar favourites.

Beethoven's Ninth Symphony

With Beethoven's Ninth Symphony alone they could not get on, though it was considered a point of honour to give that work every year. I had copied the score for myself, and made a pianoforte arrangement for two hands; but I was so much astonished at the utterly confused and bewildering effect of the *Gewandhaus* performance that I lost courage, and gave up the study of Beethoven for some time. Later, I found it instructive to note how I came to take true delight in performances of Mozart's instrumental works: it was when I had a chance to conduct them myself, and when I could indulge my feelings as to the expressive rendering of Mozart's *cantilena*. I received a good lesson at Paris in 1839, when I heard the orchestra of the Conservatoire rehearse the enigmatical Ninth Symphony. The scales fell from my eyes; I came to understand the value of correct execution, and the secret of a good performance. The orchestra had learnt to look for Beethoven's melody in every bar—that melody which the worthy Leipzig musicians had failed to discover; and the orchestra *sang* that melody.

This was the secret. Habeneck, who solved the difficulty, and to whom the great credit for this performance is due, was not a conductor of special genius. Whilst rehearsing the symphony, during an entire winter season, he had felt it to be incomprehensible and ineffective (would German conductors have confessed as much?), but he persisted throughout a second and a third season (!) until Beethoven's new *melos* was understood and correctly rendered by each member of the orchestra. Habeneck was a conductor of the old stamp; *he* was the master—and everyone obeyed him. [...]

I cannot attempt to describe the beauty of this performance.

[...] Even with first class orchestras I have never been able to get the passage in the first movement performed with such equable perfection as I then (thirty years ago) heard it played by the musicians of the Paris *Orchestre du Conservatoire*. [...] Often in later life have I recalled this passage, and tried by its aid to enumerate the desiderata in the execution of orchestral music: it comprises movement and sustained tone, with a definite degree of power. The masterly execution of this passage by the Paris orchestra consisted in the fact that they played it *exactly* as it is written. [...]

Keeping my further practical experience in view, I would ask how did the musicians of Paris arrive at so perfect a solution of the difficult problem?

By the most conscientious diligence. They were not content with mutual admiration and congratulation nor did they assume that difficulties must disappear before them as a matter of course. French musicians in the main belong to the Italian school; its influence upon them has been beneficial in as much as they have thus been taught to approach music mainly through the medium of the human voice. The French idea of playing an instrument well is to be able to *sing* well upon it. And (as already said) that superb orchestra *sang* the symphony.

The possibility of its being well sung implies that the true tempo had been found: and this is the second point which impressed me at the time. Old Habeneck was not the medium of any abstract aesthetical inspiration—he was devoid of "genius": But he found the right tempo while persistently fixing the attention of his orchestra upon the *melos* of the symphony.

The right comprehension of the *melos* is the sole guide to the right tempo; these two things are inseparable: the one implies and qualifies the other. As a proof of my assertion that the majority of performances of instrumental music with us are faulty it is sufficient to point out that our conductors so frequently fail to find the right tempo because they are ignorant of *singing*.

I have not yet met with a German Kapellmeister or Musik-

140

director who, be it with good or bad voice, can really sing a melody. These people look upon music as a singularly abstract sort of thing, an amalgam of grammar, arithmetic, and digital gymnastics;—to be an adept in which may fit a man for a mastership at a conservatory or a musical gymnasium; but it does not follow from this that he will be able to put life and soul into a musical performance.

Personal experiences

The whole duty of a conductor is comprised in his ability always to indicate the right tempo. His choice of tempi will show whether he understands the piece or not. With good players again the true tempo induces correct phrasing and expression, and conversely, with a conductor, the idea of appropriate phrasing and expression will induce the conception of the true tempo. This, however, is by no means so simple a matter as it appears. Older composers probably felt so, for they are content with the simplest general indications. Haydn and Mozart made use of the term *andante* as the mean between *allegro* and *adagio*, and thought it sufficient to indicate a few gradations and modifications of these terms.

Bach, as a rule, does not indicate tempo at all, which in a truly musical sense is perhaps best. He may have said to himself: whoever does not understand my themes and figures, and does not feel their character and expression, will not be much the wiser for an Italian indication of tempo.

Let me be permitted to mention a few facts which concern me personally. In my earlier operas I gave detailed directions as to the tempi, and indicated them (as I thought) accurately, by means of the metronome. Subsequently, whenever I had occasion to protest against a particularly absurd tempo, in *Tannhäuser* for instance, I was assured that the metronome had been consulted and carefully followed. In my later works I omitted the metronome and merely described the main tempi in general

141

terms, paying, however, particular attention to the various modifications of tempo.

It would appear that general directions also tend to vex and confuse Kapellmeisters, especially when they are expressed in plain German words. Accustomed to the conventional Italian terms these gentlemen are apt to lose their wits when, for instance, I write "moderate". Not long ago a Kapellmeister complained of that term (*mäßig*) which I employed in the score of *Das Rheingold*; the music, (it was reported) lasted exactly two hours and a half at rehearsals under a conductor whom I had personally instructed; whereas, at the performances and under the beat of the official Kapellmeister, it lasted fully three hours! (according to the report of the *Allgemeine Zeitung*). Wherefore, indeed, did I write *mäßig* [moderato]? To match this I have been informed that the overture to *Tannhäuser*, which, when I conducted it at Dresden, used to last twelve minutes, now lasts twenty. No doubt I am here alluding to thoroughly incompetent persons who are particularly shy of *alla breve* time, and who stick to their correct and normal crotchet beats, four in a bar, merely to show they are present and conscious of doing something. Heaven knows how such "quadrupeds" find their way from the village to our opera theatres.

Elegant conductors

"Dragging" is not a characteristic of the elegant conductors of these latter days; on the contrary they have a fatal tendency to hurry and to run away with the tempi. [...] Robert Schumann once complained to me at Dresden that he could not enjoy the Ninth Symphony at the Leipzig *Gewandhaus* concerts because of the quick tempi Mendelssohn chose to take, particularly in the first movement. [...] Mendelssohn himself once remarked to me, with regard to conducting, that he thought most harm was done by taking a tempo too slow; and that on the contrary, he always recommended quick tempi as being less detrimental. Really good execution, he thought, was at all times a rare thing, but shortcomings might be disguised if care was taken that they should not appear very prominent; and the best way to do this was "to get over the ground quickly". This can hardly have been a casual view, accidentally mentioned in conversation. The master's pupils must have received further and more detailed instruction; for, subsequently, I have, on various occasions, noticed the consequences of that maxim "take quick tempi", and have, I think, discovered the reasons which may have led to its adoption.

I remembered it well, when I came to lead the orchestra of the Philharmonic Society in London, 1855. Mendelssohn had conducted the concerts during several seasons, and the tradition of his readings was carefully preserved. It appears likely that the habits and peculiarities of the Philharmonic Society suggested to Mendelssohn his favourite style of performance (*Vortragsweise*)— certainly it was admirably adapted to meet their wants. An unusual amount of instrumental music is consumed at these concerts; but, as a rule, each piece is rehearsed once only. Thus in many instances, I could not avoid letting the orchestra follow its traditions, and so I became acquainted with a style of performance which called up a lively recollection of Mendelssohn's remarks. The music gushed forth like water from a fountain; there was no arresting it, and every *allegro* ended as an undeniable *presto*.

It was troublesome and difficult to interfere; for when correct tempi and proper modifications of these were taken the defects of style which the flood had carried along or concealed became painfully apparent.

Beethoven's Eighth Symphony

I have often been astonished at the singularly slight sense for tempo and execution evinced by leading musicians. I found it impossible, for instance, to communicate to Mendelssohn what

I felt to be a perverse piece of negligence with regard to the tempo of the third movement in Beethoven's Symphony in F major, No. 8. [...] Now, the late Kapellmeister Reissiger, of Dresden, once conducted this symphony there, and I happened to be present at the performance together with Mendelssohn; we talked about the dilemma just described, and its proper solution; concerning which I told Mendelssohn that I believed I had convinced Reissiger, who had promised that he would take the tempo slower than usual. Mendelssohn perfectly agreed with me.

We listened. The third movement began and I was terrified on hearing precisely the old *Ländler* tempo; but before I could give vent to my annoyance Mendelssohn smiled, and pleasantly nodded his head, as if to say "now it's all right! Bravo!" So my terror changed to astonishment. Reissiger [...] may not have been so very much to blame for persisting in the old tempo; but Mendelssohn's indifference, with regard to this queer artistic contretemps, raised doubts in my mind whether he saw any distinction and difference in the case at all. I fancied myself standing before an abyss of superficiality, a veritable void.

It would have been very indiscreet to risk a change of tempo which had not been rehearsed. For the orchestra, accustomed to play the piece in a quick tempo, would have been disturbed by the sudden imposition of a more moderate pace; which, as a matter of course, demands a totally different style of playing.

Holding sounds

We have now reached an important and decisive point, an appreciation of which is indispensable if we care to arrive at a satisfactory conclusion regarding the execution of classical music. Injudicious tempi might be defended with some show of reason inasmuch as a factitious style of delivery has arisen in conformity with them, and to the uninitiated such conformity of style and tempo might appear as a proof that all was right. [...] our orchestras nowadays hardly know what is meant by equally sustained tone. Let any conductor ask any orchestral instrument, no matter which, for a full and prolonged *forte*, and he will find the player puzzled, and will be astonished at the trouble it takes to get what he asks for.

Yet tone sustained with equal power is the basis of all expression, with the voice as with the orchestra: the manifold modifications of the power of tone, which constitute one of the principal elements of musical expression, rest upon it.

The conductors of the day care little about a sustained forte, but they are particularly fond of an exaggerated *piano*. Now the strings produce the latter with ease, but the wind instruments, particularly the wood winds do not. It is almost impossible to get a delicately sustained *piano* from wind instruments. [...]

This drawback, which exists in our best orchestras, suggests the question: why, at least, do not conductors try to equalise matters by demanding a somewhat fuller piano from the strings? But the conductors do not seem to notice any discrepancy. [...]

The sustained soft tone here spoken of, and the sustained powerful tone mentioned above, are the two poles of orchestral expression. But what about orchestral execution if neither the one nor the other is properly forthcoming? Where are the modifications of expression to come from if the very means of expression are defective? Thus, the Mendelssohnian rule of "getting over the ground" suggested a happy expedient; conductors gladly adopted the maxim, and turned it into a veritable dogma; so that, nowadays, attempts to perform classical music correctly are openly denounced as heretical!

The character of the performance

I am persistently returning to the question of tempo because, as I said above, this is the point at which it becomes evident whether a conductor understands his business or not. Obviously the proper pace of a piece of music is determined by the particular character of the rendering it requires; the question, therefore, comes to this: does the sustained tone, the vocal element, the *cantilena* predominate, or the rhythmical movement (figuration)? The conductor should lead accordingly.

The *adagio* stands to the *allegro* as the sustained tone stands to the rhythmical movement. The sustained tone regulates the *tempo adagio*: here the rhythm is as it were dissolved in pure tone, the tone per se suffices for the musical expression. In a certain delicate sense it may be said of the pure *adagio* that it cannot be taken too slow. A rapt confidence in the sufficiency of pure musical speech should reign here; the languor of feeling grows to ecstasy; that which in the Allegro was expressed by changes of figuration, is now conveyed by means of variously inflected tone. Thus the least change of harmony may call forth a sense of surprise; and again, the most remote harmonic progressions prove acceptable to our expectant feelings.

None of our conductors are courageous enough to take an *adagio* in this manner; they always begin by looking for some bit of figuration, and arrange their tempo to match. I am, perhaps, the only conductor who has ventured to take the *adagio* section of the third movement of the Ninth Symphony at the pace proper to its peculiar character.

The difference between the Mozartian and Beethovenian allegro

We have seen that sustained tone with its modifications is the basis of all musical execution. Similarly the *adagio*, developed, as Beethoven has developed it in the third movement of his Ninth Symphony, may be taken as the basis of all regulations as to musical time. In a certain delicate sense the Allegro may be regarded as the final result of a refraction of the pure *adagio*-character by the more restless moving figuration. On careful examination of the principal motives of the *allegro* it will be found that the melody derived from the *adagio*, predominates. The most important *allegro* movements of Beethoven are ruled by a predominant melody which exhibits some of the characteristics of the *adagio*; and in this wise Beethoven's *allegros* receive the emotional sentimental significance which distinguishes them from the earlier naive species of *allegro*. [...] It is enough to state here that I take Mozart's quick *alla breve* movements as representative of the naive allegro. The *allegros* of the overtures to his operas, particularly to *Figaro* and *Don Giovanni* are the most perfect specimens. [...] As I have said of the pure *adagio* that, in an ideal sense, it cannot be taken too slowly, so this pure unmixed *allegro* cannot be given too quickly.[...]

Let us merely consider it established that the character of the older classical or, as I call it, naive *allegro* differs greatly from the new emotional sentimental *allegro*, peculiar to Beethoven. Now, how does the true Beethovenian Allegro appear with regard to this? To take the boldest and most inspired example of Beethoven's unheard-of innovation in this direction, the first movement of his *Eroica* Symphony: how does this movement appear if played in the strict tempo of one of the *allegros* of Mozart's overtures? But do our conductors ever dream of taking it otherwise? Do they not always proceed monotonously from the first bar to the last? With the members of the 2elegant" tribe of Kapellmeisters the "conception" of the tempo consists of an application of the Mendelssohnian maxim *"chi va presto va sano."* [...]

We have now reached the point in our discussion from which we can judge the music of the day. It will have been noticed that I have approached this point with some circumspection. I was anxious to expose the dilemma, and to make everyone see and feel that since Beethoven there has been a very considerable change in the treatment and the execution of instrumental music.

Things which formerly existed in separate and opposite forms, each complete in itself, are now placed in juxtaposition, and further developed, one from the other, so as to form a whole. It is essential that the style of execution shall agree with the matter set forth— that the tempo shall be imbued with life as delicate as the life of the thematic tissue.

Modification of tempo

We may consider it established that in classical music written in the later style modification of tempo is a sine qua non. No doubt very great difficulties will have to be overcome. Summing up my experiences I do not hesitate to assert that, as far as public performances go, Beethoven is still a pure chimera with us. I shall now attempt to describe what I conceive to be the right way of performing Beethoven, and music akin to his. In this respect also the subject seems inexhaustible, and I shall again confine myself to a few salient points.

Variation

One of the principal musical forms consists of a series of variations upon a theme. Haydn, and eventually Beethoven, have improved this form, and rendered it artistically significant, by the originality of their devices, and particularly, by connecting the single variations one with the other, and establishing relations of mutual dependence between them. This is accomplished with the happiest results in cases where one variation is developed from another—that is to say, when a degree of movement, suggested in the one is carried further in the other, or when a certain satisfactory sense of surprise is occasioned by one variation supplying a complementary form of movement, which was wanting in the one before it. The real weakness of the variation-form, however, becomes apparent when strongly contrasting parts are placed in juxtaposition, without any link to connect them. Beethoven often contrives to convert this same weakness into a source of strength; and he manages to do so in a manner which excludes all sense of accident or of awkwardness: namely—at the point which I have described above as marking the limits of the laws of beauty with regard to the sustained tone (in the *adagio*), and the unfettered movement (in the *allegro*)— he contrives to satisfy, in a seemingly abrupt way, the extreme

148

longing after an antithesis; which antithesis, by means of a different and contrasting movement, is now made to serve as a relief.

This can be observed in the master's greatest works. The last movement of the *Eroica* Symphony, for instance, affords excellent instruction in this respect; it should be understood as a movement consisting of a greatly expanded series of variations; and accordingly it should be interpreted with as much variety as possible.

To do this properly, here as in all similar cases, the above mentioned weakness of the variation-form, and the disadvantage which is felt to result from it, must be taken into account. Single and separate variations are frequently seen to have had each an independent origin, and to have merely been strung together in a conventional manner. The unpleasant effects of such fortuitous juxtaposition are particularly felt in cases where a quiet and sustained theme is followed by an exceptionally lively variation. The first variation on that most wonderful theme in Beethoven's grand Sonata in A major for piano and violin (Kreutzer) is an example. Virtuosi always treat this as "a first variation" of the common type—i.e., a mere display of musical gymnastics, which destroys all desire to listen any further. [...] When the composer invented it he could hardly have thought of it as immediately following the theme, or as being in direct contact with it. The component parts of the variation-form are each complete in themselves, and perhaps the composer was unconsciously influenced by this fact. But, when the entire piece is played, the parts appear in uninterrupted succession. [...]

When the parts are conceived as standing in immediate connection, how deftly and delicately the links between the different variations can be contrived. [...]

I may have been too circumstantial, but the matter is of incalculable importance. Let us now proceed to look still more closely into the wants and requirements of a proper performance of classical music. In the foregoing investigations I hoped to have elucidated the problem of the modification of tempo, and to have

149

shown how a discerning mind will recognise and solve the difficulties inherent in modern classical music. Beethoven has furnished the immortal type of what I may call emotional, sentimental music—it unites all the separate and peculiar constituents of the earlier essentially naive types; sustained and interrupted tone, *cantilena* and figurations, are no longer kept formally asunder—the manifold changes of a series of variations are not merely strung together, but are now brought into immediate contact, and made to merge one into the other. Assuredly, the novel and infinitely various combinations of a symphonic movement must be set in motion in an adequate and appropriate manner if the whole is not to appear as a monstrosity. I remember in my young days to have heard older musicians make very dubious remarks about the *Eroica*. Dionys Weber, at Prague, simply treated it as a nonentity. The man was right in his way; he chose to recognise nothing but the Mozartian *allegro*; and in the strict tempo peculiar to that *allegro*, he taught his pupils at the Conservatorium to play the *Eroica*! The result was such that one could not help agreeing with him.

The power of the Eroica

Yet everywhere else the work was thus played, and it is still so played to this day! True, the symphony is now received with universal acclamations; but, if we are not to laugh at the whole thing, the real reasons for its success must be sought in the fact that Beethoven's music is studied apart from the concert-rooms—particularly at the piano— and its irresistible power is thus fully felt, though in rather a round-about way. If fate had not furnished such a path of safety, and if our noblest music depended solely upon the conductors, it would have perished long ago. [...]

This worrying and driving to death of the principal theme at the close of a piece is a habit common to all our orchestras—very frequently indeed nothing is wanting but the sound of the great horse-whip to complete the resemblance to the effects at a circus. No doubt increase of speed at the close of an overture is frequently demanded by composers; it is a matter of course in those cases where the true *allegro* theme, as it were, remains in possession of the field, and finally celebrates its apotheosis. [...]

However, it is difficult to understand why the close of the *Freischütz* overture should be thus hurried and worried by Germans, who are supposed to possess some delicacy of feeling. Perhaps the blunder will appear less inexplicable, if it is remembered that this second *cantilena*, which towards the close is treated as a chant of joy, was, already at its very first appearance, made to trot on at the pace of the principal *allegro*. [...] An indescribably repulsive effect is produced by this trivial reading of a passage [...] Truly, certain people [...] sit and listen again and again to a vulgar effect such as this, whenever and wherever the Freischutz overture is performed, and approve of it, and talk of "the wonted excellence of our orchestral performances" [...] — such people, I say, are in the right position to warn the public against "the absurdities of a mistaken idealism"—and "to point towards that which is artistically genuine, true and eternally valid, as an antidote to all sorts of half-true or half-mad doctrines and maxims".

As I have related, a number of Viennese amateurs who attended a performance of this poor maltreated overture, heard it rendered in a very different manner. The effect of that performance is still felt at Vienna. People asserted that they could hardly recognize the piece, and wanted to know what I had done to it. They could not conceive how the novel and surprising effect at the close had been produced, and scarcely credited my assertion that a moderate tempo was the sole cause. [...]

À la Wagner

Our Kapellmeisters are not particularly pleased at a success such as this. Herr Dessof, however, whose business it was afterwards to conduct *Der Freischuütz* at the Viennese opera, thought it advisable to leave the members of the orchestra undisturbed in the possession of the new reading. He announced this to them, with a smile, saying: "Well, gentlemen, let us take the overture 'à la Wagner'". Indeed, I believe, it would do no harm if everything were to be performed "à la Wagner". It has repeatedly been pointed out that our conductors dislike attempts at modification of tempo, for the sake of perspicuity in the rendering of Beethoven and other classical music.

Modification of the sound

It has repeatedly been pointed out that our conductors dislike attempts at modification of tempo, for the sake of perspicuity in the rendering of Beethoven and other classical music. I have shown that plausible objections can be urged against such modifications, so long as they are not accompanied by corresponding modifications of tone and expression; and I have further shown that such objections have no foundation other than the incompetence of conductors, who attempt to perform functions for which they are not fit.

In fact, there is but one valid objection which can be urged against the mode of procedure I advocate, namely this: nothing can be more detrimental to a piece of music than arbitrary nuances of tempo, etc., such as are likely to be introduced by this or that self-willed and conceited time-beater, for the sake of what he may deem "effective". In that way, certainly, the very existence of our classical music might, in course of time, be undermined. [...]

Inertia and incapacity

The first performances of classical compositions with us have, as a rule, been very imperfect. [...] A good deal also has, from the first, been brought before the German public in an absolutely incorrect manner. [...] This being so, how can the current style of execution appear other than it is? In Germany the "conservators" of such works are both ignorant and incompetent. And, on the other hand, suppose one were to take an unprejudiced and impartial view of the manner in which a master like Mendelssohn led such works! How can it be expected that lesser musicians, not to speak of musical mediocrities generally, should really comprehend things which have remained doubtful to their master? For average people, who are not specially gifted, there is but one good guide to excellence—a good example; and a guiding example was not to be found in the path chosen by the host of mediocrities. Unfortunately, they entirely occupy this path or pass, at present, —without a guide or leader—and any other person who might, perchance, be capable of setting up a proper example, has no room left. [...]

As I have said at the outset this new musical Areopagus consists of two distinct species: Germans of the old type, who have managed to hold out in the South of Germany, but are now gradually disappearing; and the elegant Cosmopolites, who have arisen from the school of Mendelssohn in the North, and are now in the ascendant. Formerly the two species did not think much of each other; but latterly, in the face of certain disturbances which seem to threaten their nourishing business, they have united in mutual admiration; so that in the South the Mendelssohnian school, with all that pertains to it, is now lauded and protected—whilst, in the North, the prototype of South-German sterility is welcomed. [...]

Thus to ensure their prosperity the two species are shaking hands. Perhaps at the outset such an alliance was rather repugnant to those of the old native type; but they got over the difficulty by the aid of that not particularly laudable propensity of Germans: namely, a timid feeling of jealousy which accompanies a sense of helplessness. [...] The opposition of the more subordinate musicians signifies nothing beyond this: "we cannot advance, we do not want others to advance, and we are annoyed to see them advance in spite of us". This is at least honest Philistinism; dishonest only under provocation.

In the newly-formed camp, however, things are not so simple. Most complicated maxims have there been evolved from the queer ramifications of personal, social, and even national interests. Without going into details, I will only touch one prominent point, that here there is a good deal to conceal, a good deal to hide and suppress. The members of the fraternity hardly think it desirable to show that they are "musicians" at all; and they have sufficient reason for this.

The musician, half-wild, half-child

Our true German musician was originally a man difficult to associate with. In days gone by the social position of musicians in Germany, as in France and England, was far from good. {...} Musicians remained peculiar half-wild, half-childish beings, and were treated as such by their employers. [...]

The new species of conductors did not grow up among the musical guilds—they would have shrunk from the hard work there. They simply took the lead of the guilds—much as the bankers take the lead in our industrial society. To be able to do this creditably conductors had to show themselves possessed of something that was lacking to the musicians from the ranks— something at least very difficult to acquire in a sufficient degree, if it was not altogether lacking: namely, a certain varnish of culture.

I say pseudo-culture, not *culture*, for whoever really possesses the latter is a superior person and above ridicule. But there can be no harm in discussing our varnished and elegant friends. I have not met with a case in which the results of true culture, an open mind and a free spirit, have become apparent amongst them.

Even Mendelssohn, whose manifold gifts had been cultivated most assiduously, never got over a certain anxious timidity; and

154

in spite of all his well-merited successes, he remained outside the pale of German art-life. It seems probable that a feeling of isolation and constraint was a source of much pain to him, and shortened his life.

Pseudo-culture

The reason for this is to be found in the fact that the motives of a desire for culture, such as his, lack spontaneity and arise from a desire to cover and conceal some part of a man's individuality, rather than to develop it freely. But true culture is not the result of such a process: a man may grow extremely intelligent in certain ways; yet the point at which these ways meet may be other than that of "pure intelligence". [...] if we are not inclined to grin in return, as superficial observers of our civilization are wont to do, we may indeed grow seriously indignant. And German musicians nowadays have good reason to be indignant if this miserable sham culture presumes to judge of the spirit and significance of our glorious music.

Generally speaking, it is a characteristic trait of pseudo- culture not to insist too much, not to enter deeply into a subject or, as the phrase goes, not to make much fuss about anything. Thus, whatever is high, great and deep, is treated as a matter of course, a commonplace, naturally at everybody's beck and call; something that can be readily acquired, and, if need be, imitated.

Goethe's aesthetic

Again, that which is sublime, god-like, demonic, must not be dwelt upon, simply because it is impossible or difficult to copy. Pseudo-culture accordingly talks of "excrescences", "exaggerations", and the like—and sets up a novel system of aesthetics, which professes to rest upon Goethe— since he, too, was averse to prodigious monstrosities, and was good enough to invent

155

"artistic calm and beauty" in lieu thereof. The "guileless innocence of art" becomes an object of laudation; and Schiller, who now and then was too violent, is treated rather contemptuously; so, in sage accord with the Philistines of the day, a new conception of classicality is evolved. In other departments of art, too, the Greeks are pressed into service, on the ground that Greece was the very home of "clear transparent serenity".

Such shallow meddling with all that is most earnest and terrible in the existence of man, is gathered together in a full and novel philosophical system wherein our varnished musical heroes find a comfortable and undisputed place of honour.

Mendelssohn and dissimulation

How the latter heroes treat great musical works I have shown by the aid of a few representative examples. It remains to explain the serene and cheerful Greek sense of that "getting over the ground" which Mendelssohn so earnestly recommended. This will be best shown by a reference to his disciples and successors. Mendelssohn wished to hide the inevitable shortcomings of the execution, and also, in case of need, the shortcomings of that which is executed; to this, his disciples and successors superadded the specific motive of their "culture": namely, "to hide and cover up in general", to escape attention, to create no disturbance. [...]

A large part of their education has ever since consisted in learning to watch their behaviour, and to suppress any indications of passion; much as one who naturally lisps and stammers, is careful to keep quiet, lest he should be overcome by a fit of hissing and stuttering. Such continuous watchfulness has assisted in the removal of much that was unpleasant, and the general humane amalgamation has gone on much more smoothly; which, again, has brought it about that many a stiff and poorly developed element of our home-growth has been refreshed and rejuvenated. I have already mentioned that amongst musicians, roughness of speech and behaviour are going out, that delicate details in musical execution are more carefully attended to, etc. But it is a very different thing to allow the necessity for reticence, and for the suppression of certain personal characteristics, to be converted into a principle for the treatment of our art! Germans are stiff and awkward when they want to appear mannerly: but they are noble and superior when they grow warm. And are we to suppress our fire to please those reticent persons? [...]

Bach performed by Liszt

The first result of the new doctrine, and the most important for our investigations, came to light in the execution of classical music. Everything here was governed by the fear of exaggeration. I have, for instance, hitherto not found any traces that those later pianoforte works of Beethoven, in which the master's peculiar style is best developed, have actually been studied and played by the converts to that doctrine. For a long time I earnestly wished to meet with someone who could play the great Sonata in B flat (Op. 106) as it should be played. At length my wish was gratified—but by a person who came from a camp wherein those doctrines do *not* prevail. Franz Liszt, also, gratified my longing to hear Bach. [...] I begged Liszt for once to cleanse my musical soul of the painful impression: he played the fourth Prelude and Fugue (C sharp minor). Now, I knew what to expect from Liszt at the piano; but I had not expected anything like what I came to hear from Bach, though I had studied him well; I saw how study is eclipsed by genius. By his rendering of this single fugue of Bach's, Liszt revealed Bach to me; so that I henceforth knew for certain what to make of Bach, and how to solve all doubts concerning him.

I was convinced, also, that those people know nothing of Bach; and if anyone chooses to doubt my assertion, I answer: "request them to play a piece of Bach's". I would like further to question any member of that musical temperance society and, if it has ever been his lot to hear Liszt play Beethoven's great B flat Sonata. I would ask him to testify honestly whether he had before really known and understood that sonata. [...]

But now what becomes of our great and glorious German music? It is the fate of our music that really concerns us. We have little reason to grieve if, after a century of wondrous productivity, nothing particular happens to come to light for some little time. But there is every reason to beware of suspicious persons who set themselves up as the trustees and conservators of the "true German spirit2 of our inheritance.

Regarded as individuals, there is not much to blame in these musicians; most of them compose very well. [...] In any case we must protest against any presentation of our great warm-hearted Beethoven in the guise of such sanctity. If *they* cannot bring out the difference between Beethoven, whom they do not comprehend and therefore pervert, and Schumann, who, for very simple reasons, *is* incomprehensible, they shall, at least, not be permitted to assume that no difference exists.

State of sanctity

I have already indicated sundry special aspects of this sanctimoniousness. Following its aspirations a little further we shall come upon a new field, across which our investigation on and about conducting must now lead us. [...]

If a single member [of this ascetic musical temperance society] for once only, were to achieve a success with an opera, it is more than probable that the entire "school" would explode. But, somehow, no such success has hitherto been achieved, and this keeps the school together; for, every attempt that happens to fail, can be made to appear as a conscious effort of abstinence, in the sense of the exercises of the lower grades; and "the opera", which beckons in the distance like a forlorn bride, can be made to figure as a symbol of the temptation, which is to be finally resisted—so that the authors of operatic failures may be glorified as special saints.

Seriously speaking, how do these musical gentlemen stand with regard to "the opera"? Having paid them a visit in the concert- room to which they belong, and from which they started, we shall now, for the sake of "conducting", look after them at the theatre.

Herr Eduard Devrient, in his memoirs, given us an account of the difficulties his friend Mendelssohn met with in the search for a textbook to an opera. It was to be a truly "German" opera, and the master's friends were to find the materials wherewith to construct it. Unfortunately, they did not succeed in the quest.

I suspect there were very simple reasons for this. A good deal can be got at by means of discussion and arrangement; but a "German" and "nobly-serene" opera, such as Mendelssohn in his delicate ambition dreamt of, is not exactly a thing that can be manufactured—nor old nor new testamentary recipes will serve the purpose. The master did not live to reach the goal: but his companions and apprentices continued their efforts.

Herr Hiller believed he could force on a success, simply by dint of cheerful and unflagging perseverance. Everything, he thought, depends upon a "lucky hit", such as others had made in his very presence, and which steady perseverance, as in a game of chance, must, sooner or later, bring round to him. But the "lucky hit" invariably missed. Schumann also did not succeed, and many other members of the church of abstinence, both adepts and neophytes, have since stretched forth their "chaste and innocent" hands in search of an operatic success—they troubled greatly—but their efforts proved fruitless—"the fortunate grip" failed. Now, such experiences are apt to embitter the most harmless persons. All the more so, since Kapellmeisters and Musikdirectors are daily occupied at the theatres, and are bound to serve in a sphere in which they are absolutely helpless and impotent. And the causes of their impotence, with regard to the composition of an opera, are also the causes of their inability to conduct an opera properly. Yet such is the fate of our public art, that gentlemen who are not even able to conduct concert music, are the sole leaders in the very complicated business of the opera theatres! Let a reader of discretion imagine the condition of things there!

The habits of operatic directors

I have been prolix in showing the weakness of our conductors, in the very field, where, by rights, they ought to feel at home. I can be brief now with regard to the opera. Here it simply comes to this: "Father, forgive them; for they know not what they do". To characterize their disgraceful doings, I should have to show how much that is good and significant *might* be done at the theatres, and this would lead me too far. Let it be reserved for another occasion. For the present I shall only say a little about their ways as operatic conductors.

In the concert room these gentlemen go to work with the most serious mien; at the opera they deem it becoming to put on a nonchalant, sceptical, cleverly-frivolous air. They concede with a smile that they are not quite at home in the opera, and do not profess to understand much about things which they do not particularly esteem. Accordingly, they are very accommodating and complaisant towards vocalists, female and male, for whom they are glad to make matters comfortable; they arrange the tempo, introduce fermatas, *ritardandos*, *accelerandos*, transpositions, and, above all, "cuts", whenever and wherever a vocalist chooses to call for such.

Whence indeed are they to derive the authority to resist this or that absurd demand? If, perchance, a pedantically disposed conductor should incline to insist upon this or that detail, he will, as a rule, be found in the wrong. For vocalists are at least at home and, in their own frivolous way, at ease in the opera; they know well enough what they can do, and how to do it; so that, if anything worthy of admiration is produced in the operatic world it is generally due to the right instincts of the vocalists,

160

just as in the orchestra the merit lies almost entirely in the good sense of the musicians. [...]

The aesthetic principle

Our conductors [...] have no notion that a perfectly correct performance, be it of the most insignificant opera can produce an excellent impression upon an educated mind, simply by reason of its correctness. Even the shallowest theatrical concoctions, at the smallest Parisian theatres, can produce a pleasant aesthetical effect, since, as a rule, they are carefully rehearsed, and correctly rendered. The power of the artistic principle is, in fact, so great that an aesthetic result is at once attained, if only some part of that principle be properly applied, and its conditions fulfilled: and such is true art, although it may be on a very low level.

But we do not get such aesthetic results in Germany, unless it be at performances of ballets, in Vienna, or Berlin. Here the whole matter is in the hands of one man—the ballet-master—and that man knows his business. [...] In this way the stage manager might lend his aid to the ensemble of the opera. But, singularly enough, the fiction that the opera is a branch of absolute music is everywhere kept up; every vocalist is aware of the musical director's ignorance of the business of an opera; yet—if it should happen that the right instincts of gifted singers, musicians and executants generally are aroused by a fine work, and bring about a successful performance—are we not accustomed to see the Herr Kapellmeister called to the front, and otherwise rewarded, as the representative of the total artistic achievement? Ought he not himself to be surprised at this? Is he not, in his turn, in a position to pray, "Forgive them, they know not what they do"?

But as I wished to speak of conducting proper, and do not want to lose my way in the operatic wilderness, I have only to confess that I have come to the end of this chapter. I cannot dis-

161

pute about the conducting of our Kapellmeisters at the theatres. Singers may do so, when they have to complain that this conductor is not accommodating enough, or that the other one does not give them their cues properly: in short, from the stand-point of vulgar journeyman-work, a discussion may be possible. But from the point of view of truly artistic work this sort of conducting cannot be taken into account at all. Among Germans, now living, I am, perhaps, the only person who can venture openly to pronounce so general a condemnation, and I maintain that I am not exceeding the limits of my province when I do so.

The Prelude to Die Meistersinger

If I try to sum up my experiences, regarding performances of my own operas, I am at a loss to distinguish with which of the qualities of our conductors I am concerned. Is it the spirit in which they treat German music in the concert rooms, or the spirit in which they deal with the opera at the theatres? I believe it to be my particular and personal misfortune that the two spirits meet in my operas, and mutually encourage one another in a rather dubious kind of way. Whenever the former spirit, which practices upon our classical concert music, gets a chance—as in the instrumental introductions to my operas—I have invariably discovered the disastrous consequences of the bad habits already described at such length.

I need only speak of the tempo, which is either absurdly hurried [...], or muddled [...], or both dragged and muddled [...], yet never with those well-considered modifications of the tempo, upon which I must count as much as upon the correct intonation of the notes themselves, if an intelligible rendering is to be obtained.

To convey some notion of faulty performances of the latter sort it will suffice to point to the way in which the overture to Die Meistersinger is usually given. [...] This overture was first performed at a concert at Leipzig, when I conducted it as described above. It was so well played by the orchestra that the small audience, consisting for the most part of non-resident friends, demanded an immediate repetition, which the musicians, who agreed with the audience, gladly accorded. The favourable impression thus created was much talked of, and the directors of the *Gewandhaus* Concerts decided to give the native Leipzig public a chance to hear the new overture.

In this instance Herr Kapellmeister Reinecke, who had heard the piece under my direction, conducted it, and the very same orchestra played it—in such wise that the audience hissed! I do not care to investigate how far this result was due to the straightforward honesty of the persons concerned; let it suffice that competent musicians, who were present at the performance, described to me the sort of time the Herr Kapellmeister had thought fit to beat to the overture—and therewith I knew enough. [...]

Safely bedded thus, not only the overture, but, as will appear in the sequel, the entire opera of *Die Meistersinger*, or as much of it as was left after the Kapellmeister's cuts, was presented to the public of Dresden. [...] The ultimate results were as follows: I had made use of the combination of the two main themes under an ideal tempo *andante alla breve* to form a pleasant and cheerful conclusion to the entire opera, something after the manner of a burden to some old popular song: I had augmented and enlarged the treatment of the thematic combination for this purpose, and now employed it as a sort of accompaniment to Hans Sachs's epilogising praise of the "Mastersingers", and to his consolatory rhymes upon German art, with which the work ends.

Though the words are serious, the closing apostrophe is none the less meant to have a cheering and hopeful effect; and, to produce this, I counted upon that simple thematic combination, the rhythmical movement of which was intended to proceed smoothly, and was not meant to assume a pompous character, except just before the end, when the chorus enters. Now in the overture, the conductor had failed to see the necessity of a modification of the original march-like tempo in the direction of an *andante alla breve*; and, of course, here—at the close of the opera—he equally failed to feel that the movement was not directly connected with the march tempo—his first mistake was therefore continued, and he proceeded to confine and hold fast the warmly-feeling singer of the part of Hans Sachs in rigid 4/4 time, and to compel him to deliver his final address in the stiffest and most awkward manner possible.

The "cuts"

Friends of mine requested me to permit a large "cut" for Dresden, as the effect of the close was so very depressing. I declined. [...]

"Cut! Cut!"—this is the ultimo ratio of our conductors; by its aid they establish a satisfactory equilibrium between their own incompetence, and the proper execution of the artistic tasks before them. They remember the proverb: "What I know not, burns me not!", and the public cannot object to an arrangement so eminently practical. It only remains for me to consider what I am to say to a performance of my work, which thus appears enclosed between a failure at Alpha, and a failure at Omega?

Outwardly things look very pleasant: An unusually animated audience, and an ovation for the Herr Kapellmeister—to join in which the royal father of my country returns to the front of his box. But, subsequently, ominous reports about cuts which had been made, and further changes and abbreviations super-added. [...]

On the other hand there is some little consolation in the fact that in spite of all ill-treatment the work retains some of its power—that fatal power and "effect" against which the professors of the Leipzig conservatorium so earnestly warn their pupils, and against which all sorts of destructive tactics are applied in vain!. [...] I am content to accept the "success" of the work as a consolatory example illustrating the fate of our classical music in the hands of our conducting musicians. Classical music retains its warmth, and continues to exist in spite of the maltreatment they subject it to. It appears truly indestructible: and the Spirit of German art may accept this indestructibility as a consoling fact, and may fearlessly continue its efforts in future.

It might be asked: But what do the marvellous conductors with celebrated names amount to, considered simply as practical musicians? Looking at their perfect unanimity in every practical matter one might be led to think that, after all, they understand their business properly, and that, in spite of the protest of one's feelings, their ways might even be "classical". The general public is so ready to take the excellence of their doings for granted, and to accept it as a matter of course, that the middle- class musical people are not troubled with the slightest doubt as to who is to beat time at their musical festivals, or on any other great occasion when the nation desires to hear some music. [...] On the other hand, I am sorry to say I know of no one to whom I would confidently entrust a single tempo in one of my operas; certainly to no member of the staff of our army of time-beaters.

The poor devils

Now and then I have met with some poor devil who showed real skill and talent for conducting: but such rare fellows find it difficult to get on, because they are apt not only to see through the incompetence of the celebrities, but imprudent enough to speak about it. [...] Such gifted poor fellows are destined to perish like the heretics of old. As everything is thus apparently in good order, and seems likely to remain so, I am again tempted to ask how can this be? We entertain lurking doubts whether these gentlemen really are musicians; evidently they do not evince the slightest musical; yet, in fact, they hear very accurately (with mathematical, not ideal, accuracy; contretemps like that of the faulty orchestra parts do not happen to everyone); they are quick at a score, read and play at sight (many of them, at least, do so); in short, they prove true professionals; but, alongside of this, their general education —in spite of all efforts – is such as can pass muster in the case of a musician only; so that, if music were struck from the list of their attainments, there would be little left—least of all, a man of spirit and sense.

No, no! They certainly *are* musicians and very competent musicians, who know and can do everything that pertains to music. Well, then? As soon as they begin to perform music they muddle matters […]. That which makes our great music great is the very thing which confuses these people; unfortunately, this cannot be expressed in words and concepts, nor in arithmetical figures. Yet, what is it other than music? and music only! What, then, can be the reason of this barrenness, dryness, coldness, this complete inability to feel the influence of true music, and, in its presence, to forget any little vexation, any small jealous distress, or any mistaken personal notion? […]

If then our celebrated and uncelebrated conductors happen to be born for music only under the sign of Numbers, it would seem very desirable that some new school might be able to teach them the proper tempo for our music by the rule of three. I doubt whether they will ever acquire it in the simple way of musical feeling; wherefore, I believe, I have now reached the end of my task.

Perhaps the new school is already in sight.

CHARLES GOUNOD

The interpretation of Mozart's music – 1890

*The Conductor is the centre of the musical per-
formance. This word, in itself, shows the importance and responsibility of his functions.*

Charles Gounod

*In 1890, Charles Gounod (1818-1893) published in an appendix to
his* Mozart's Don Giovanni, *a commentary on the work of the great
Austrian composer, a short essay on the interpretation of his music and
operas. Among the six aspects he considers, Gounod dwells on the figure
of the conductor, defining him as the "centre of the musical performance"
and underscoring his fundamental importance.*

Mozart's music, so clear, true, natural, and penetrating, is,
notwithstanding, seldom perfectly performed. What is the reason? This is the question I propose to examine, and, if possible,
to make comprehensible to my readers in this Appendix.

In the execution of the works of Mozart, it is necessary, before everything, to avoid seeking for effect. I mean here by the
word effect not the impression produced on the listener by the
work itself, an impression of charm, grace, tenderness, terror—
in a word, all the feelings which the musical text offers, or, at
least, should offer, by itself in the form and portrayal — but that
exaggeration of accent, light and shade, and time which too often
lead the executants to substitute their own ideas for those of the
author, and to distort the nature of his thoughts instead of reproducing them simply and faithfully.

When a great musician has written a work, and such a musician as Mozart, the least that one can do him the honour to suppose is that he has wished to write what he has written, and there are very strong presumptive reasons for saying that in trying to express more than Mozart has done they would express less. What would be thought of an engraver who should replace by outlines and figures of his own those of a picture by Raphael? Does an actor dare to introduce a phrase, a verse, a word of his own invention in a work of Racine or Molière? Why should the language of sounds be treated with less respect than that of words? Is the truth of expression less an obligation in one than the other? What remains of a musical thought if executants distort accents, nuances, and the respective values of notes? Absolutely nothing. Many singers do not give the least thought to these matters. Preoccupied as they too often are with the idea of gaining admiration for their voices, they sacrifice without scruple the demands of expression to the success of the virtuoso and the lasting triumph of truth to the empty and evanescent gratification of vanity.

It is hardly necessary to say that in thus permitting personal whims to replace obedience to the text, a gulf is created between the author and the auditor. What meaning is there, for example, in a prolonged pause on certain notes, to the detriment of the rhythm and the balance of the music phrase? Do they reflect for an instant on the perpetual irritation caused to the listener — to say nothing of the insupportable monotony of the proceeding itself. And then what becomes of the orchestral design in this constant subordination to the singer's caprice?

It is impossible to draw up a complete catalogue of abuses and licences of all sorts which in the execution alter the nature of the sense and compromise the impression of a musical phrase. One may be permitted to remind musicians that want of attention to the following points causes nearly all the usual infractions of the rules of art and of good taste:

The rate of movement – The light and shade – The breathing – The pronunciation – The conductor.

The Rate of Movement.

Whenever the real expression, the true character, the just sentiment of a piece depends upon the ensemble, the most important, the most indispensable condition is, undoubtedly, the exact and scrupulous observance of the time in which the composer has conceived it.

The speed determines its general character and, as this character is an essential part of the idea, to alter the time is to alter the idea itself to such a degree as to destroy sometimes the sense and expression. It cannot be denied that a musical phrase may be absolutely travestied and disfigured by an excess of slowness or rapidity of the time in which it is performed. I could quote many examples.

Here is one which I shall never forget, it shocked me so much. At a ball given by the Minister of State during the winter of 1854-55, if I mistake not, the old contredanse (quadrille) was still in existence, or, rather, was just dying out. All of a sudden I heard the orchestra strike up the first figure. Horror! Abomination! Sacrilege! It was the sublime air of the High Priest of Isis in Mozart's *Il Flauto Magico* falling from the height of its solemn and sacred rhythm into the grotesque stamping of satin shoes and patent leather boots. I fled as if I had the devil at my heels!

However, a very incomplete idea of the importance of the musical movement would be formed if it were considered purely from a mathematical point of view only, and I shall now endeavour to consider the circumstances which might cause mathematical differences in the time, the music nevertheless retaining its identity of character and expression:

The size of the building in which the performance is held. This is a question of acoustics and proportion. In a very large hall, a movement would bear to be taken less quickly than if executed in a smaller one. The style of the executant, the amplitude of delivery, and the production of the voice.

I will cite here two famous examples — Duprez and Fauré. When Duprez came to the *Opéra* and filled the place which

Nourrit had occupied with so much brilliancy and distinction for fifteen years, it was a complete revolution in lyrical declamation. Nourrit was a great artist; the dignity of his character, the culture of his intelligence, a constant care of truth in his varied and numerous roles of the repertoire of that period — these qualities obtained for him not only the favour and esteem of the public, but an influence at the theatre which was felt by all around him. With rare talent as an artist he played the principal parts in all the grand operas, from *La Vestale, Masaniello,* and *Guillaume Tell,* to *Robert le Diable, La Juive,* and *Les Huguenots,* in the last of which he created the part of Raoul de Nangis, stamping it with an ineffaceable impression. His powerful acting so held his audience that he succeeded in making them forget that his voice was a little thin and guttural, and that he used the falsetto register too frequently. The coming of Duprez took everybody by storm. I was present at his debut which took place in the part of Arnold (*Guillaume Tell*). Duprez returned from Italy preceded by a great reputation and the well-known story of the chest C, which was to raise a tempest of applause at the end of the celebrated air of the last act. It was unnecessary to wait till then to know that the success of the great singer was assured. In two bars it was made. From the first verse of the recitative, *"Il me parle d' hymen ! Jamais, jamais le mien!"* One felt that this was a transformation in the art of singing, and when Duprez finished the phrase of the duet in the second act, *"Oh, Mathilde ! Idole de mon âme",* there was a frenzy of enthusiasm throughout the house. He had a breadth of declamation and volume of tone which captivated the hearer, and the admirable melodies of the great Italian master shone with a new lustre owing to the marvellous notes of his voice. The use of the chest voice and the amplitude of his declamation, permitted Duprez to take the time slower than his illustrious predecessor had done without appearing to alter it, so well did he know how to captivate the ear by the fullness of his voice, and to move the audience by his dramatic powers.

Fauré in our day has been a new and striking example of the same thing. He produces the sounds with such richness and fullness, he gives them such interest by a continual modulation of the tone [...] that one forgets the duration which he gives them, and which is hidden under his admirable method and his unrivalled pronunciation.

To these illustrious names must be added those of Pauline Viardot, Miolan-Carvalho, Gabrielle Krauss, the brothers De Reszke, Lassalle, and others who have understood the importance of declamation.

But the preceding remarks on time have nothing to do with the accent, which is also, from an entirely different point of view, a matter of great importance. Unfortunately, many singers of today do not sufficiently consider this subject, great detriment being thus caused to the music and considerable annoyance to both composer and conductor. Much might be said upon this topic. I must be satisfied to touch lightly upon it, as this is not the place to set forth a complete course of musical education.

The bar and the accent

Disregard of the accent is one of the modern faults, it entirely destroys the musical equilibrium. Many singers regard the bar as an insupportable yoke, and as an obstacle to feeling and expression. They think that it makes machines of them, and that it takes away all grace, charm, warmth, and freedom in performance. Now it is exactly the reverse. The bar, instead of being the enemy to the musical phrase, gives protection and freedom to it. It is not difficult to demonstrate this. Let us consider it first as a principle of unanimity of performance.

The essential character of the bar is the equality of the duration of the beats which compose it. If, then, inequality is introduced, the unity which is essential to the phrase, and which alone permits one to feel it, is destroyed.

If the misrepresentation of the bar is injurious to such an extent upon an isolated phrase, what confusion will it not bring in the execution of an ensemble? The effect would be indescribable.

There is still the orchestra to be considered. It presents a multitude of figures of accompaniment subjected to the laws of accent, and from which laws there can be no deviation under penalty of abominable confusion. Sixty or eighty musicians cannot be left in a state of constant uncertainty. Deprived of the word of command, they will not know what to do in order to avoid disorder and cacophony.

But the bar, which is a principle of order with regard to the rhythm, is no less essential to the expression. The idea of the bar includes that of rhythm, which is its characteristic sub-division. To neglect the bar and its regulating influence injures the rhythm and the prosody.

These few reflections are sufficient to give an idea of the detrimental effects which disregard of the accent may cause to musical works. Another question of extreme importance in the matter of musical expression is that of light and shade.

Light and shade (the "nuances")

We understand by the word "nuance" the degree of intensity of any sound, whether it be produced by a voice or instrument. That is to say, the gradations of tone play in musical art a part analogous to that of proportion in the art of painting.

We see by this how the true observation of the nuances is indispensable to the faithful rendering of a musical phrase, and to what degree the thoughtless caprice of the executant can alter the sense and character to such an extent as to make it unrecognisable by substituting for the author's intentions and indications the nuances and accents of pure fancy. It is here that the independence of the singer most frequently finds the opportunity of giving free scope to his imagination, and Heaven knows how he uses it. It matters little whether the accent be neglected, whether the prosody be sacrificed, whether the melodic figure be altered, or whether affectation destroys the logical and natural movement of the musical phrase, provided that the sound be no-

172

ticed and applauded for itself. These performers are entirely mistaken as to the function and role of the voice. They take the means for the end and the servant for the master. They forget that fundamentally there is but one art, (the word) and one function, (to express) and that consequently a great singer ought to be first of all a great orator, and that is utterly impossible without absolutely truthful accent. When singers, especially on the stage, think only of displaying the voice, they should be reminded that that is a sure and infallible means of falling into monotony; truth alone has the privilege of infinite and inexhaustible variety.

The breathing

This important question of the breathing may be regarded under two distinct aspects — the one purely physical, the other purely expressive. Under the first it devolves upon the composer to write in such a way as not to exceed the power of the respiratory organs, under the penalty of seeing his musical phrase divided into fragments, which would disfigure it.

But, as regards the expression, it is another thing. Here it is prosody and punctuation which determine and regulate the expression. Unfortunately this rule is seldom observed. A singer does not scruple to divide a section of a phrase, often even a word, in order to take breath, for the sake of a sound to which they wish to give exaggerated power and duration, to the detriment of the musical sense and the prosody, which ought to be the first consideration. It is ridiculous to introduce, for example, a respiration between "my" and " love" in the phrase "To thee I give my love! " — a respiration which nothing can justify; but then the singer has had the pleasure of showing off on a short syllable until all the breath has been used, just for the sake of gaining a noisy demonstration of conventional applause. Such licences simply disfigure the form of the musical idea, and are revolting to common sense.

The Pronunciation.

There are two special points to observe in the pronunciation:
– It should be clear, neat, distinct, and exact; that is to say, the ear ought not to be left in any uncertainty as to the word pronounced
– It should be expressive; that is to say, to paint in the mind the feeling enunciated by the word itself.

All that concerns clearness, neatness, and exactness may be more properly classed as articulation. Articulation relates to the due formation of every sound in the word. Everything else may be described as pronunciation. It is by the latter that we make the word picture the thought, the feeling, the passion which it envelops. In short, the function of articulation is to form the material sounds of a word, whereas that of pronunciation is to reveal its inner meaning. Articulation gives clearness to the word; pronunciation gives it eloquence. True instinct, though lacking culture, can make all these distinctions apparent. One cannot insist too much upon the value and interest which clear articulation and expressive pronunciation give to singing, so important are they. By the force of expression, they exercise such a power over the listener that they make him forget the insufficiency or the mediocrity of the vocal organ; whilst the absence of these qualities, though the voice may be the most beautiful in the world, leaves him unmoved.

The foregoing considerations show how much depends upon simplicity, sincerity, and freedom from all preoccupation as to personal success. Can there be a higher ambition for a performer than to be an artist capable and worthy of interpreting Mozart's music, so pure and so true; or a more noble dream than to inspire love for the works of such a master, and thus contribute to the sacred and salutary devotion to the true and the beautiful? But, alas! in art, as in everything else, the abnegation of self is rare, although it is the condition of all true greatness.

It remains only to speak now of the conductor, who plays such an important part in the performance.

The Conductor

The conductor is the centre of the musical performance. This word, in itself, shows the importance and responsibility of his functions. First of all, the unity of the movement, without which there is no possible ensemble, is in the hands of the conductor. That is self-evident, and does not need demonstration. It is on this point most necessary, and at the same time most easy, for the conductor to make his authority felt; his baton is one of command. But, apart from the ensembles, how often does this command degenerate into servitude? What compliance there is to the caprices of the singers, and what fatal neglect of the interests of art and the real value of the works performed!

However, it is not necessary that the rule of the conductor should amount to an unyielding and mechanical rigidity, which would be the absurd triumph of the letter over the spirit. A conductor who would be like an inflexible metronome throughout a musical composition would be guilty of an excess of strictness as unbearable as an excess of laxity.

The great art of the conductor is that power which may be called suggestive, and which elicits from the singer an unconscious obedience, whilst making him believe that it is his own will that he follows. In short, the singer must be persuaded and not constrained. Power is not in the will, but in the intelligence; it is not questioned, but it is felt. It behoves the conductor, then, to understand, and to make others understand, how much he will concede to them in the matter of time without altering the character of the movement. It is his duty to seize upon the difference between elasticity and stiffness, and to atone, without abruptness, for any momentary retardation by an imperceptible return to the normal and regular time. It is also essential that the conductor should not mistake precipitation for warmth —

175

the result would be to sacrifice the rhythmical power of the declamation and the fullness of tone.

It is commonly imagined that a *crescendo* ought to be hurried, and a *diminuendo* gradually slackened. Now, it is precisely the contrary which is nearly always the case. It stands to reason that one feels inclined to lengthen a sound in augmenting its intensity, and vice versa. But this is not all.

It is an error to think that the conductor can make himself entirely understood by means of the baton or the bow which he holds in his hand. His whole demeanour should instruct and animate those who obey him. His attitude, his physiognomy, his glance should prepare the singers for that which is demanded of them ; his expression should cause them to anticipate his intentions, and should enlighten the executants. Yet it is not necessary for him to indulge in wild gesticulations.

True power is calm, and when the poet of antiquity wished to express the might of Jupiter, he represented him as making the whole of Olympus tremble at his nod. In short, the conductor is the ambassador of the thought of the composer and he is responsible for it before the artists and audience – he has to be its living expression, its faithful mirror, its incorruptible repository. Entire volumes could be written about this important function of the conductor and I am convinced that it should be the subject of an educational course, which would fit naturally within the curriculum of our music schools. There is a gap here, which will hopefully be filled in future. Apart from the considerable benefits for the musical works themselves, it would act as a kind of foretaste of all the special, rare and essential skills required and a guarantee of authority for all the performers the conductor is called upon to direct.

FELIX WEINGARTNER

On conducting

The role of the conductor should never dominate
that of the composer

F. Weingartner

It is no coincidence that essay by Felix Weingartner (1863-1942) on conducting has the same title as Wagner's treatise of 1869. Weingartner presents his text, which appeared for the first time in 1895, "not as plagiarism of Wagner's study, as it has been defined, but rather as counterpoint to it, or its effective continuation. [...] if Wagner's writings tended towards liberation from bland formalism", asserts the Austrian composer, "mine is a cry of alarm against absence of form, which, wishing to be too ingenious, is equally bland. Formalism and absence of form both betoken the death of art". For this reason, Weingartner warns against slavish imitation of the most famous conductor of the time, Hans von Bülow, of whom he gives a more balanced evaluation, going against contemporary trends and attracting much criticism on himself. The aim of his essay is to put an end to the whims of conductors who, driven by the cult of personality, take the liberty of modifying or misinterpreting the works of the great composers simply for personal gain. Indeed, the role of the conductor is essential for the artistic performance, but it should never dominate that of the composer.

When I first published this essay in 1895 it cannot be said to have been received favourably. At the time delusion about Bülow's infallibility was at its height and it was considered unconscionable for a young artist to dare to oppose him. Even my right to pursue a literary activity was questioned, to which I re-

177

sponded by publishing a second polemical article dealing with the infallibility delusion in vogue in Bayreuth. Now that the ball was rolling, there could not be enough nasty words for what I did and said. Unperturbed, I tried to find my way through the throng, working and observing, clinging to Goethe's opinion about a virtuous man – it is more proper to do what is just than worry whether justice has been achieved. And I found my way. When in 1905 a third edition of my essay on conducting became necessary, I based it on the experience I had meanwhile acquired: thus a considerable enlargement was called for. The present fourth edition differs from the third chiefly in a clearer arrangement of the material

Under the same title as that of the present volume, Richard Wagner published in 1869 his well-known brochure, which, assailing as it did with uncompromising candour the most famous conductors of that epoch, drew upon him the furious enmity of the persons he attacked.

In spite, however, of the hatred, open or concealed, of the music-popes whose infallibility was assailed, Wagner's book laid the foundation for a new understanding of the function of the conductor, in whom we now recognise not only the external factor that holds together an orchestral, choral or operatic performance, but above all the spiritualising internal factor that gives the performance its very soul. Wagner was certainly not the first to realise how much depends on the way a piece of music is rendered.

He opines that the reason Bach rarely marked tempi in his scores was because he said to himself, as it were, "If anyone does not understand my theme and my figuration, has no feeling for their character and their expression, of what use will an Italian tempo-indication be to him"? I maintain, on the contrary, that the vigorous old master would have been incapable of looking at art in this resigned way. I believe rather that he so rarely indicated the tempo or gave any dynamic marks only because he always had in view his own presence at the performances. If we picture to ourselves a Bach performance in his own lifetime we must think of himself at the organ with his little band of musicians round him. How many of his innumerable cantatas, now assured of immortality, must in his own day have been sung just once, on the Feast-day for which they were composed, whereupon the manuscript went into the drawer "with the others", and for the next Feast-day the inexhaustible Cantor wrote a new one! His Suites and Concertos, again, are to be regarded as chamber-music works at whose production he himself or a privileged pupil sat at the clavicembalo; the "Well-tempered Clavier" and the Sonatas were intended as studies. Why should he waste time in noting down instructions for execution? It always rested with him to give the correct tempo, and to explain to the musicians the interpretation he wanted. The mighty teacher of the Thomas-School certainly never anticipated a collected edition of his works [...] nor did he anticipate concert productions of them with large orchestras and choruses.

Also in the early works of Mozart and Haydn we find, for similar reasons, few indication about the execution. Only in the wake of greater dissemination of the works was the necessity felt by these maestri for more detailed guidance which, especially at the time of Mozart's maturity, attained a high level of precision. We know that not only Mozart, but Weber, Mendelssohn and Spohr were excellent conductors, and that each of them, from his own artistic standpoint, fought energetically against abuses and errors of taste. How Wagner did this is shown among other things in the book of his I have mentioned. This, however, with all its perfect outspokenness, seems quite mild when we read the flaming words with which Berlioz opens his treatise on "The theory of the conductor's art". He says:

Singers have often been reproached with being the most dangerous of the factors concerned in the production of music; but, I think, unjustly. The most formidable intermediary is in my opinion the conductor. A bad singer can spoil only his own part, while an incompetent or malicious conductor

179

can spoil everything. The composer must indeed count himself fortunate when the conductor into whose hands he has fallen is not both incompetent and malicious; for against the destructive influence of such a man nothing can avail. The most excellent orchestra is crippled by him; the finest singers are perplexed and exhausted; there is no longer any ardour or precision in the rendering. Under conducting of this kind the composer's finest audacities become mere oddities; enthusiasm is killed; inspiration comes precipitately to earth; the angel's wings are clipped; a genius is made to look like an eccentric or a madman; the godlike statue is thrown from its pedestal and dragged in the mud. The worst of it is that the public, no matter how good its musical education may be, is not in a position, at the first performance of a new work, to detect the mutilations, stupidities, errors and sins against art that such a conductor has on his conscience.

What experiences Berlioz must have had for this wild cry to be drawn from him can be estimated from the single fact that a conductor who in the first half of the nineteenth century occupied a really foremost position, and of whom both Wagner and Berlioz spoke with the warmest acknowledgement, that Habeneck of Paris, as Berlioz tells us, conducted not from the score but from a violin part, a custom today confined to beer-garden concerts with their waltzes and pot-pourris. Yet Habeneck, by means of diligent rehearsals with the orchestra of the Conservatoire, must have given performances of a technical perfection that as a rule could not be met with in Germany at the same time; Wagner confesses that it was from Habeneck's rendering that he first really understood Beethoven's Ninth Symphony, after having received at the Leipzig *Gewandhaus* such confused impressions of it that for a time he "had his doubts" even about Beethoven himself.

Like so many things in Wagner's writings, these "doubts" must not be taken literally, for a musician of his rank must have been able to judge from his knowledge of the score of which indeed he had made a manuscript copy for himself how much of the confused impression was due to the work and how much to the rendering. The fact remains, however, that a bad interpretation can not only completely deceive the uninstructed but also prevent the instructed from listening with full sympathy. I still remember in the early eighties, when I was a pupil at the Leipzig Conservatoire, to have heard some performances by the splendid *Gewandhaus* Orchestra, which, through the fault of its half solid, half elegant conductor, answered so little to the ideas I had formed for myself of the works in question, that I preferred not to stay to the end of many of the performances, so as not to have my precious picture marred.

Bülow's "performances"

Of course I did not "have doubts" about any of our masters. Only my longing increased to be able at some time to render the works as I felt them. As I gave imprudently outspoken expression to this desire and to my dissatisfaction with what I heard, it was looked upon as unwarrantable self-glorification on my part. However, as Bülow soon afterwards appeared with the Meiningen orchestra, people then realised what was meant by a finely-balanced ensemble, and I heard much agreement expressed with what I had previously maintained.

The impression of Bülow's interpretations must have kindled in our Leipzig conductor a spark of that temperament that had been long extinguished under the ashes of convention, for at one of the concerts given after the visit of the Meiningen band he played the great *Fidelio* Overture (*Leonore*) in a quite surprising way. It was especially noticeable, however, that he did not imitate Bülow's arbitrarinesses, of which I shall speak later but let the work unfold itself in great- featured simplicity.

And as his was the larger and better orchestra, the effect was such that the generally rather reserved audience broke out into a huge exclamation of joy, that even surpassed the storms of applause that had been given to Bülow. In a few minutes the affectedness was blown away as by a breeze from heaven, all arbitrariness was banished, and Beethoven spoke to us without commentary. This experience was very instructive to me.

When Wagner, after his first Parisian sojourn, came to Dresden as conductor, he had learned from Habeneck to what perfection orchestral performances can attain under conscientious guidance; and from all we have learned of him as conductor, from himself and from others, he obviously aimed in his own performances not only at correctness but at bringing out that to which the sounds and notes are only the means. He sought for the unifying thread, the psychological line, the revelation of which suddenly transforms, as if by magic, a more or less indefinite sound-picture into a beautifully shaped, heart-moving vision, making people ask themselves in astonishment how it is that this work, which they had long thought they knew, should have all at once become quite another thing, and the unprejudiced mind joyfully confesses, "Yes, thus, thus-; must it really be". Out of the garment of tone there emerges the genius of the artwork; its noble countenance, formerly only confusedly visible, is now unveiled, and enraptures those who are privileged to behold it. Wagner calls this form, this quintessence, this spirit of the artwork its *melos*, which term, later on, was perverted by inability to understand Wagner's own creations into "endless melody". His desire to make this *melos* stand out clearly carried him so far that in some places in Beethoven's works where he held the evident purpose of the composer to be not fully realised in the orchestration, whether because the instruments at Beethoven's disposal were imperfect, or because his increasing deafness sometimes clouded his perception of the relations of the various orchestral timbres, he discreetly altered the orchestration, touching it up so as to bring the hitherto unclear melody into due prominence.

Of course the music-popes and wretched literalists screamed anathema. It is certainly open to question whether all these retouchings were happy and deserving of imitation; there is no doubt however that he very often hit upon the right thing. I believe, for example, that nowadays no conductor who can think at all will play the Ninth Symphony without Wagner's instrumental emendations.

Added to this desire for clarity in Wagner was the passionate temperament with which, aided by a keen understanding, he threw himself into his work; he brought to it also a faculty of immediate communication with the players and imposition of his will on them, in a word that genius which, in spite of other acknowledgements, he had to deny to Habeneck, but which made some of his own performances historically memorable, in spite of the perishable nature of all reproductive art.

I regret that I never saw Wagner conduct. He was described to me; the body, of no more than middle-height, with its stiff deportment, the movement of the arms not immoderately great or sweeping, but decisive and very much to the point; showing no restlessness, in spite of his vivacity; usually not needing the score at the concert; fixing his expressive glance on the players and ruling the orchestra imperially, like the Weber he used to admire as a boy. The old flautist Fürstenau of Dresden told me that often, when Wagner conducted, the players had no sense of being led. Each believed himself to be following "freely his own feeling, yet they all worked together wonderfully. It was Wagner's mighty will that powerfully but unperceived had overborne their single wills, so that each thought himself free, while in reality he only followed the leader, whose artistic force lived and worked in him. "Everything went so easily and beautifully that it was the height of enjoyment", said Fürstenau; and the eyes of the old artist gleamed with joyful enthusiasm.

After Wagner had given up regular conducting he sought to transfer his feeling, his insight and his power to some younger, plastic spirits in whom they might live on. His plan of an ideal school, where singers and conductors of the type he desired should be trained, was not realised owing to the indolence of his contemporaries. A few young musicians associated themselves with him, to whom he now imparted of his spirit. Of these, the

183

oldest is the most significant his intimate friend, at that time his most faithful champion, his alter ego, as he himself once called him the master-conductor Hans von Bülow. After a comparatively short co-operation, they had to part company, and Bülow's star first shone brilliantly again when in 1880 he became chief of the Meiningen orchestra. A year later the Duke, whose scenic art had already effectively influenced the dramatic theatre, sent him off with the orchestra on a grand concert- tour through Germany, Austria and Russia.

Seldom has such a victory of mind over matter been seen. A rather poorly-appointed orchestra, by no means absolutely excellent in its proportions, conquered everywhere the large orchestras, famous the whole world over as possessing the best artists; this was the work of the eminent conductor, who – a second Leonidas – had the courage to defy with a small troop of admirably schooled players the big musical armies that were mostly led by ordinary time-beaters. By dint of diligent, indefatigable practice he had so infused into the orchestra his own conception of the works as to get a perfection of ensemble at that time unknown. The most scrupulous rhythmical exactitude was united with so artistic a balance of the various timbres, that the question whether this or that player was the better, or whether this or that peculiarity of the conductor was justifiable, could scarcely be raised. The orchestra seemed to be a single instrument, on which Bülow played as on a pianoforte.

These concert-tours of the Meiningen orchestra were of inestimable significance. Those whom it concerned recognised that it would not do to go on simply beating time and playing away with the old reprehensible carelessness and thoughtlessness, for that would certainly lower them in the eyes of the public, which, after once having nibbled dainties at the table of the great, would no longer be content with canteen-fare.

Rehearsals

So these people first of all took pains to cultivate the orchestra better on the technical side, held more rehearsals, followed more conscientiously the dynamic indications, and in general gave more attention to accurate ensemble. The capability of orchestras has since then greatly increased, and composers today can set problems that even a few years ago would have seemed insoluble, while at the same time a better rendering of the works of the old masters has been made possible.

These things represent the gain from Bülow's work, and make his name an ineradicable landmark in the evolution of the art of conducting; to him alone, after those great composers who themselves were notable conductors , we owe the diffusion and the strengthening of the consciousness that conducting is an art and not a handicraft. But Bülow's work had also its harmful features, for which the guilt lies both with himself and a number of his followers; and to expose these and attack them is as much a duty of sincerity as to acknowledge the gains with frank delight.

In the first place, it cannot be denied that even while he was leader of the Meiningen orchestra there was often to be detected a pedagogic element in Bülow's renderings. It was clearly seen that he wished to deal a blow on the one side at philistine, metronomic time-beating, on the other side at a certain elegant off-handedness. Where a modification of the tempo was necessary to get expressive phrasing, it happened that in order to make this modification quite clear to his hearers he exaggerated it; indeed, he fell into a quite new tempo that was a negation of the main one; the *Egmont* overture was a case in point. Wagner tells us, apropos of this motive:

which, as he says, "is so drastic an epitome of terrific earnestness and placid self-confidence", and which, as a rule, "was tossed about like a withered leaf in the uncontrollable rush of the *allegro*" that he induced Bülow to play it in the true sense of the composer, modifying "ever so little" the hitherto passionate tempo, "so that the orchestra might have a proper chance to accentuate this dual theme, with its rapid fluctuation between great energy and thoughtful self-content".

All who have heard this overture under Bülow must agree with me that at the place in question he by no means made "ever so little" a modification, but leaped at once from the *allegro* into an *andante grave*, thereby destroying the uniform tempo that should be preserved in the *allegro* of the overture, as in general in every piece of music that has a uniform tempo-mark at the beginning. The proper expression can be obtained without any change of the main tempo, be it "ever so little" if the strings, who have the first two bars of the theme, are told to bring them out energetically and very precisely by a uniform down-bowing of the crotchets, thus preventing the last quaver of the first bar from being turned, as often happens, into a semiquaver, whereby indeed, as Wagner says, the effect of a dance-step is given; and when we consider that the tempo of the main part of the overture is just *allegro*, not *vivace*, there can be no danger of an "uncontrollable *allegro*-rush" if the tempo is correct.

It is a common source of trouble that introductions are taken very slowly and the main sections very fast, and the numerous gradations of these broad tempo-differences scarcely observed. We often hear the beginning of the Seventh Symphony taken *adagio*, whereas it is marked *poco sostenuto*; the finale of the Fourth Symphony is usually taken *presto*, whereas the humour of the movement only comes out when attention is given to Beethoven's marking, which is *"allegro ma non tanto"* . The introduction to the *Egmont* overture is marked *sostenuto, ma non troppo*, which does not at all signify an actually slow tempo; while the next section is marked *allegro*, that only increases to *allegro con brio* at the end, which again, however, does not imply an immod-

186

erately rapid tempo. The maintenance of an essentially easy tempo just suits the tragic weight of the work, which is completely destroyed by hurrying.

The only way I can express the distinction between the introduction (that should be taken with three moderate beats), and the main portion, is that one bar of the 3/4 section is about equivalent to a minim, and so to a third of a bar in the 3/2 section, whereby the crotchets at the entry of the *allegro* do not become about half what they are in the introduction. In this way any *ritenuto* at the place in question is superfluous, and the "terrific earnestness" of the chords

and the "calm self-confidence" of the two following bars are made perfectly clear.

Wagner quite rightly contended against the *scherzo*-tempo in which it had become usual to take the third movement of the Eighth Symphony, and claimed that it should go in comfortable minuet-time. Under Bülow, however, I heard this movement played so slowly that its humorous cheerfulness was replaced by an almost disagreeable seriousness.

It certainly belies the titanic character of the *Coriolan* Overture when, as usually happens, the chief theme and all that follows it are taken in a flying *presto* instead of *allegro con brio*, but Bülow began it almost *andante* and then increased the tempo until the pause in the seventh bar, to begin again *andante* and accelerate the sequence in the same way. In the first place, taking the incredibly characteristic theme in this way robs it of its monumental strength; in the second place, I hold that if Beethoven had wanted these subtleties he would have indicated them, since he always gave his directions for performance with the greatest precision.

Bülow's purpose as such was always clearly recognisable and also quite correct. It was as if he said to his audience, and more especially to the players: "This extremely significant passage in the *Egmont* Overture must not be scrambled through thoughtlessly; the comfortable, easy-going minuet of the Eighth Symphony must not be turned into a *scherzo*; the main theme of the *Coriolan* Overture must be given out in a way conformable to the dignity of the work".

But in the effort to be excessively clear, he often went too far. His quondam hearers and admirers will recollect that often when he had worked out a passage in an especially plastic form, he turned round to the public, perhaps expecting to see some astonished faces, chiefly, however, to say "See, that's how it should be done!" But if the Venus de Milo, for example, were suddenly to begin to speak, and to give us a lecture on the laws of her conformation, we should be a good deal sobered down. Artworks and art-performances exist only for the sake of themselves and their own beauty. If they pursue a "tendentious" aim, even though this should be instructive in the best sense, the bloom goes off them. From "tendencies" of this kind Bülow's interpretations were seldom quite free. Thence came also his proneness to make details excessively prominent. In an art-work, indeed, no one part is of less significance than another, and each detail has its full raison d'etre, but only in so far as it is subordinated to a homogeneous conception of the essential nature of the whole work, a continuous conception that dominates all detail.

It is this homogeneous conception of the essential nature of a musical work that constitutes what there is of specially artistic in its interpretation; it originates in a deep feeling that is not dependent on the intellect, that cannot, indeed, even be influenced by this, while it itself must dominate everything that pertains to the intellect, such as routine, technique, and calculation of effects. If this feeling is not strong enough, then the intellect usurps the foremost place and leads, as was often the case with Bülow, to a propensity to ingenious analysis. In the contrary case the feeling becomes unwholesomely powerful and leads to unclearness, false sentimentality and emotional vagueness. If neither feeling nor intellect is strong enough, then we get, according to the prevailing fashion, either mere metronomic time-beating or a senseless mania for nuance, a mania that chiefly prompted me to write this book. Neither, however, has anything to do with art, which is at its best when that exceedingly delicate balance, more a matter of intuition than of calculation, is attained between the feeling and the intellect, which alone can give a performance true vitality and veracity.

Concerts or lessons?

The pedagogic element I have referred to in Bülow's performances became more prominent in the last years of his life; it was linked with a capriciousness that was probably increased by his physical sufferings and his consequent spiritual distemper. This capriciousness led him into eccentricities that had no object, not even a pedagogic one, and that could have been thought fine only by those who, having quite lost the capacity for thinking for themselves, fell at Bülow's feet in blind idolatry, and pocketed his insults submissively when he now and then treated them as they deserved.

Through his habit of making speeches at his concerts he committed such errors of taste that it was difficult to maintain unimpaired the feeling of esteem that could in the most heart-felt way be given to the earlier Bülow. It was sad to see the public rushing to his concerts with the question "What will he be up to today?"

All this "hamminess" in music and the pernicious cult of personality (extremely widespread and taken to ridiculous lengths today) began with Bülow, driving every mediocre Tom, Dick and Harry to assert special rights – so long as he behaves rudely – and blinding even the effeminate, eccentric genius to the extent that he commits all manner of tomfoolery. If, on the contrary, we consider the example of great men, we see that the noblest and most distinctive mark of a great personality is precisely the awareness of measure, even when facing daring challenges. Bülow did not grasp this sense of measure and opened the doors to the worst extravagances, which today would be even more difficult to accept, since there no longer exist personalities in whom such extravagances one might be able to tolerate up to a certain point.

What Bülow did, however, was interesting, simply because he *was* a personality, though a misguided one. Where could you find a Bülow today? I would gladly spare myself the ungrateful work of enumerating some examples I myself saw of his eccentricities, if it were not necessary later on to speak of their results.

In a performance of the Ninth Symphony in Berlin he began the first movement remarkably fast, and not until the entry of the main theme did he adopt a broader tempo. In these chords, however he suddenly became almost twice as slow, and remained so until he came to the following passage, when he just as suddenly went off again into quite a fast tempo.

What was the object of these unmotivated, spasmodic derangements of the tempo? In the same performance of the Ninth Symphony I heard him render the wonderful, passion-free andante melody of the third movement with the following nuances:

making it sound like some ardent love-lament out of an Italian opera. The truth is that Beethoven's markings of *espressivo* and *crescendo* are to be interpreted discreetly, in a delicate sense consistent with the nature of the whole movement – any disturbance of the tempo must be completely bad.

One of those idolaters I have mentioned, to whom I expressed my surprise at this downright odious treatment of the divine melody, replied to me, "Yes, yes, you are right, but Bülow is Bülow; he may do anything". O blind fetish-worship and uncritical adulation, what harm have you not done!

The Eighth Symphony he once began very quickly, took the 5th, 6th, and 7th bars quite slowly, then in the 8th bar came back to his opening tempo. And so on. The impression given by performances of this kind was that not the work but the conductor was the chief thing, and that he wanted to divert the attention of the audience from the music to himself.

The readiness of the orchestra

So that finally there was nothing to admire but the readiness with which the orchestra followed him in his sometimes singular fancies. One of these was the cause of a complete rupture between Bülow and myself. I made his personal acquaintance in Eisenach, where he and the Meiningen orchestra gave a concert I shall never forget, at which there was a very impressive rendering of Beethoven's C minor Symphony. Here I had the honour to be presented to him by Liszt. He interested himself in me, later on gave a little composition of mine for string orchestra, and, the post of conductor at Hanover being then vacant through the death of Ernst Frank, recommended me without success. When the post of second conductor in Meiningen became open through the departure of Mannstaedt, I applied for it, hoping to learn a good deal by working under Bülow. I went to see him in Berlin about it. He spoke at once of my application, and said to me literally: "I cannot make use of you; you are too independent for me. I must have someone who will do absolutely only what I wish. This you could not and would not do."

Carmen

I fully agreed with him, of course. He then advised me not to turn up my nose at the most unimportant post if only I were independent so far as this is possible in the theatre and above all had no other conductor over me. Thereupon we separated. Two years later we met in Hamburg. He had engaged himself to the director Pollini to conduct thirty opera-performances in the season 1887/8; I was engaged as permanent conductor there. The first opera that he took up was *Carmen*. I am still convinced, and was so from the first moment, that at that time he was bent on the joke of trying what you can palm off on the public if you bear a famous name, a practice that has unfortunately found its counterpart to-day in the field of composition. He took almost all *Carmen*, that is so full of passion and piquancy, in a tempo that was often intolerably slow and dragging, the beginning, for example, almost andante, and Escamillo's song downright *adagio*. He further foisted on the work so many nuances, "breath-pauses", and the like, that it would have greatly astonished Bizet to have heard his opera thus given. Bülow had the satisfaction of knowing that his joke succeeded completely. His admirers and the critics agreed that now for the first time the true and only right conception of *Carmen* was given to the world. This opinion indeed found some support in the fact that the ensemble was faultless and the opera given without cuts, which were unusual things at the Hamburg *Stadttheater*. When questioned about his remarkably slow tempi, Bülow replied that "he intended in this way to suggest the dignity of the Spaniards". This remark, that was merely a jest and not a particularly good one, also met with general admiration, except from me. I soon found an opportunity to confirm my opinion by acts. Bülow being prevented from conducting *Carmen* once, it fell to my lot to do so, and later on to alternate with him. It was absolutely impossible for me to imitate him, and, against my own convictions, to take the opera in his style. I therefore held a rehearsal of my own, and conducted as I felt was right, in accordance with the instructions of the composer, in a generally lively tempo, without any affected nuances, to the joy of the orchestra and of such singers as dared to express their opinion.

After I had conducted two performances, Bülow ran to Pollini, complained that by my "arbitrary notions" I would spoil the opera for him, and insisted that I should not conduct it any more. Pollini told me of this in the friendliest way, and, with the excuse that he did not want to fall out with the always irritated Bülow, turned *Carmen* over to a colleague, who was very proud to take the opera "just like Bülow".

Could Bülow really not see from this much-discussed affair that he was blaming me for his own fault, since not I, who restored the unequivocal directions of Bizet, was the arbitrary one, but he, who had disregarded them? At any rate he never forgave me for having been sharp enough to see through his joke, and having dared to be "independent" with regard to him; and whereas on my arrival in Hamburg he had received me very cordially, he now lost no opportunity of showing his displeasure with me, which culminated in a public expression of his antipathy to me in full view of the audience, during some performances that I conducted.

Nor was his temper towards me any more friendly when

some years later in Berlin I tried to exert an influence on the symphony concerts; his jeering remarks, however, in which he gave free play to his wrath against me, and which his friends took good care should be spread abroad, necessarily kept me out of his company, much to my regret.

The greatness of Bülow

Nothing could prejudice the admiration I had for what was great in him. In the present book, however, I hope that by separating the insignificant and the paltry I have shown his greatness in its true light; and while I steadfastly maintain a standpoint in many respects contrary to his, I render what objective history will someday render to this most successful furtherer of that art of conducting that Wagner brought into new being honour and respect.

II

I once saw this aphorism in a humorous paper: "Nothing misleads us more than when a wise man does something stupid, since it is just this that we are apt to imitate in him". A true saying, true at all times and especially in the' present day. It characterises in vigorous words that epigonism that is not able to comprehend a great personality as a whole, yet wants to do as it does, and believes it can attain this by imitating this or that feature of it. But it is just the significant and characteristic features that cannot be imitated, since these pertain to genius alone, and to each genius again in a particular way. So much the more zealously, however, are the seeming and often even the real weaknesses of eminent minds imitated, since it is only in these that the great man has any actual affinity with the dullard.

It almost goes without saying that the striking phenomenon of such a conductor as Hans von Bülow was bound to lead to imitations. A whole tribe of "little Billows" sprang up, who copied the great Bülow in everything they could his nervous movements, his imperial pose, his stabs with the baton, his furious glances at the audience when anything disturbed him, his half instinctive, half demonstrative look round at some special nuance, and finally the nuances themselves. Every last gesture was imitated, even his concert-speeches were plagiarised, as I had the occasion to note in New York.

Tempo rubato conductors

I have ventured to label this kind of conductor, whose manner was a more or less complete caricature of his master's, the "tempo-rubato conductor" [*Temporubatodirigenten*].

Wagner speaks of "elegant" conductors, at the head of whom, whether with justice I rather doubt, he puts Mendelssohn: conductors who skip in the fastest possible tempo over passages that are difficult and at first sight obscure. The tempo-rubato conductors were the exact opposite to these; they sought to make the clearest passages obscure by hunting out insignificant details. Now an inner part of minor importance would be given a significance that by no means belonged to it; now an accent that should have been just lightly marked came out in a sharp *sforzato*; often a so-called "breath-pause" would be inserted, particularly in the case of a *crescendo* immediately followed by a piano, as if the music were sprinkled with *fermate*.

These little tricks were helped out by continual alterations and dislocations of the tempo. Where a gradual animation or a gentle and delicate slowing-off is required often however without even that pretext, a violent, spasmodic *accelerando* or *ritenuto* was made. The latter was more frequent than the former, since as a rule the tendency to drag, thanks to the sport that has been for some time carried on in Bayreuth with drawn-out tempi was stronger than the passion for whipping-up. When the tempo was whipped up, however, one received about the same confused impression of the poor dishevelled work that one gets of the parts of the landscape lying nearest the railway track when one whizzes past in an express.

The rhythmic distortions to which I have referred were in no way justified by any marks of the composer, but always originated with the conductor. With reference to the *sforzati* I have mentioned, however, I will cite the apt remarks of Berlioz:

> A conductor often demands from his players an exaggeration of the dynamic nuances, either in this way to give proof of his ardour, or because he lacks fineness of musical perception. Simple shadings then become thick blurs, accents become passionate shrieks. The effects intended by the poor composer are quite distorted and coarsened, and the attempts of the conductor to be artistic, however honest they may be, remind us of the tenderness of the ass in the fable, who knocked his master down in trying to caress him.

If many of the above-mentioned errors could be supposed to be "proofs of ardour" and of good intention, [...] of the works played in this eccentric way, however there was often little more left than of a plant that the professor of botany has dissected, and whose torn leaves, stamens, and pistils, after being demonstrated to the students of the college, lie scattered about on the desk.

Fingal's Cave by Mendelssohn

Thus I once heard the *Hebrides* Overture of Mendelssohn played with literally not one bar in the same tempo as the rest. Even the second and fourth bars, which are repetitions of the first and the third were "characterised" as against these by means of a pointedly different tempo; and the same kind of thing went on to the end. All that was humanly possible in the way of the unnatural was done, with the result that the lovely work was deformed and its real character obliterated. Certainly it would be just as false to play one crotchet after another with metronomic uniformity; but the modifications of the tempo, some of which Mendelssohn himself has indicated, should be done in such a way as not to dismember the organic character of the whole thing its *melos*, the right comprehension of which, as Wagner aptly says, gives also the right tempo.

At one moment the sea flows quietly round the rocks of Fingal's Cave, at another a stronger wind produces higher waves and the white foam of the breakers beats more strongly against the beach, but the picture of the landscape remains the same, and there is nothing in Mendelssohn's overture of an actual, formidable storm that could imprint on the scenery a radically different stamp. The atmosphere of gentle, noble melancholy that lends the Hebrides their peculiar charm is also preserved in the music. Is it then not a matter for vigorous censure when something that a master has sincerely felt and expressed in faultlessly beautiful music is distorted by the irresponsible additions of a conductor?

"To what end is all this?" I asked myself in amazement on these and many other occasions. Why this inordinate desire of some conductors to turn musical works into something other than what they really are? Whence this aversion to maintaining a uniform tempo for any length of time? Whence this rage for introducing nuances of which the composer never thought? The reason for these curious phenomena was mostly the personal vanity that was not satisfied with rendering a work in the spirit of its author, but must needs show the audience what it "could make out of this work".

The conductor's mania for notoriety was thus put above the spirit of the composer. The parading of this vanity was due partly to a misconception of the better side of Bülow's work, which founded on Wagner; partly to a clumsy imitation of the palpable weaknesses and uncalled-for caprices of his later years.

Mozart's G Minor Symphony and Beethoven's Sixth Symphony

Even what is good can be performed badly. The following instance was communicated to me by a friend. Bülow had played the G minor Symphony of Mozart with the Meiningen Orchestra, and had produced a deep impression by his temperate handling of the chief theme that is sometimes taken thoughtlessly fast, and by his very expressive phrasing throughout the movement. The permanent conductor of the town in question, plainly stimulated by Bülow's success, having later on to conduct the same symphony, informed his acquaintances that he would now take the tempi exactly like Bülow, and at the performance, at which my friend was present, played the first movement andante throughout. The beautiful butterfly, fluttering gently on a summer's day over the sadly inclined campanula, was transformed into a clumsy grasshopper! This was a case of misunderstanding and an overdoing, probably well-meant, of Bülow's version. But it was otherwise with what, to my horror, I had to listen to in the Pastoral Symphony. In the "Scene at the Brook", for example, in the following passage the conductor made in the second bar a strong *ritenuto* and after the last quaver quite a "breath-pause", so that a complete interruption ensued, and the third bar, detached from the second, came in without any connection.

The same thing happened again in the corresponding passage in the recapitulation. After the performance I tried to convince the conductor of the wrongness of his interpretation, pointing out to him that just as it would be impossible for a rippling brook suddenly to be made to stand still, so it was unnatural to interrupt arbitrarily the flow of the music at this point. To my astonishment I got the answer: "I really don't like it myself, but the people here are so accustomed to it like this from Bülow that I take it in the same way". I thought it useless to make any further effort on behalf of truth and nature, since here it was not a case of misunderstanding, but of a conscious imitation of an admitted fault.

This is a sample of the most evil feature of that manner of conducting against which I am contending, since the man's own conviction was here sacrificed and the work knowingly disfigured to comply with the habit of the public, and in fear of incurring displeasure by flying in the face of this habit. In many other cases the trouble mostly came from unconscious defect of artistic feeling, and a certain fumbling after something fine without being quite able to achieve it.

To make their own, however, just that in virtue of which Bülow was really great, the deep seriousness with which he took his calling, the prodigious zeal and the restless devotion with which, even in his last years, when his powers were no longer at their height, he strove to give the most finished performances possible, which were indeed often so perfect that one could forget his personal peculiarities: all this was certainly denied to his imitators.

Indeed I have often doubted whether those who wanted to be so "ingenious" really knew properly the works they were playing. When I saw that somebody was incapable of letting one tempo grow out of another, but made every change with a jerk, or that he began what should have been a long and slow *crescendo* with an explosive *fortissimo*, so that nothing was left over for the finish, this in my opinion pointed not only to a want of proper feeling but also to an insufficient study of the work; being surprised and confused by some passage he had not properly thought out the conductor either flew over it, or else, through would-be "temperament", made too sudden a rush at the crescendo and spoilt it.

Difficulty of obtaining a good ensemble

The difficulty of getting a good ensemble in the *tempo rubato* manner is all the greater when the conductor goes touring. Bülow for some years directed only the Meiningen Orchestra, and afterwards only the Philharmonic orchestras in Hamburg and Berlin. He knew these through and through, and the players, who understood him thoroughly, followed him in every detail, so that even his caprices were rendered with faultless technique. But a conductor who comes before a strange orchestra and wants to take the works not in their natural way (wherein the feeling of the players will always assist him) but to distort them, has not the time, in the few rehearsals that are usually allowed him, to elaborate properly all these *ritenuti, accelerandi,* little *fermate,* and breath-pauses by which he hopes to make an effect; and so it may happen that some of the players follow the conductor and the others their natural feelings, and the greatest ambiguity results. It has struck me that eccentricity of this kind has been carried to further extremes in foreign tours than in our own country, apparently because the public abroad is supposed to be more easily imposed on. At least I have found in the orchestral parts abroad some markings which, had I not seen them with my own eyes, I should have thought impossible. Having often been asked by the players, before the rehearsal, whether I would adopt this or that peculiar nuance of one of my predecessors, I generally found it necessary to say categorically: "Ignore all markings; follow only the printed instructions as to phrasing".

Since in spite of this there were misunderstandings, owing to the parts being in many places so covered with "readings" that the original was obliterated, I often protected myself later on by taking my own copies with me.

The saddest part of the business was that the chief arena chosen for all these varieties and experiments was our glorious classical music, especially the holiest of all, that of Beethoven, since Bülow had acquired the reputation of a master-conductor of Beethoven, and his followers wanted to outbid him, even there; though one would have thought that reverence to say nothing of love for this unique genius would have put all vain thoughts of this kind to flight.

Beethoven's Fifth Symphony

To take only one example, how the C minor Symphony has been tampered with! Already the gigantic opening has brought into being a whole crowd of readings, notably that according to which the first five bars (with the two *fermate*) are to be taken quite slowly. Even the "spirit of Beethoven" was cited to justify this misguided attempt at emendation, for which, however, not Beethoven's spirit but that of his first biographer, Schindler, is entirely responsible. Schindler, the key to whose character, I think, is sufficiently given by the fact that after the master's death he had visiting cards printed with the title *"Ami de Beethoven"*, has told in his biography so many anecdotes whose untruth has been proved by Thayer, that we may unhesitatingly reckon among them the story that Beethoven wanted the opening of the C minor symphony to be taken *andante*, and the faster tempo to come only after the second *fermata*. Is there even a moderately satisfactory explanation why Beethoven, instead of specifying so extremely important a change of tempo, should have marked the passage *allegro con brio* when what he wanted was andante? Liszt's opinion on the point will be of interest. In the previously-mentioned concert of the Meiningen Orchestra in Eisenach, where I made Bülow's personal acquaintance, he took the opening of the C minor symphony, that time at least,

201

in a brisk *allegro*, Liszt told me that the "ignorant" and further-more "mischievous fellow" Schindler turned up one fine day at Mendelssohn's, and tried to stuff him that Beethoven wished the opening to be andante: pom, pom, pom, pom. "Mendelssohn, who was usually so amiable", said Liszt laugh-ingly, "got so enraged that he threw Schindler out — pom, pom, pom, pom!"

Near the end of the first movement there is at one place a five-bar group. Now whether we look upon the fourth bar of the second group (the pause) as a short fermata and the first bar of the succeeding five-bar group as the up-take – according to which there then comes another four-bar sentence or whether we take it that the opening theme of the allegro occurs in the recapitulation the first time thus:

and the second time with an extra bar, thus:

however we calculate the thing mathematically, in either case the short breathless silence and the ensuing outburst of the chord of the diminished seventh become, just by their prolon-gation, terrific, gigantic, powerful, menacing, overwhelming, vol-canic. It is like a giant's fist rising from the earth. Will it be be-lieved that almost everywhere I found the indescribable effect of this passage simply destroyed, either by a bar of the diminished-seventh chord or by the pause itself being struck out?

The most tasteless rhythmic distortions, the most absurd breath-pauses, have been calmly indulged in in order to appear interesting; the result has been, however, to turn a supreme stroke of genius into a mere piece of irregularity; because the thing must go as a four-bar phrase. O sancta simplicitas! The offenders always father their audacities on Bülow. I cannot believe he had so many sins so answer for.

Towards the end of the same movement, in the passage where the chords come rattling down like devastating masses of rock, I found the two *sforzati* corrected to an elegant *piano*, and a delicate *diminuendo* marked before them, making the passage like an elegiac sigh.

Andante con moto

I freely admit that I have never been fully satisfied with the rendering of the second movement of this symphony under any conductor but Bülow. Beethoven marks it *andante con moto*. The older conductors overlooked the *con moto* and played the movement *andante*, the modern ones, on the other hand, appear to see only the *con moto*, and drop into an *allegretto*, thus giving the wonderful theme:

a dance-like character that is quite alien to its nature. My own conception of it, in which the *andante* is maintained while the *con moto* is regarded as the spiritual breath that unites and animates the movement, I cannot adequately express in words; I must refer to the performances I am permitted to give of the work.

I may mention a tragi-comic incident I once witnessed in this movement. After the conductor had begun in the usual *allegretto*, he played these bars –

in so slow a tempo that he had to beat each semiquaver of the triplet separately! But enough of these examples.

Wagner's new bases

[In this essay] my object is to try to show how much the art of conducting has developed since the time when Wagner gave it a new basis both by his deeds and his words. If on the one hand a decided progress can be noted, greater competence in the orchestra, a more perfect ensemble, more feeling for vital phrasing than hitherto, thanks to Bülow and some excellent conductors who had become great under Wagner's direct influence, on the other hand there is imminent danger that the vanity, egoism and caprice of younger conductors (under the sway of the more negative aspects of Bülow) should make fashionable a style in which the masterpieces of music should be merely pegs on which to hang a conductor's own personal caprices. This is all the more dangerous as an audience with little artistic education may, in its astonishment, take the arbitrary for the genuine thing, and, its healthy feeling once perverted, always hanker after these unsound piquancies, so that finally it thinks the trickiest performance the best.

Wagner's treatise combated the philistinism that suffocated every modification of tempo and therefore all vitality of phrasing in a rigid metronomism; my own book on the other hand combated the errors that had arisen through exaggeration of these modifications after the necessity for them had gradually come to be admitted. It was therefore no plagiarism of Wagner's, as was of course asserted, but its counterpart, or, if you will, its continuation in the spirit of our own day. If Wagner opened new paths, I believed it my duty to warn people against mistaking a senseless trampling of the grass for progress along new paths. If Wagner's essay tended to free one from bland formalism, mine is a cry of alarm against the absence of form, which, in seeking to be too ingenious, is equally bland. Formalism and lack of form both betoken the death of art. Splendid form is inseparable from the living art, which, since it is nourished by the spirit of art, makes this spirit sensitive to the world. As with every kind of art, this truth is also valid for the art of conducting.

III

A poor conductor remains a poor conductor

There remain some special points for me to discuss.

Here I must digress to contradict sharply an opinion that has considerable vogue. The interpreter – in our case the conductor – is not able to increase the worth of a work; he can merely diminish this occasionally, since the best that he can give is simply a rendering on a par with the real value of the work. He has done the best that is possible if his performance expresses just what the composer meant; anything more there is not and cannot be, since no conductor in the world can, by his interpretation, make a good work out of a bad one. What is bad remains bad, no matter how well it is played; indeed, a particularly good performance will bring out the defects of a work more clearly than an inferior one. The remark: "The work owed its success to its excellent interpretation" contains a half-truth, since the interpreter is entitled to the recognition of his undoubted deserts; but the composer has a still higher right, for it was he who made it possible for the interpreter to achieve a success with the work. If however the critic inserts in the above sentence a "solely" or "exclusively", then he either falls into an error arising from the preconceived opinion I have spoken of, or else he indulges in a piece of dishonesty in order to depreciate the success of composers he does not like unless, which is indeed the more convenient course, he prefers to ignore this success altogether. How often, for example, have we heard this ludicrous phrase repeated, since some modern conductors recognised their duty and played Berlioz' works in a proper manner? The deeper impression now made by the works could of course not be denied; but the credit for the greater effect they made had to go entirely to the conductors, not to the works themselves, to which people were, and indeed in some quarters still are, as unfavourably disposed as of yore. But what had the conductors done, except by means of their interpretation brought something into the light that had really been there all the time? That of course is a great merit; but it must not be exploited to the disadvantage of the composer, who made what the interpreter could only reproduce.

"We can listen to Beethoven and Mozart even when badly played; but Berlioz is only enjoyable when so-and-so conducts him." This, I take leave to say, is another great mistake, for in the first place Beethoven and Mozart, badly played, are likewise unenjoyable; the public, however, has heard these works so often and played them more or less efficiently on the piano, that it can discover the familiar beloved features even in a performance that disfigures them can even perhaps imagine these features when they are barely recognisable; which is naturally impossible in the case of a work it does not know, such as a rarely-given composition of Berlioz or a novelty. But how feeble is the applause one usually hears after an indifferently played classical symphony, in comparison with the uncontrollable enthusiasm aroused by an artistic interpretation of the same work! Then the masterpiece appears in its true form; to be able to make this true form visible, however, is the sacred task of the conductor, and to have fulfilled it is his only honourable, nay, his only possible glory. A good performance of a poor work is of no artistic consequence, and regrettable both because it furthers bad taste and because it means time and labour unprofitably squandered. The reverse case to perform a good work badly is inexcusable. Equally inexcusable is it, however, to set up off-hand the interpretation against the work in cases where both have contributed to make the artistic impression. To do this is to exhibit the conductor's function in a wholly false light, to put him, in comparison with the composer, disproportionately into the foreground, and merely serves to inflict as much harm as possible on the latter.

Memory

This makes a great impression on the audience, but I do not place too high a value on it. In my opinion a conductor may really know a work by heart and yet fear that his memory may play him a trick, either through pardonable excitement or some other disturbing influence. In such cases it is always better to use the score; the audience is there to enjoy the work, not to admire the memory of the conductor; I recommend doing without the score only when knowledge of it is combined with such a mastery of oneself that reference to it is more a hindrance than a help, and the conductor, though he may read a page now and then, yet feels that to use the score throughout the whole work would be putting a needless fetter on himself. (The French use for this the gracious expression *diriger par cœur.*) It is all a purely personal matter, however, that has nothing to do with the perfection of the performance. If the conductor is so dependent on the score that he can never take his eyes from it to look at the players, he is of course a mere time-beater, a bungler, with no pretension to the title of artist. Conducting from memory, however, that makes a parade of virtuosity is also inartistic, since it diverts attention from the work to the conductor. Now and then we see a conductor put a score on the stand although he conducts from memory, his object being not to attract too much attention a proceeding that I think commendable. But I hold that it is entirely the conductor's own concern whether he will use the score or not.

A good performance conducted with a score has value; a bad one done from memory has none. For instrumental artists also, playing from memory is in my opinion a matter of quite secondary importance; it can be done by anyone who has a quick and reliable memory. But if a player has difficulty in learning by heart, it is better for him to devote his time to mastering the intellectual and technical structure of the piece and to play from a copy at the concert, than to be in continual dread of a lapse of memory and of having either to stop or to pad with something of his own, which means disfiguring the work. I have even heard Bülow, who had a remarkable memory, "improvising" in this way in his piano recitals. Here, as in so many other cases, it only needs someone with the courage to begin and the others will follow.

Bülow, in his witty way, divided conductors into those who have their heads in the score and those who have the score in their heads. I might distinguish them, perhaps rather more deeply, by means of the following antithesis some conductors see only the notes, others see what is *behind* the notes. Then again there are conductors who destroy the unity of a work that is one and indivisible, and others who can shape the apparently fragmentary into a unity.

The dancing conductor

Some conductors are reproached with making too many gestures – not without reason, for the mechanical element in conducting is by no means beautiful in itself, and the black dress-coated figure with the baton-wielding arm can easily become ludicrous if the arm gesticulates wildly instead of leading the men, and the body also twists and curves in uncontrollable emotion. A pose of assumed quiet is however just as repellent. In our music there are, thank God, moments when the conductor must let himself go if he has any blood in his veins. An excess of movement is therefore always better than its opposite, since at any rate, as a rule, it indicates temperament, without which there is no art. Temperament, however, can be given neither by education, nor conscientiousness, nor, by the way, by favour; it must be inborn, the free gift of nature.

Therefore performances of genius can only receive recognition either by another genius, just as the height and beauty of a mountain are best appreciated from another summit, or by that naive instinct, often found among non-artists and the people, that gives itself up spontaneously to the beautiful. But they are quite incomprehensible to those "aesthetes" who consider them as problems of the understanding and would solve them, like a mathematical problem, by analysis, incomprehensible not only because temperament is an endowment of the heart, not of the understanding, but also because the curb that the artist has to put on his temperament has to be directed by head and heart, not by the former alone.

Hence in most cases critical aesthetic and aestheticising criticism pass undeserved censure honest as the intention may be, on performances of genius, and only gradually attain to the correct view when the naive instinct to which I have referred has given its final verdict, and disparagement would now be like flying in the face of a plebiscite.

Temperament itself should not be blamed, but excesses of it. We should not laugh at a talented young conductor whose vehemence prevents him bridling himself, but exhort him in a friendly way to keep his body quiet, and to train himself not to make any more movements than are necessary. The expression of each passage will then generate an appropriately great or small motion of the baton. A complete harmony between music and gesture will indeed only come with the years; but as a general thing it may be pointed out that short, quick motions ensure greater precision than very extensive ones, since in the time taken up by the latter the strictness of the rhythm may easily be deranged.

Ideally, one should aim for the most faithful compliance of the gesture to the music being played.

Fixing the tempo

I would here insert a rule, the observance of which I hold to be indispensable for a right apprehension of the limits of tempo: no slow tempo must be so slow that the melody of the piece is not yet recognisable, and no fast tempo so fast that the melody is no longer recognisable.

Another general rule regards dynamics: "*Diminuendo* signifies *forte, crescendo* signifies *piano*" said Bülow. This is only a seeming contradiction, since to play *forte* at the beginning of a *crescendo*, and *piano* at the beginning of a *diminuendo*, really means the negation of *crescendo* and *diminuendo*. It is not improbable that in Mannheim Mozart heard for the first time an orchestra that could really play *crescendo* and *diminuendo*. Even our best orchestras of today need to be constantly told that the increase and decrease of tone is to be done evenly and gradually, not suddenly; and the difficulty of doing this increases with the number of bars over which these variations in volume have to be extended.

IV

Conducting in the theatre

I have so far spoken only of conducting in the concert-room, not of that in the theatre. That is a chapter in itself, and unfortunately not a pleasant one. The conductor of a small concert-society in a small town has generally at his command a fair if not a strong orchestra and a tolerably well-taught chorus, with which two factors, given much industry and some ability in the conductor, really good performances can often be given. Now and then such performances in the smaller towns, not so-called "music-centres", are surprisingly good.

The relatively greatest possibility of artistic achievement exists in the richly subsidised court and other theatres, whose chief, employed by the town, is not forced to work for his pocket and in addition to worry about meeting his rent. Yet even here there are some extremely serious defects. In the first place, only in a very few towns, and even there not entirely, is it fully recognised that the supreme direction of opera should be in the hands of an artist – of a musician, in fact, with an administrative committee under him that shall have no power of veto against him in artistic matters. Then again at all theatres, the large as well as the small, too much is played. This is the incurable pestilence of our theatrical scene, which should immediately be rectified if one wished to give a healthy impulse to the art.

No theatre is in a position to give daily performances of equal value; it would need at least more than twice as many soloists, chorus and orchestra, and more than twice as many adequate rooms for rehearsal, to allow of a sufficient number of rehearsals taking place without over-fatiguing everyone. An opera that has been put aside and then revived is bound to suffer if it is not carefully and critically rehearsed afresh, especially when long intervals elapse between these unrehearsed repetitions. The ensemble that has been produced by such vigilant care is imperilled when, owing to the absence of the players of one or more chief roles , other singers who have studied only their own parts, and who, supposing them to have been present at the preliminary rehearsals, have been merely looking on, are put in with a cursory stage rehearsal. Guest-visits of foreign artists are the absolute enemies of finished, artistically rounded performances. But how often we find that even the largest theatres have such a poor disposition of personnel that guest appearances are essential to prevent the cancellation of performances. Every attempt at bettering this situation is wrecked by the absolutely frightening necessity of opening the portals of the "temple of art" to the public every evening, and often in the afternoon as well. There is never a heart-felt mature performance! Breathlessness, overexertion, living-from-hand-to-mouth, getting through one chore so at to go on to another one – these are the dispiriting signs of that theatrical heavy industry of ours which mercilessly crushes all finer art. Who among older actors and singers does

211

not recall the time when the theatre was sometimes closed at night so a rehearsal could be conducted? We were glad to rehearse from five to midnight! Is there anyone old enough to have experienced the friendly charm of these evening rehearsals who can forget them? And how fresh and ready for action we were the next day! All gone, a thing of the past! A bad performance that takes in a few marks is preferred to a good rehearsal!

Need there be a performance every day? This question opens up further questions, the answers to which nowadays, when money-making is the war-cry and the box-office statement trumps, look rather utopian. Nevertheless I will try to give the answers, in spite of their uselessness. Could not the public be gradually made to see that it would be better, for the same money that is spent on the average in going to the theatre, to go less often and pay higher entrance-prices, but have thus the certainty of seeing only first-class performances, and so get more real elevation instead of often very superficial enjoyment? Fewer but better-prepared performances would then yield about the same receipts. Or, and here indeed I touch upon the province of the apparently impossible will courts, states and towns never comprehend that the theatre must be a place not of luxury and thoughtless amusement, but of popular education like the school, only in a more spiritualised sense, with that lofty, ethical, indeed religious significance associated with it by the Greeks?

Will people "above" cease to obstruct the perception that noble dramatic and musical plays which, if the grievous concept "deficit" no longer existed, could be made accessible also to the lower classes, would perform a powerful culture-work, weaken the lower instincts and strengthen the higher, to the good of the nation that cultivates them? Let the man who altogether lacks feeling for any higher artistic urge amuse himself daily with music halls, bad operettas and the like, as far as I am concerned. Let the theatre of noble character open its doors less frequently, but then only onto perfect performances. Is it not unpardonable that the worthiest works are rarely given, because the public has lost touch with them? But why? Simply because it hardly ever gets a chance of hearing them. Gluck and Weber no longer arouse interest. *Fidelio* is often greeted by semi-empty halls. Wagner, whose whole life was devoted to ennobling the German stage, is today lost beyond recall to the snob element. New compositions of a fine nature have little chance. *The Barber of Baghdad* slumbered for decades. Berlioz' operas are as good as forgotten. Great singers, who could re-establish our master composers on the stage, are fewer every year, and when they appear, America snaps them up. We poor Europeans are left with the mediocre, which we must be contented with, while dramatic art resembles a funeral adorned with song, mime and dance.

"*Mundus vult Schundus*" [the world wants rubbish], jested Liszt with bitter irony; and our theatres take the greatest pains to avoid bettering this state of affairs.

Conviction, conviction a theatrical director should prove he possesses this. He can only do so, however, if he is independent of daily receipts and press scribblers, and can fully and freely fulfil his task of educating the public in the noblest sense of the word the – that does indeed too easily incline towards the bad and the superficial, but still has enough freshness and naivety to receive the good willingly if it is only offered to it. Of course, to this end a man who is an artist and at the same time has a strong character, who not only know what he wants, but means to fight for it and get it, must be given a firm guarantee for years to come that money will play no role and that no incompetent person will stand in his way. Then, perhaps, an exemplary theatre would be possible.

But I stop dreaming

As for the special function of the conductor in the theatre, Wagner says very truly that just as the right comprehension of the *melos* of a piece of music suggests the right tempo for it, so the right way of conducting an opera presupposes the true comprehension of the dramatic situation on the part of the conductor.

213

As a matter of fact he must before all things have the stage in his eye. This will give him, consistently with due fidelity to the markings of the composer, the criterion as to whether he shall take the tempo faster or slower, how he shall modify it, and where he shall expand or contract the volume of orchestral tone. He will not allow himself to draw a melody out at length when the phrasing should be free and animated; he will not beat out a fast tempo, effective as this may be from the merely musical point of view, where the dramatic development goes more slowly; nor will he elaborate orchestral nuances that drown the singers or divert people's attention from the events on the stage.

Of special importance is his relation to the singers. Only a significant individuality can create a significant performance, and this only when the individuality can express itself in the performance fully and without hindrance. Drill counts for nothing; it may be necessary with the less endowed singers, who for better or for worse are just put into their proper places in the frame of the whole. Admirable artists however must have, within this frame, room for the free play of their own conceptions, indeed, they must be held to the necessity of thinking out their parts for themselves. At the piano rehearsals the conductor should in the first place impress it strongly on the singers that they must learn their parts correctly down to the smallest detail, which is the only way to attain precise co-operation between orchestra and stage, and so secure the fundamental condition of any good performance a faultless ensemble. When, after thorough study, individual liberties begin to be taken by the singers, he should see that these do not contradict the spirit of the whole work — which he must have completely assimilated, or the character of the particular passage. The artistic perception of the conductor and of the singers may be measured by the degree in which they secure the fine medium between rigid correctness and living freedom.

I must mention one more defect which, in the light of pure reason and of all that Wagner has said and done, seems really ludicrous, but which, notwithstanding, is rooted in our theatres so deeply as to be almost beyond the possibility of extirpation, namely the complete separation of the stage management, the machinist's department and the musical direction.

New works

If a new opera is given on which the theatre does not mind spending a little, a commission is sent to a scene- painter – often to a foreign firm of repute – along with a text-book, while the stage manager arranges his book and the conductor rehearses the singers. When the scenery comes to be set up, the stage-manager generally finds that he will have to alter his business, since a good deal that he had planned will not fit in with that particular scenery. Then when the conductor comes in with singers and orchestra it is clear that, e. g. such and such a chorus cannot do its musical work properly if it stands with its back to the audience, that such and such an actor requires a lot of room for his action in a rather long *ritornello*, while he has been allowed only about four square feet; and so on.

Then bad temper, a scramble, and the best face possible put on it, which however only leads to further mischief; and at the last rehearsal but one the end of it is that they would all, if they could, gladly begin again from the beginning. But the day of production is fixed, the booking guaranteed, the mere idea of a postponement therefore monstrous; so let it go as best it can. This system of work often results in some good stories; for example, at three large theatres I have known Brunhilde to wake up in quite another stage-setting than the one she went to sleep in. Years had elapsed between the staging of the *Valkyrie* and of *Siegfried*. The scenery had been ordered of different painters, who had not come to an understanding as to the identity of the scenes in the two works. The proposal, however, simply to use in *Siegfried* the scenery of the *Valkyrie* was vetoed by the chief machinist, on the grounds that for technical reasons this scenery could not be put in after the fire-transformation. With the careless remark "The public does not notice" they went on to the order of the day, and the enchanted Brunhilde was spirited away each time to another sleeping-place.

Since, however, an operatic performance can be artistic only when all the factors work together, the proper distribution of the labour is this: when the stage management and the music are not in the hands of the same man, which is not much to be recommended, since the conductor, when he is in the orchestra, cannot possibly attend to every detail of the stage picture, then stage manager and conductor, before the rehearsals begin, must come to a perfect understanding between themselves as to how the work is to be done. Both must be clear and of one mind as to the atmosphere of the opera, the action, the scenic pictures, the tempi, and the dynamic effects, so that later on at the rehearsals only trifling changes may be necessary.

Only after this preliminary work should the scenic artist and the machinist receive from stage manager and conductor their precise orders, compliance with which, however, does not mean the paralysis of their own imagination, which can work more freely and fruitfully within the artistic boundaries prescribed by the work in question than outside them.

An eye for the stage

For this understanding between stage manager and conductor two things are necessary. In the first place the conductor must have a knowledge of, an eye for, and an interest in the stage, and not merely bury himself in his orchestra to the ignoring of everything else; in the second place the stage manager must be a man of musical perception and musical education, who is just as conversant with the score as the conductor is. In my opinion no conductor should be appointed to a theatre who has not shown that he can stage an opera, and no stage manager who cannot rehearse the musical part of the work. It is perfectly nonsensical that sometimes people should be made operatic stage managers who are not at all musical. But the nonsensical is always destined to prevail in life, alas.

V

The suggestive power of a conductor

More and more I have come to think that what decides the worth of conducting is the degree of suggestive power that the conductor can exercise over the performers. At the rehearsals he is mostly nothing more than a workman, who schools the men under him so conscientiously and precisely that each of them knows his place and what he has to do there; he first becomes an artist when the moment comes for the production of the work. Not even the most assiduous rehearsing, so necessary a pre-requisite as this is, can so stimulate the capacities of the players as the force of imagination of the conductor. It is not the transference of his personal will, but the mysterious act of creation that called the work itself into being takes place again in him, and, transcending the narrow limits of reproduction, he becomes a new-creator, a self-creator.

The more however his personality disappears so as to get quite behind the personality that created the work, to identify itself, indeed, with this the greater will his performance be.

The requisites of the conductor who wished to be considered a true artist are, in my view, the following:

– he should be sincere towards the work he is playing, towards himself and towards the public;

– when he is preparing a score, he should not think: "What can I do with this piece?", but rather, "What was the author's intention with this piece?";

– he should study the composition in depth so that, during the

217

performance the score only serves as an aid to memory, but is no longer a hindrance;

— if, while studying the work he has come up with a particular idea relating to it, he should elaborate this in a unified, and not fragmentary, way;

— he should bear in mind that he is, in the musical sphere, the most authoritative and responsible figure; with faultless executions he can educate the public and occasion an overall refinement of its artistic sensibility; with mediocre executions that satisfy only his own vanity, however, he can make the subject ill-suited for the practice of;

— performing a work well should be his main triumph; his own success should rightfully be the success of the composer.

Wagner also was afraid of his remarks on this point being misunderstood and thereby giving occasion for exaggerated phrasing. After having devoted to the necessity of artistic modifications of tempo almost the whole of his treatise on conducting and many other passages in his writings, he expresses the following opinion, in which, we must admire his prescience:

It is certainly a really valid warning against these (to me) necessary modifications in the cases I have named, that nothing could harm the works more than capricious nuances in phrasing and tempo, which, by opening the door to the whims of every vain and self-complacent time-beater who aims at "effect", would in time deform our classical music beyond recognition. To this, of course, no reply is possible except that our music must be in a bad way when such fears can be entertained; since it is as good as admitting that we have no belief in a power of true artistic consciousness among us, against which these caprices would at once be broken.

Anarchy, a dangerous enemy

What Wagner feared came to pass. Today the days are open to fantastic caprices, and not only (since fantastic presupposes the presence of imagination), but also to arbitrariness, coupled with complete lack of imagination; and this is true not only in conducting, but in every art. The most irremediable idiocy can count on at least one clique that will howl its praises in every key and outlaw all who do not howl along. Just as anarchy has become a dangerous enemy in the existence of nations, so in the existence of art there is a threat of anarchistic confusion unless the true consciousness of art comes to life and grows into a force that will destroy the anti-artistic breeding of senseless and vain caprices as surely as healthy blood kills the bacilli that endanger life.

We have had to absorb too much that is morbid; too much that is repellent, trivial and irrelevant has diverted our art from its true path for recovery to be able to occur quickly and for our defunct consciousness of art to be able to develop again all at once. We are so firmly set on impossible possibilities and possible impossibilities, so hemmed in by luxuriating weeds, that we should be happy to discover a narrow path that would at least offer us the hope of leading us out of the swamp and jungle onto the road to grandeur and beauty. This road we have abandoned, so that we can no longer enter the sacred temple of art, can no longer even catch sight of it. Instead we build straw huts and fill them with idols which we worship with a devotion directly proportional to their hideousness, while from all side specious hymns numb our sense with the lying assertion that things are not only absolutely splendid as they are, but are a thousand times more splendid than they ever were. And yet again and again they appear before us, the sad countenances with the hesitant question in their sun ken eyes and on their pale whispering lips: "Will things never ever be different? Is a fresh breeze never to blow in this fearsome sultriness that robs us of breath? Is a genuine sunbeam never again to warm us in place of these smouldering torches set up before the idols with which the false priests wish to give us the illusion of daylight?"

Let the darkness subside

Then for a moment it becomes light. Some glowing passes by overhead, whose glittering rays play upon the leaves of the jungle, through which all at once a bit of blue sky becomes visible. But something wondrous resounds within our hearing, a long-absent, delightful, melodious song. The pale countenances listen, alarmed and delighted at the same time. But, as if by pre-arrangement, the hymns and prayers to the idols swell to a furious roar, so that it is no longer possible to hear the music descending from above. The glowing vision passes on toward other, more beautiful countries far away, and things remain just as they were with us.

It is not the modern conductor, nor even the modern writer who will lead us for good out of that labyrinth of the arts into which we have strayed. This will be the lot only of the creative artist who will be the true and genuine – and probably also the crucified – saviour. But both the writer and the conductor can do much to help; the writer if he is manly and fearless; the conductor if he regards it as his sacred task to present the works of our great classical masters to us with purity of style and with emotion that grows out of their own spirit. Of course he will first have to cleanse himself thoroughly of all he has acquired from a false tradition. Only there, in those great creations of the classical age, still so near to us in time, but already so far away in spirit, does that pure heavenly fire gleam with which a chosen man can kindle the Promethean torch so that he can set ablaze our straw huts and idols along with all the jungle plants surrounding them. Thus he will drain the noxious swamp and allow fresh air to blow once more over a healthful, fertile soil. Then there will also be room for the development of the true consciousness of art that Wagner longed for, and a period of painful

220

transition like ours today could hardly recur. Or has our era already become so inartistic and industrialised that the Promethean torch can no longer catch fire? "Terrible if you were right", says Max in *Der Freischütz*. Let us hope that this time Kaspar's answer holds true: "Strange that you ask!"

LAZARE SAMINSKY

The new art of orchestra conducting – 1932

In the section – of which we include an extract – on orchestra conducting in his Music of our Day: Essentials and Prophecies *(1932), the Ukrainian composer Lazare Saminsky (1882-1959) focuses on the gestures and movements that the conductor has to master to achieve perfect communication with the orchestra.*

The art of conducting belongs to a dark domain of performance. The mechanism and resources of either are still vaguely understood and not at all systematized. The absence of a scientific theory aggravates a dimness in the understanding of conducting by the layman, the professional musician and sometimes by the conductor himself. We are still unable to define precisely what part in the rendition is due to the conductor's craft and what to the competence of the players. It may occur, that having in his hands a flexible orchestra, able reader of old and new repertory, a bold and technically clever conductor, externally energetic and aided by the right measure of cabotinage, will acquire the reputation of a valuable and inspired leader, possibly that of a great one, when being mediocre, even ignorant as a musician.

One finds confusion and incertitude as to the very qualities and their measure, necessary for conducting. Equilibrium is rare. Often one requisite dominates to the detriment of others. Sometimes an excellent performing gift and a fine general musicianship is coupled with a lack of the technical and physical qualities indispensable to a leader. All his attention is then absorbed by his struggle with the technical problems of leadership; his interpretive plans can be realized only in part and casually. Then again, the reverse may be true: a great technical gift united with mediocre performing talent and an inferior type of musical mentality. Many a celebrated man has belonged to this type.

The rhythmic ensemble

Our visual field embraces not only objects on which our visual axis focuses, but includes also things placed somewhat outside the focus of vision. The latter objects are perceived by our lateral sight. His direct vision the orchestra musician uses for the music on his desk. He focuses on that his conscious attention, reads the notes and reproduces them on his instrument. He achieves the literal performance of the musical work. But owing to the lateral vision directed by subconscious attention, he adapts himself to the movement and gesture of the conductor. Through the half-conscious attention and through other subconscious psychic forces, the orchestra musician perceives the intentions of the conductor, intimated by his facial and bodily movement.

If the musicians should focus their conscious attention on the conductor's gestures, try in this manner to gather his design, the literal performance of the work, that is the reproducing of the musical signs, would become impossible. The unity of the orchestral mass would immediately decompose. The individual rhythmic sensitiveness, each trait of individual perception of each instrumentalist, would begin then to count. Then the orchestra would have ceased to be a performing entity and would have become an assembly of individual performers, feeling the music, judging the leader's intention and responding to it each in his own way. There are exceptions, however, to the principle of subconscious attention. In certain cases the transfer of that submerged attention to the conscious mind is a necessity. If the orchestra ensemble is shaken by a lack of skill in its leader or by accident, the instrumentalists are forced to restore the unity themselves. They consciously observe the conductor's gesture to find out what is wrong. Again should the instrumentalists know their part by memory, then their conscious scrutiny, no longer occupying itself with literal performance, is focused on the leader and follows his movement.

The following experiment will clarify the special role of the subconscious perception. At the end of the introduction of the *Oberon* overture, the divided violas sustain *piano* a second which the full orchestra breaks up suddenly with a short, cutting *forte*:

Then we indicate the *fortissimo* re-entrance of the full orchestral *tutti* not with the habitual downbeat but with a brisk jerk of the wrist toward the orchestra, a sort of swift rejecting gesture. Such a dry and cutting movement of the conductor will provoke, under the circumstances, an immediate and unanimous reaction from the orchestra, and we shall have obtained a perfectly concise and neat chord.

In order that the subconscious attention might have full sway, it is necessary that the movement of the conductor be perceived by the orchestra with the least possible engagement of their conscious effort. The perception must then be a will-less one, effected with all possible ease. To economize the psychic strength of the orchestra, is imperative. The proper role of the conscious attention is concern for the higher, interpretive part of the performance. An effortless grasp of the director's action is possible only when his rhythm-setting gesture emanates from a certain fixed and single centre, a focus, so to speak, radiating rhythm. Such a centre should be permitted to revolve in but very narrow limits, so that the instrumentalists may have it always within their lateral visual field and perceive it without strain. The centre of the rhythmic radiation is the wrist of the leader's right hand. From the technical point of view, there is nothing more disconcerting, and also nothing more disagreeable to the spectator, than a conductor who continually marks rhythm with both hands or one who paces his podium, forcing his musicians to waste their psychic energy on superfluous watching.

The rhythm being marked by the right wrist, its movement must be confined to a triangle or a rhombus with the sharp angle pointed to the focus, where the initial downbeat originates. The right hand alone is the legitimate organ of rhythm; the left must be considered chiefly a signifier for shading.

As the rhythmic focus of conducting must displace itself as little as possible, and the expense of attention be reduced to a minimum, the latter normally addressed to a reading of the notes, it is evident that the gesture which generates rhythm, should not be over-large. The entries of the instruments should therefore be indicated not by a jerk of the body or by a large gesture of the right hand but by a slight sign from the left hand or from the head, or even better, by a glance. One never forgets the incomparable ease and grace of Nikisch's indicating of the entries. Showing the entries must by no means upset the right hand and detract it from its principal role, directing of the ensemble's rhythmic life.

From this point of view, it seems that the baton has a special value, and it is scarcely wise to abolish the use of it. The gesture of a batonless hand grows less concise. It loses the neatness of rhythmic punctuation which the movement from the wrist transmits to the baton-point with such clarity. The ensemble feels the absence of the baton at once.

It follows that the other means of a leader's action, his posture, facial expression, gestures reflecting his emotion, should be applied solely to the details of the performance. Only conductors of a primitive type, technically uncouth, try to interfere everywhere, to show everything with their stick: the entries, the shades and the general conception. They understand nothing of conducting the phrasing and the dynamics of a work.

The time-beaters are not aware of the axiom that the leader's gesture must reflect the spirit, the rhythmic life of a work, not its arithmetic.

There are certain qualities indispensable to a ruler of orchestral rhythmic life. These might be enumerated as:

– *a faithful sense of rhythm, a faculty for maintaining the rhythm adopted and for modifying it at will and in the right measure, when necessary;*

– *a flawless memory for tempos and an instinct for the right movement, in other words, a capacity for determining without fault the only inherent tempo of the given piece;*

– *natural technical facilities, such as a flexible and well developed wrist, a certain pliability of body.*

Cheironomic technique

I have not mentioned here the hearing, as a keen analytical listening and auditory perception are indispensable only to the rehearsing and the handling of the orchestral sonority, and not to the directing of the rhythmic ensemble. A memory for tempo and an instinct for the true *melos* of a given work, are of prime importance. We appreciate these gifts when we hear great masters such as Nikolai Andreyevich Rimsky-Korsakov and Joseph Willem Mengelberg: both of them always determined the metronomic indication of each piece with the utmost precision. When one listens to one of the Mengelberg's finest performances – that of Beethoven's *Eroica* – and notes its perfect rhythmical plan, one understands the paramount importance of intuiting the exact movements in the orchestral art.

227

Orchestral sonority

The working out and the control of orchestral sonority, a meeting of its requirements, is a very special domain in the labours of a director. It partakes of the same nature as that of any virtuoso's exercise of his instrument. But unfortunately conducting has not as yet established definite written methods to guide this work. Its *Gradus ad Parnassum* or "School of Velocity" do not yet exist. Before setting himself to work with his orchestra, the leader must be in possession of not only a rhythmic plan of the performance, a full chart of the main rhythmic movements in the composition, but he must also have a plan for its sonority to aid him in the working out of the sheer sound of the orchestral ensemble. He should not fail to know in advance, to hear clearly in imagination how the piece should resound, and he must be sure of how to obtain the desired sonority.

The treatment of the orchestral sonority and its control present a double aspect. One observes first an ensemble of means definitely aiming at cohesion and equilibrium within the various groups forming the orchestral mass. Then the balance and true tonal colour of the whole ensemble has to be established. Systematic and general labour is not sufficient to accomplish this. Each composition has its special exigencies. The orchestral sonority of a work may be well conceived by the composer in his day, yet its actual equilibrium may demand modification for present-time performance; even the scoring may need change. This may be caused by a difference in the technique and composition of the orchestra, variances due to the time of birth of the piece and the present period. To revise some of the orchestration or to effect changes, so modifying the equilibrium within some of the instrumental groups and underlining certain shades or designs, is sometimes a necessity.

Thus, in some of Beethoven's symphonies a sustained note of a woodwind instrument or even its solo is too feeble to penetrate the dense chord of the tremendous string group of our day. In the canon of the *allegretto* of the Seventh Symphony, for instance, the strings would surely strangle the clarinet part if we were to follow Beethoven's shading. It is necessary then either to alter the shading, or to double the woodwind, or to diminish the number of strings. In this symphony, the violas and cellos execute an uncharacteristic rhythmical pattern that has no need to be emphasised. But the great number of string instruments in our orchestras dulls the sonority of this phrase:

Systematic work on orchestral sonority begins with the tuning of the orchestra and a correcting of the intonation of various groups and instruments. The conductor must obtain a neatness in the melodic design and a balance of the various groups in the orchestral chord. He must secure a harmonic clarity of the latter. To this end the bass of the instrumental chord should be made distinctly transparent and yet it must not overshadow other voices. When the composer's intentions require it, the orchestra leader must be able to screen or to submerge secondary designs and sonorities, such as pedal points supporting the flux of changing harmonies, polyphonic voices of the subordinate kind, etc. The conductor must also control the uniform and conscientious bowing of the strings and the embouchure of the wind instruments.

Every conductor knows, for instance, how the natural inertia of the orchestral mass manifests itself in a tendency to play all music in a neutral *mezzo forte,* for this requires the least effort from the players. The conductor is compelled to exert real pressure to get his instrumentalists to execute a veritable *forte,* a real *piano* and to obtain the gradual, true *crescendo* and *diminuendo*. The instinctive tendency of the ensemble to play every *calando* also as *diminuendo*, and to add to an *accelerando* some degree of *crescendo*, is always to be combated.

An Italian sociologist has ingeniously shown in a treatise on mass-psychology that the decisions of an assembly or a parliament, composed even of talented intellectuals, must inevitably be mediocre and banal. For the particular taste, the individual talent is levelled and smothered in the resultant of common instinct and habit which gains supremacy in any mass-assembly. This is true also of orchestras.

The strings are naturally less inert. With them the tendency to retard their response to the conductor's gesture is less manifest than with the wind-group. But there are cases when short strokes of the wrist somewhat anticipating the beat, would also yield good results, in directing string players. In the *adagio* of the Emperor Concerto of Beethoven, the strings double the harmonies of the piano part with chords *pizzicato*.

The conductor has to follow not only all the expressive deviations of the pianist, but he is also to obtain a perfect cohesion of the pizzicato chords and their flawless dropping at the proper instant. The slightest incertitude would be felt immediately in this transparent web. The best way to achieve a perfect ensemble is to indicate the *pizzicato* chords with dry, brief strokes preceding by a smallest fraction of time the accentuation of the pianist.

Interpretation

The manning of the rhythmic ensemble and of the orchestral sonority lies in the elementary sphere of orchestral leading. Its superior domain embraces ways and means to achieve unity of plan, to animate the performance and to bring out the true character of the composition which the conductor senses. This is, of course, the task of every interpreter, but the special character of the instrument handled by an orchestra leader, confronts us with some peculiar problems of execution.

The gesture of the conductor and his pose should be addressed solely to the instrumentalists. These are justified only when, and as long as they are useful to the orchestra. The mimoplastic art of the directing musician is only similar to, not identical with that of an actor. Drama is differently addressed. Both the gesture and attitude of a conductor are basically wrong when they act on the public directly, and so transform listeners into spectators.

Grace, elegance in the leader's gesticulation and attitude are legitimate when necessary for the performance. A concise gesture, gracefully executed, will evoke an automatically exact and elegant orchestral response. A plastic movement of the conductor, aesthetically significant, will achieve the desired shade and detail with magic fidelity.

But if the conductor, even remotely, half-consciously, addresses himself to the audience as spectators, his authority loses at once some of its power, and the performance suffers even technically. A sensitive listener perceives immediately a subtle incoordination between the conductor's gesture and the orchestral response; a blemish is apparent in the spiritual ensemble of the orchestra. They are eminently mistaken, those conductors who think to hypnotize their listeners with other proceedings than that of addressing themselves to the orchestra. Many more or less unconsciously pose. They mean to follow Celibidache, whose gesture and attitude, however, had always technical significance. Conductors of bad taste do not or do not wish to understand the true role of their mimoplastic medium and the principle of its application. The "touch" of the *chef d'orchestre*, that is, the inner nature of his gesture, must be such as to bear on nothing but the mere regulation of the orchestral performance. In no task is the conductor's regulating role observed with such clarity, as in his guiding of the orchestral accompaniment to soloists, and nowhere is a leader's over-directing more absurd.

From the preceding study of gesture and its action on the subconscious mind of the instrumentalists, we may draw the following inferences:

– The movement of the director must conserve the orchestra's energy so that at a needed moment all its power may be summoned. In this respect monotony of gesture is especially harmful. The abuse of large and expressive gesticulation which certain orchestra leaders bring to the verge of hysterical exaggeration, exhausts quickly the psychic strength and the enthusiasm of the players. Only a wisely diversified gesticulation, when it is also restrained and centred, is capable of keeping the ensemble's attention watchful without fatiguing it.

– The conductor must constantly be aware of the fact that his gesture is his natural instrument of action on the subconscious mind of his players, and that the word, the address to their conscious sphere, is but a secondary means of communication.

A union of all the qualities demanded for an orchestra leader is rare. One meets combinations of very diversified traits, at times contradictory, even. Therefore, what follows must be considered as schematic.

Conductors of an inferior type usually lack self-control. They are constantly in a state of feverish agitation, sometimes simulated, and this is often mistaken for temperament. Their interpretation consists of a wandering through primitive sequences of orchestral *crescendos* and *diminuendos*, in an abuse of *piano subito*, in a setting up of orchestral climaxes at random, by instinct. Now and then such leaders intuitively find a happy detail but their execution is mainly haphazard improvisation. They abuse shading, are apt to lose themselves in detail. The opposite type is not more valuable. Now the interpretation is studied, cerebral and sometimes artificially impassive.

One should apply the general rule "to govern means to foresee" to the superior sphere of orchestra leading, just as methodically, as it is applied when creating a plan for directing the rhythmic ensemble or for handling the orchestral sonority. In conductors of a superior type one finds a close union of the dynamic, passionate forces with the intellectual element. The latter moulds the execution into concise form, brings the essence of the composition into relief and co-ordinates the various plans for performance, those for rhythm, tone-colour, etc., with the conception of the whole. The Apollonian principle, plan, control, consciousness, and the Dionysian element, temperament, intuition, in the elevated type of a conductor, stand in inverse relationship to those in the inferior type. Caprice and intuition may govern details of an interpretation of a supreme nature; improvising may find a place there. But the general form, in great reading, an idea of the work as a whole, is preconceived. Such a formal conception may also be considered as springing from intuition, but it is ingrained in the interpretation by the Apollonian forces of the leader, no matter how often impulse may generate detail. Passion, impetus, exaltation do not upset, nor confuse a conductor of this type. They elevate, illuminate his faculties to the highest degree; a fiery creation of detail would be incapable of dissipating his vision of the whole. These leaders have digested the advice of genius given by Flaubert to a friend: "*Méfiez-vous de l'inspiration*". Do not trust to inspiration!

These qualities acquire a special significance in the interpretation of modern works. Intricacy and the colouristic display in present-day composition are apt to lure the conductor into an overdressed kind of rendition, overabundant in detail and gaudy. Today more than ever, unity demands a preconceived executive plan. To counteract by a simplicity of general conception the richness and multiplicity of detail, is now imperative.

233

I have shown, then, that conducting comprises the direction of the rhythmic life of the orchestral ensemble, a control of the latter's sonority, and an unfoldment of the plan and spirit of the work. A conductor is therefore a very peculiar complex of artists. He is all in one: a psychophysical metronome; a pedagogue amalgamated with a virtuoso handling a gigantic instrument; a mime, but one whose gesture is for the orchestra only. .

WILHELM FURTWÄNGLER

Conversations about music

*Technique cannot and must not become an end in
itself without killing the spirit of the work of art.*

Wilhelm Furtwängler

Among the names of artists and academics who produced
writings on orchestral direction in the twentieth century, that of
Wilhelm Furtwängler is incontestably the most authoritative.
This essay, however, published in 1949 by Ulstein of Berlin, does
not deal with technique and practice. The conversations are
predicated thus: a question from Walter Abendroth – "Was the
audience's enthusiasm for yesterday's concert at the Philharmonic justified?" And Furtwängler's answers: no, there were
certain effects, but the effects were illicit. One cannot expect the
public to know the right dosage of effects or be able to judge
their legitimacy. The public is an amorphous mass that suc-
cumbs, in its reactions, to momentary, instinctive impulses, in
which suggestion can play... Music is at the mercy of the one
who performs it, its fate, if we are talking about "innovation",
is entrusted to the conductor's baton or the singer's voice. It is
quite unusual for a performer to make a mediocre work sound
good; but it is extremely common for an exquisite work to be
played badly. So the listener cannot judge whether a missing or
negative effect is to be attributed to the composer or the performer.

In *Conversation I*, Furtwängler is invited to consider his
favourite works on the basis of statistics gleaned from the Berlin
audiences: Beethoven's symphonies, Schubert's *Unfinished*, some
Tchaikovsky pieces – which on account of their brilliance, plasticity and wealth of inventiveness (one might also add the innate
laziness of the audience who know them off by heart), can even

withstand mediocre playing; and he observes that other works, on the contrary, greeted with clamorous success at their appearance, are gradually abandoned: many works by Liszt, some of Berlioz and Strauss and some of Wagner and Tchaikovsky. These are nearly always works that aim unscrupulously for success, for cheap immediate effect, for what Wagner called effect without cause, which accompanied right from the outset the era of the conductor virtuosi. But Furtwängler did not in any way believe that popularity with the audience was a sign of the inferiority of a work. And he cites the example of Beethoven, whose compositions always triumph through their content, and not surface appearance; and this comes about via the brilliance and clarity with which they are presented – which is the only means the artist has at his disposal for winning over the public. "For it to mean anything to me, it has to be played in the clearest and simplest way possible. As far as problems are concerned, I've got enough of my own to deal with".

Conversation II focuses on the tricky issue of *style*. Furtwängler says that there is no justification for classical style to be tantamount to boredom. Tchaikovsky and Verdi do not demand greater passion or sensuality that Beethoven; Bach does not have a less fiery soul than Puccini – he has a more intimate soul, which is more difficult to attain and render. Anyone who can direct the true Beethoven well can also conduct Tchaikovsky and Verdi equally finely. So-called "classical" music (which embraces the whole romantic repertoire) is made up of around fifty "numbers" which are repeated in all the world's symphonic concerts; they constitute a musical architecture that, in terms of solidity and plasticity of ideas, building materials and clarity of design and distribution of masses of colour and shade, of is a match for any system of logical reasoning. From Liszt onwards, and with a steady progression up to our days, this solidity and compactness of construction loosens and is dispersed. Now it is the details, the decoration, the thematic cells that take on great importance. In Reger the composition advances bar by bar, or even just by a fraction of one. The "detail" absorbs all the attention and care of the performers – who indeed lose the ability to recognise the great lines, the monumental architecture of the musical work, and they find themselves uncomfortable with works of the past which are entirely architecture, cohesion, logic. The performance standard of of classical works is generally very poor and current prejudices regarding style make for a enormous confusion of ideas. For the performer every piece of music that seems simple and well-constructed, one of Haydn's symphonies, for instance, is difficult, for the above reasons; while art that drifts away from human content, focusing on the particular, the characteristic, on virtuosity, and that does not speak from the heart is easy, as are the complications and problems of blending, rhythm, technique and phonic equilibria with which it is studded. An adequate technical exercise triumphs over any mechanical problem. But true art, the authentic creative power, requires of those who wish to deliver it worthily quite other gifts, which have nothing to do with technical practice.

In *Conversation III*, Furtwängler opines that "pure" music does not achieve really tragic effects, yet in any of Beethoven's sonatas or quartets, one can recognise the playing out of a drama, a real tragedy. Beethoven's themes are like characters in a play, immersed in a particular atmosphere, subject to various vicissitudes tied up with their destiny. This Conversation is dedicated to Beethoven, and in particular, to to the less performed even-numbered symphonies, which the public does not appreciate for what they are. The main responsibility for this incomprehension is to be attributed to the modern performers, whom Furtwängler brands as "incompetent".

Conversation IV is a fine piece of criticism devoted almost exclusively to the Ninth Symphony, including a fascinating page in which Furtwängler explains the intervention of human voices in the last movement as being dictated by a purely musical need. He makes this telling observation: he notes the constant effort made by Beethoven to simplify the first draft of a theme and ascertains that Beethoven's creative process nearly always goes from chaos to form, from the complicated to the simple.

In *Conversation V*, we find something relevant to our subject. It is true, says Furtwängler, answering Abendroth's question, when Bülow said that bad orchestras do not exist, only bad conductors, he was not just trying to be witty. Nor is it true that the more rehearsals that take place, the better the performance will be. There are conductors who don't know how to make best use of rehearsals. Rehearsals should be used to iron out details, practise the technically difficult passages, the flights of virtuosity; one must have a sense of measure, not asking for less than is necessary, nor indeed more than is necessary, paralysing the whole work and removing, at the moment of performance, that pulse of human warmth, that controlled impetus of inspiration, that only the players can instil. In order to achieve this "felicitous improvisation", it is essential that the conductor identifies with the work he is executing. If spirit is form, form must be spirit. Technique cannot and must not become an end in itself without killing the spirit of the work of art.

In *Conversation VI*, after a lengthy digression on the opportunities for exchange of artists and music among various European countries, and on the need for every composer to preserve in his music the distinctive, spontaneous features of his country's art, he goes into full polemical mode. Furtwängler concludes that this travesty sows the seeds of fierce hatred, even among people of the same country. Many composers, for fear of falling into the "sentimental", are afraid of themselves. As if making music did not imply the full acceptance of oneself.

In *Conversation VII*, appended just after the war (1947) to the other six dialogues of 1937, he reiterates and develops, in the light of recent post-war experience, the concepts and stances set out in *Conversation VI*. There must be some reason, he argues, why the musical public has rejected avant-garde music for forty years. Strenuous organisational efforts and propaganda campaigns have done little to remedy this situation.

The personal experiences he has lived through as conductor confirm this state of affairs. He has noted that many new ultramodern works had resounding success on their first performance in such and such a festival, at the SIMC (International Society for Contemporary Music) or the Venice Festival. The same works, however, played in "normal" concerts alongside classical music or contemporary music free from any extreme or "weird" tendencies, failed completely to arouse the public's interest.

In short, concludes the maestro, new contemporary works have to prove that they can exist in a normal everyday musical context. Art has to assert itself freely and spontaneously, going beyond any prejudice or technical-compositional conditioning.

TULLIO SERAFIN

The Conductor – 1940
(To young people intending to embark on a conducting career)

In the text that follows, which appeared for the first time in 1940 in
The Art of Orchestra conducting *by Adriano Lualdi, Tullio Serafin*
(1878-1968) addresses young people who wish to become conductors and
offers them some invaluable advice.

What particular talents should a young musician have to become a conductor? I am often asked this question and I think I
can answer that there are three indispensable requirements for
a conductor:
- they have to know what they want
- they have to want what is right
- they have to get what they want.

While the first two concern the musician generally, the third
refers exclusively to the conductor. It refers to that force that
obliges all players not just to obey you, but also to express themselves as you want them to and to pull along artists, ensembles
and audiences with you. If you don't have this captivating power,
then don't bother trying to become a conductor.

I remember when I was a student for a few years at the Milan
Conservatoire. The Director Antonio Bazzini (1818-1897) was
loved by everyone, teachers and students alike, and by me in particular, since I enjoyed his personal and affectionate attention.
How much he taught me, how much advice he gave me, which
I have never forgotten: "Remember always to seek beauty wherever it is to be found, without prejudice of school, nationality or
epoch. Finding flaws in a work is easy; discovering the good
qualities and assigning them appropriate value is much more
difficult".

One morning the dear teacher came to the school wreathed in smiles and told us that a lady had been to see him, on the recommendation of a very dear friend. The lady had brought her eight-year-old son with her and wanted him to embark on music studies. She knew nothing whatsoever about music. Antonio Bazzini asked her which instrument she had in mind and she replied very simply: "I want him to be a composer". It was impossible to explain to her that to be a composer certain special gifts are required, above all creativity, which would emerge at a later stage – in the meantime he should learn to play an instrument. A waste of breath: "He has to be a composer".

This is exactly how many (even excellent) musicians think they will become conductors, without having any special disposition – essential for anyone wishing to take up the art of conducting. They might be able to pull off "correct" performances, but they will lack that enlivening spark. They will be *batteurs de baton*, but never conductors.

So how can a young person go about becoming a conductor? Who will guide him in his his studies? Not the conservatoires, which only offer some drills and practice. No syllabus in any of the major music schools offers the study of eighteenth and nineteenth century operas (Mozart, Rossini, Bellini, Verdi and Wagner). Verdi, in his project for the reform of conservatoires presented to Cavour, said that one could not expect opera composers to emerge without first making them study the works of numerous composers, *excluding* opera composers.

The best school for budding composers is undoubtedly the orchestra itself. Evidence shows that our most eminent conductors were all previously instrumentalists. Angelo Mariani was a violinist, Franco Faccio a violist, Arturo Toscanini a cellist, Leopoldo Mugnone a violinist, Luigi Mancinelli a cellist, while Victor de Sabata played just about every instrument. In the absence of such an opportunity, only the major opera houses and symphonic organisations can be of help to young people who might be worthy of their attention. When, among students of composition (a fundamental subject for aspiring conductors),

242

someone is found who, while directing orchestra practice, shows outstanding ability, he is invited to attend rehearsals and practices, as well as the staging for the theatre – the whole process. This will be invaluable preparation for him.

It is important to distinguish between conductors of symphonic music and directors of operas. For the latter the situation is more complex. With opera, we also have the vocal part, which is usually the most important, but the orchestra is still crucial. The melodrama is played out on the stage and descends from the stage to the orchestra; it does not ascend from the orchestra pit to the stage, as some would have us believe. In conceiving the poem *Tristan und Isolde*, Wagner first created the characters: Tristan, Isolde, Brangäne, Kurwenal, King Marke, right down to the little shepherd, all have to stand out in all their fullness – without this there would be absolutely no drama. Everyone knows that, for an artist, the most effective and direct means of expression is the voice. Without this divine instrument it is difficult for the character to stand out, with the consequent loss of drama. It is thus essential that young people pay maximum attention to the voice. They should attend singing lessons (there are still some fine teachers around) and learn how one sings. How can a conductor give instructions to an artist if he cannot indicate the best way to sing? Advice for singers: articulation gives clarity, pronunciation gives eloquence. The conductor who, while directing, does not sing along with the artist will never bring about the perfect fusion – undoubtedly, this is one of the main aims of a conductor. Remember that this aim will only be achieved if one is also a good pianist. Unfortunately, nowadays many have picked up the atrocious habit of letting the singers join the orchestra without first preparing them well. Big mistake! The finest performances are achieved by rehearsing beforehand with the orchestra alone; the singers are trained meticulously and in great detail, separately, accompanied at the piano. Get your players and singers to practice separately, and practise well, before bringing them together. If you have instructed the orchestra with the same intentions and precise rhythms, you will see that at the communal rehearsal, perfect fusion will be rapidly attained. In this way you won't tire out the orchestra, you won't waste money or time in useless practices that enfeeble the performance.

Remember that the artist is one of the main responsibilities of the rendering of the composer's ideas; so take care of him. Love him. Is his training insufficient? Guide him. Does he tend to be overexpressive, to "ham it up"? Such a tendency is more common than you might think. Stop this, with firm persuasion. Gounod, in his book on Mozart's *Don Giovanni*, says that one of the primary skills of the conductor is ensuring that the artist executes and interprets his part as the composer intended, but leaving the illusion that it is he himself who is interpreting it.

In melodrama there is still a highly relevant part for the conductor: the mise-en-scene. Stage sets, costumes, lighting, movement – the conductor should not ignore anything. Today there are directors who take care of all the preparation and coordination of these elements, but the conductor should be aware of all that is going on and intervene if necessary. Indeed, nobody more than he – since he is a musician – has to know what colour on the stage is suitable for a particular musical passage, or how far a given stage movement should be pushed. Don't forget that you have to be the repository of the composer's intentions and you have to ensure that these are respected. All this is neither easy nor simple, but it is indispensable if you want to call yourself an opera director.

Finally, the most delicate and important point: the interpretation, wanting it to be just right. A certain composer, on making an observation to a conductor about his way of interpreting one of his works, received the answer: "I feel it like this". That composer felt nothing. One only has to feel how the composer felt it. Interpreting means: interpreting the composer's thought through one's own personality (this is a sine qua non), but always inspired by the will of the composer. Before beginning the study of the opera to be directed, study all the composer's works; try to understand his artistic temperament by reading what he has written about himself and his art. Only then will you be spiritually close to the composer and able to interpret his musical ideas soundly.

"Serve art with humility", a great conductor said. Be careful, however, that the modesty which can appear stupidity is not concealed in these words. Quite the opposite – a noble pride lies therein. Conveying to the audience the composer's though, confident in having understood all its creative force, with the faith of an apostle. Being a high priest of Art: what mission could be more magnificent for a musician?

The things I have said are all well-known, but since some people still ignore them and many pretend to ignore them, I thought it might be useful to repeat them.

VICTOR DE SABATA

A concert in Salzburg – 1953
A conversation with Adriano Lualdi

> *We have to be able to understand what Beethoven intended, where he was satisfied with the instruments at his disposal, and where he was not.*
>
> Victor de Sabata

"With regard to some "tricks of the trade", I recall a conversation I had last November with Victor de Sabata concerning the recollection I had of one of his recent concerts: that of Salzburg, summer 1953", writes Adriano Lualdi in the third edition of his The Art of Conducting the Orchestra *(1957). It was 1 August 1953 when Victor de Sabata (1892-1967) was directing the Vienna Philharmonic in a programme that included Berlioz' overture,* Le Carnaval Romain, *Richard Strauss' tone poem,* Tod und Verklärung, Ravel's *La Valse,* Stravinsky's *Le Chant du Rossignol and Verdi's* Vespri Siciliani. *Just a few weeks after the Salzburg concert, an illness forced de Sabata to abandon the podium and his position as Artistic director of La Scala. Thus ended the career of one the greatest performers of the twentieth century.*

Launched precociously into music studies at the Milan Conservatoire, de Sabata immediately demonstrated outstanding ability in mastering several instruments (piano, violin, wind, woodwind and brass instruments and the harp) and an extraordinary talent for the art of composition. He was only seventeen when he presented and directed his first composition, in 1909. His proper debut was not until 1916, the year in which Ettore Panizza directed at La Scala the opera Il Macigno *(which was to become* Driada *in 1935), with music by de Sabata and libretto by Alberto Colantuoni. There followed* Melodia per Violino *(1918), the symphonic poem* Juventus *(1919), the never performed opera* Lisistrata *(1920),*

247

the symphonic sketch for orchestra La Notte di Platòn *(1923), the con-
templative poem* Gethsemani *(1925, the ballet* Le Mille e Una Notte
(1931) and incidental music for Shakespeare's Merchant of Venice
*(1934). But around that time his career as a composer was taken over by
that of conductor: the first night of Wagner's* Tristan und Isolde, *directed by him, at La Scala on 11 December 1930 was a resounding triumph, consecrating him as one of the most important conductors of the
time. The next day the "Secolo Sera" newspaper had this to say:*

*Victor de Sabata has given us, with this masterpiece, an interpretation
that is the most faithful to the spirit of the opera, the most complete and
balanced, the most ardent and the most musical that we can remember.
Every page of the magnificent score has found in him a profound and passionate exegete; every word of Tristan's legendary love story has found in
de Sabata's heart the the means to relive and re-suffer it and to express
its immense wealth of humanity, universality and poetry.*

*He distances himself, it is true, from what are believed (or purported)
to be the "traditional" movements of the score. But he was able to stamp
such a sense of urgency and expressive force into every beat, every caesura,
every elastic sinuosity of rhythm that once more the true or false tradition
(which is often reduced to nothing but the foolish and convenient habit of
retracing old steps; to the inability to see, to read, to intuit the spiritual
and fiery content beyond the material notation) is left incinerated by the
ardour of a new soul and by the intimate emotion of a truly great artist.
De Sabata's execution was heart-rending and moving, from the first to the
last bar – and when we say from the first to the last bar, we include the
pages that usually appear veiled somewhat by a greyness, a degree of
lethargy, but which yesterday seemed splendid and necessary for integrating
the musical and dramatic elements of the opera. This came about through
the tone of discretion de Sabata employed, ensuring that the orchestra was
not an obstacle between the characters on stage and the audience; on account of the prominence that de Sabata was able to constantly give to the
voices, mindful of the fact that it is not enough for a score to bear the name
of Wagner or Strauss to stop a melodrama mutating into a ... symphonic
poem: it came about thanks to the intellect and love of an artists and musician who allowed de Sabata to identify and fully emphasise, at every junc-
ture, the* melos, *that is, the the very soul of the mighty composition.*

The ardour of a new soul, it has been said. And this appeared quite evident not only in the fresh sensibility, full of wonder and enthusiasm, that de Sabata brought to Tristan und Isolde, *which is already so garlanded with glory and well-known in every detail, as well as so terribly hampered by all manner of short-sighted critical barbs levelled against it by critics and performers. It was also evident in the fact that for the first time since the opera has been presented, the public was able to understand and feel what Wagner had in mind when he asserted that he had composed* Tristan und Isolde *"for Italian singers and conductors". He was obviously thinking of singers who could fully express the passionate, sensual, wholesale abandonment to the miracle of love that animates his music and which last night, as never before, was brilliantly realised, in both the perfect prominence given to the voices in relation to the orchestra and the atmosphere of abandonment, sensuality, amorous languor and nervy vibration created by de Sabata in this superb execution – this is the true, unique atmosphere of* Tristan und Isolde.

Twenty years later, Renato Mariani thus described de Sabata's art in the pages of "La Scala" magazine:

With regard to Victor de Sabata – the most brilliant and generous conductor of our times – I would not say that the final goal, the sublime aspiration, is "perfection". Making such an assertion would appear to diminish his marvellous qualities as an artist, to distract from a much more serious consideration. It is clear that for a sensitive artist, "perfection" – something that is extremely difficult to define critically, especially in terms of musical interpretation – may be an end but not a means, if only for the fact that the idea of something "perfect" categorically denies the presence of a living pulse, a human vibration, with unpredictable elements. The end of de Sabata is emotion. Each note is an emotional event for him. Herein lies the basis of de Sabata's interpretative behaviour. And if in his performances such emotional events reach incredible, unprecedented heights, that is because the means – and not the end – "perfection", has already been taken care of and left behind. Everything has been expended at the preliminary stage: that long, exhausting stage that de Sabata fills with in-depth study, that precious, inflexible stage when he practises with the orchestra. On the podium the maestro's target is exclusively emotion, from which he strenuously excludes any other element previously developed and experimented.

De Sabata studied with great conscientiousness and was able to count on an extraordinary memory. He was able to rewrite from memory any composition he had directed (as Lualdi also emphasised) and even corrected errors on sheet music: this is what happened during a rehearsal of Turandot; de Sabata picked up an error in the third trombone and discovered that it was a misprint in the score that had escaped even Toscanini. He also had an incredible ear for music. Nino Sanzogno recalled (in an anecdote recounted by Teodoro Celli) that, during a rehearsal in which he took part as second violin, he wanted to test de Sabata's skill by playing an octave above the other violinists (fifteen in all). It was only during the interval that de Sabata, staring him in the eye, said: "As for that joker who played everything an octave too high, do us a favour and play the notes as they were written".

On the subject of his conducting skills, Gianandrea Gavazzeni commented: "He conceived of the conductor as a demiurge, a hero, a dominator of the works of others, to be revealed through new acoustics, to be tweaked in those inventive secrets that, in some cases, even the composers themselves would never have imagined could create such significance and resonance".

Alfredo Mandinelli had a similar experience: "When I visited him we talked, naturally enough, about music. For example, about "touching up" the orchestrations of composers (even the top ones) – all the great conductors have always done it. He found it absurd that one should stop at certain limits imposed by, say, Beethoven, and not be able to insert notes that the instruments of the time could not avail themselves of.

"We have to understand what Beethoven intended, where he was satisfied with the instruments at his disposal, and where he was not".

A much healthier attitude than that prevailing today, where everyone is concerned about recreating the "original sound", which cannot be original, given that the hearing and non-silence are those of the today . He saw no conflict in the fact that there coexist instruments with a fixed sound tuned according to the tempered scale (piano, organ) and those producing a non-tempered note (strings), distinguishing between a sharp and flat.

In his view, it was part of the margin of adaptation required by our ear, even though we may not always be aware of this. He felt great respect and admiration for the technical complexity of modern music in *terms of harmony, timbres, rhythmics and the instrumental palette, and he took great pleasure in mastering it – for him it was an expressive subject, revealing the existence of a world, a world of sound that had gradually replaced the mystical aspirations of oriental music. "They haven't made progress in terms of technique". Then he would joke about the increasing bravura of composers in being descriptive, especially in describing storms, tempests and blizzards, from Vivaldi to Beethoven', on to Strauss: "The storm in the* Alpensinfonie *beats then all..." And his blue eyes twinkled".*

Universally recognised as one of the greatest conductors of the twentieth century, de Sabata directed for the last time in February 1957 on the occasion of the funeral of Arturo Toscanini, with whom he had recently buried the hatchet. In a conversation with Lualdi from two years before (1955) – which we print in full – de Sabata explains his method, referring to the Salzburg concert of 1953. At certain moments of his symphonic executions, exploiting technical means used to achieve specific, amazing effects, his authority, his powerful command, his magical, almost psychic power, which hold sway over both the orchestra and the audience, are beyond words.

LUALDI   In the concert of two years ago in Salzburg, with the stunning performance you gave of the Roman Carnival overture, you succeeded in making the piece seem beautiful, evocative, vibrant and relevant – a piece that, after countless listenings, had left me rather puzzled, almost to the point where I thought it ugly or at least not sufficiently significant to feature so often in concert programmes.

DE SABATA   Look, for example, at the beginning of this overture: the woodwinds responding on the second beat and imitating its pattern, to the energetic entry of the strings; and on the third the horns, just the starting point – we already have a nice touch. The contrast of the *allegro assai con fuoco*, which in Eulenberg's score is marked 156, a fraction that doesn't exist on Maelzel's metronome, I take rapidly, to the maximum limit allowed by, say, the trill of the four bassoons, from the fifteenth to the eighteenth beat.

This is one of the cases where practical knowledge of the instrument is very useful to the conductor. All the tempi of the overture are then played in relation to this initial one.

LUALDI   It surprised me, as if it were something new, the perfect equilibrium and the perfect clarity you obtained from the tympanum, triangle, drum and cornet, trumpets, horns, clarinets and second flute, when with their quatrains accompany the canon among cellos, violas, bassoons, first and second violins, English horn, oboe and flute.

DE SABATA   To obtain lightness of sound and precision of rhythm, of course you have to rehearse with the two groups of instruments separately.

LUALDI   But I'm talking particularly about the phonic equilibrium. You could hear them all in a light, transparent, delicate amalgam – even the triangle could be heard clearly amid the percussion.

DE SABATA   That's a practise I worked on when I studies at the conservatoire and then, with much patience, in the early years of my career, listening to the rehearsals and concerts of the great masters, in empty halls or packed auditoriums. I noticed that, of all the instruments, the percussion ones, especially the small ones like the triangle, the castanets, the small and the Basque military drums and the cymbals are the most insidious, the most difficult to deal with because the effect, the weight of sound you hear from the conductor's podium corresponds very vaguely to the sound that arrives in the auditorium. Not only that – this weight of sound varies enormously according to the orchestral mixes that accompany, or redouble, or contrast with the rhythms marked by the drums and accessories. And so I learned to dose the sounds precisely and get the desired effect. If you had heard this page from my podium, and not from the hall, you wouldn't have been satisfied because from the podium the balance between the percussion and the wind instruments appeared far from perfect. But from the hall, as you heard, it did.

LUALDI   I noticed a charming – also quite unusual – effect when after the rapid series of semitone scales by the flute and piccolo, there was a return to the first tempo and the muted violins launch into the *saltarello*...

DE SABATA   I have this entry played almost *balzato*, to achieve a *scherzoso, brillante* effect even in the pianissimo and the bow strokes the opposite to what would be more pragmatic: the quavers up, the crotchets up.

LUALDI   The entry of the first horn at 120 beats? And the trumpets and horns third and fourth at 126?

DE SABATA   Yes, I ask the horn for closed sounds, which aren't indicated in the score, which balance perfectly, also in *piano*, with the flute which has the *mezzoforte*. And I play the entry of the horns and trumpets at 126 not *forte*, as is written, but rather in a relative *forte* played cross-fingered, and I moderate the *fortissimo* of the 128 to a *forte* to give more prominence to the *fortissimos* that follow.

LUALDI   At beat 276, after the two in *fortissimo* and *crescendo* of everyone, without you opening even the slightest caesura in the movement, you could hear the *pianissimo* entry of the quartet of flute, oboe and clarinets on the resumption of the 6/8.

DE SABATA   I do the entry *mezzoforte* with a slight accent on the first note and with a hairpin of *diminuendo*; at the *pianissimo* I only get up to beat 278, which precedes the entry of the strings.

LUALDI   Let's move on to another piece in you programme: Ravel's *La Valse*. I've had the occasion to hear this peace umpteen times over various evenings, conducted by Ansermet; and I understand increasingly less how and why this mediocre piece is so adored by conductors. I think here we have one of the numerous examples of foolish ambition: this terrible sickness of the podium which – apart from the laziness virus from which it stems – we have to thank for the last forty years the repertoire of symphonic concerts being always been more or less the same. Ravel's *La Valse* doesn't lend itself to tumultuous conducting exhibitions. I think that rather we have at play a mysterious, even devious, suggestion of the subconscious, a confession, an act of contrition. I mean, not for the general public, who "drink it up", but for that section of critics and philosophers who attribute to the art of conducting powers that it doesn't possess, by which not even the most excellent of players manages, in certain cases, to make a poor wretch who can barely speak look like an amazingly eloquent orator.

DE SABATA   You're exaggerating. I love the atmosphere of Ravel's *La Valse*, for instance.

LUALDI   Yes, that atmospheric setting in the preface introducing the score: "Through whirling clouds, waltzing couples may be faintly distinguished. The clouds gradually scatter: one gradually sees an immense hall peopled with a whirling crowd...". But the starting point of the waltz, so modest and lacking in impetus is not even remotely comparable to the waltzes of Johann Strauss or Lehar or the stupendous, enthralling *Rosenkavalier*; and the development of the whole piece, so slow and plodding, and the never quite achieved effect of the vertiginous (which was the composer's declared intention); and – again – that long central part, the resumption after the fortissimo, where the same motifs and colour of the first pages are repeated with very few variations, give the entire *"poème chorégraphique"* an overall swinging movement; this, bereft of any impulses of energy, gradually reduces its movement to collapse (I'm talking about the spirit of the piece). Certainly, not even the thunderous finale succeeds in galvanising this inexplicably popular work. Especially if you consider other beautiful and momentous works by Ravel: *Le tombeau de Couperin*, for example is one of the most exquisite works of all time.

DE SABATA   Yes, that's true. There are some grey areas in that piece, especially in the central part, the resumption. But who knows? Maybe it was these that actually attracted me...

LUALDI   In the Salzburg concert you also conducted the

Chant du rossignol. That was also an exciting performance, full of a sense of awe, like a new soul before a new thing, you moulded every detail so that the listened was enthralled and astonished. With the advantage over Bulow that this poem comes from the forty-year-old Stravinsky, at the height of his powers. One moment that left me slightly puzzled about the technical aspect was where, on the *fortissimo pizzicato* chord of the double basses, cellos, violas, first and second violins, three dampered trombones come in (but the first reduplicates some of the other two's notes with an *arpeggio*). A volume of rich sound. Yet one could distinctly perceive not just the first, but also the second of the two solo cellos which, proceeding in sevenths, perform the wavy movement of the triplets.

DE SABATA   To give both prominence and balance at the same time, I ask the trombones to produce the most piercing sound possible and the two solo cellos to follow the non-*legato* triplets, without *vibrato*, mechanically. Indeed, it is precisely this proceeding by sevenths that has a particular emphatic in the orchestra, even when the position of this pattern is central and entrusted to instruments without a powerful timbre, as here.

LUALDI   Further on, after the descent with the famous, striking double effect of the two flutes and of the semitones detached from the two clarinets, I noticed a brief suspension of movement, barely a breath, of extremely evocative effect. It is spontaneous, as it seems, autonomous, or else it is also suggested by the semiquaver pause that there is in the score of the piece at a similar moment?

DE SABATA   The moment you're talking about is two beats before number 85 [de Sabata does not have the score in front of him]: oboes, clarinets, and at the end of the first movement, violins: the silent pause is of one octave. Your impression is suggested by the scrupulously observed pause. I keep it longer almost imperceptibly, almost a breath, since the woodwind motif that follows and the new pause of one octave that I respect precisely prepare better for the exquisite entrance of the flute at number 85.

255

LUALDI   Has it ever happened that you achieved, not with your first attempt, but gradually, with difficulty, amid uncertainties and perplexities, not of days, but month, even sometimes years [...], the definitive, profound expression of a particular piece, hearing it as your own creature in every moment, to feel sure, in short, that you were getting it right – in terms of tempo and its variations, colourations, accents, atmosphere?

DE SABATA   Yes, it has sometimes happened, for example with the third movement of Schumann's Third Symphony in E-flat major, the "Rhenish" [de Sabata goes to the piano and plays the opening bars of the third movement]. I found it difficult to reach that sense of the inspiration of the moment, almost of inspiration, that Schumann undoubtedly intended.

LUALDI   In one of his books, Giulio Confalonieri noted and highlighted Schumann's impulse to transcend the restraints of the classical symphony, while refusing to cancel them completely and replace them with a different model. This, in my view, is one the cases Confalonieri is referring to, and one of the most significant.

DE SABATA   Indeed, it was a real effort to convey in a live performance that sense of ardour and respect for sacred traditions at the same time.

LUALDI   How courteous your great grandfathers were towards art! Just like today. But you, in hinting at this beautiful melody, held a tempo that seemed to me an *andante moderato ma un po' mosso*: less, that is, than the *Nicht schnell* marked in the score.

DE SABATA   Your impression comes from the fact that, with extremely measured elasticity "kept secret" from the ear, I let the melody live in the *andante*, in fact, really *Nicht schnell*, though without letting it languish...

LUALDI   This reply has reminded me of another, by Antonio Guarnieri, when I asked him how he managed to obtain such effects of extraordinary beauty from the strings of his orchestras. "Me?" he replied, "I just let them play for me".

Victor de Sabata takes his seat at the piano again and resumes playing the *Nicht schnell* of the Rhenish Symphony. This time no longer hinting, almost getting excited. I think, meanwhile, of a one of Schumann's comments: "Always play with soul. It is the laws of morality that govern art. Without enthusiasm you never achieve anything great".

Profiles Of Conductors And Composers

Jean-Baptiste Lully (1632-1687)

A dancer, composer and musician, born in Florence (with the name Giovanni Battista Lulli), he made his fortune in France, particularly at the court of King Louis XIV. Here, thanks to the bounteous favours bestowed on him by the sovereign, he served first as dancer, then composer and finally as superintendent of the court music. Lully also instructed his musicians, beating time by stamping a large stick on the ground. It was through doing this that he wounded his foot, which led to complications that brought about his death.

Johann Sebastian Bach (1685-1759)

Renowned as one of the great geniuses of music history, Bach was known above all among his contemporaries as an organist, his skill as which led him to receive various appointments in German courts and churches. Bach personally directed his own compositions, guiding musician at his violin or sitting at the clavichord, singing, playing and signalling the instruments' entries authoritatively and meticulously. His works were rediscovered and reassessed only in 1829, when Felix Mendelssohn directed his *Matthäus-Passion* in Berlin.

Franz Joseph Haydn (1732-1809)

Considered one of the greatest composers of the classical age, "father" of the symphony and the string quartet, Haydn served for considerable time as *Kapellmeister*, first with Count Morzin, then at the court of the Esterhazy princes, where he stayed for almost thirty years. While he worked as music director, Haydn composed music, mounted operatic productions, conducted the musicians and choir seated at the clavichord. After leaving his position with the Esterhazy, Haydn continued to compose and direct his music, enjoying enormous success and recognition.

Wolfgang Amadeus Mozart (1756-1791)

Universally considered to be one of the greatest musical geniuses in history, Mozart began composing when he was only five. Brilliant composer and highly skilled player of the piano, organ, violin and clavichord, he was one of the first "freelance" musicians and worked in various European cities, writing and directing his music in accordance with the customs of the time. "God after Christ sent his second son down to earth" said an anonymous contemporary of him.

Ludwig van Beethoven (1770-1827)

The German composer, violist and pianist Beethoven is one of the most significant figures in the history of music. His work, midway between the classical and the romantic eras, marked a turning point in musical art and, precisely because his work was so innovative, he was often criticised and misunderstood by traditionalists. Due to his deafness, which was diagnosed when he was not even thirty and became total a few years before his death, Beethoven was not always the best conductor of his own work.

Gaspare Spontini (1774-1851)

An Italian composer and conductor. He has gone down in history as one of the major Italian composers spanning the eighteenth and nineteenth centuries (his *La vestale* is outstanding) Spontini was also a highly regarded orchestra conductor. For twenty years (1820-1840) he held the double role of *Kapellmeister* and *Generalmusikdirektor* at the Berlin *Staatsoper*. One of his admirers was Wagner, who in his autobiography recalls his authoritarian methods and use of a particular kind of baton (not light, but heavy, made of ebony and held in the middle).

Carl Maria von Weber (1786-1826)

The pianist and composer Weber was the composer of the first romantic opera: *Der Freischütz* (*The Marksman*) was a resounding success and contributed to the promotion of German melodrama. Apart from his work as a composer, Weber is considered to be the first real orchestra conductor in history, the first to conduct without playing the violin or clavichord, but conceiving of the role of conductor as one of complete autonomy.

Louis-Hector Berlioz (1803-1869)

A French composer, who with his work contributed to a radical renewal in European music. With his *Grand traité d'instrumentation et d'orchestration modernes* (1844), Berlioz revolutionised orchestral technique. Moreover, in the appendix to the second edition of the treatise (1855), he published *Le chef d'orchestre: théorie de son art*, the first theoretical essay entirely dedicated to conducting. With Berlioz, himself a distinguished conductor, the role was redefined and accorded new authority and dignity.

Michael Costa (1808-1884)

He was a British composer and conductor of Italian origin (born in Naples as Michele Costa). After studying at the Royal College of Music in Naples, he moved to England and lived first in Birmingham and subsequently in London (1830). He was appointed conductor at Her Majesty's Theatre in the West End and later at the Royal Opera House, Covent Garden, distinguishing himself for the attention, care and discipline he devoted to the players, not something that was a given at the time, and he earned the approval of Giuseppe Verdi, among others.

Jakob Ludwig Felix Mendelssohn (1809-1847)

Mendelssohn was a German pianist, organist, composer and conductor of Jewish origin, whose musical tastes were fairly conservative, unlike his contemporaries, who reflected more the romantic spirit of the age. He was among those who contributed to enhancing the reputation of the conductor, emphasising the care and attention that should be given in the preparation of the orchestra, as well as being one of the first to use the baton. Although he was much appreciated by Berlioz, Mendelssohn was fiercely criticised by Wagner.

Franz Liszt (1811-1886)

A composer, a marvellous and incomparable pianist, conductor and organist of Hungarian origin, Franz Liszt is undoubtedly one of the great masters in the history of music. He is considered to be among the most important composer-conductors of his time. Liszt contributed to the appreciation of the figure of the conductor in the romantic sense, no longer a mechanical time-beater, but a genuine interpreter of music and essential intermediary between the composer and the public.

Wilhelm Richard Wagner (1813-1883)

A genius with a will of iron, Wagner revolutionised musical theatre with his multiple roles as composer, librettist, theatre director, conductor, poet and essayist. He created a new world of fantasy and developed a potent operatic form of incredible dramatic intensity and musical expressiveness. Along with Berlioz, he is to be considered one of the greatest theoreticians of the art of conducting, as expounded in his *Über das Dirigieren*, published in 1869 and strongly influenced by the ideas of Liszt.

Giuseppe Verdi (1813-1901)

Sublime Italian composer and author of some of the most popular operas of all time, Verdi devoted himself to conducting with the Philharmonic of Busseto for a short time. His fame is inextricably linked to his operas, which enjoyed enormous success, thanks to the careful attention he paid to the tastes and trends of the time, with which he kept up to date with frequent visits to Paris.

Charles Gounod (1818-1893)

He was a French composer, creator of twelve operas, as well as oratorios, ballets, masses and motets, among other things. He was gifted with unusual melodic inspiration and graceful lyricism. He was the first conductor of the Royal Choral Society, London and author of a controversial book on the operatic works of Mozart, of which he examines six aspects: the rate of movement, the bar, the light and shade, the breathing, the pronunciation and finally the role of the conductor.

Charles Hallé (1819-1895)

Pianist and conductor of German origin, but naturalised as a British citizen. After commencing his studies in his native Germany, in 1836 he moved to Paris, where he was to stay for twelve years, coming into contact with figures of the calibre of Cherubini, Chopin, Liszt. The uprisings of 1848 prompted him to move to the United Kingdom – here he directed the "popular concerts" and the Manchester Gentlemen's Concerts and was among the first to promote the spread of Beethoven's music in England. In 1857 he founded the orchestra that bears his name (the Hallé Orchestra), based in Manchester and still going strong today.

Jules Étienne Pasdeloup (1819-1887)

French conductor. In 1851 he founded the *Société des jeunes artistes du conservatoire* and directed concerts for ten years before launching a new project, the *Concerts Populaires* (subsequently renamed the *Concerts Pasdeloup*, still the oldest French symphonic orchestra today). These continued until 1884 before being suspended until 1887, owing to the competition from the *Concerts Lamoureux* and the *Concerts Colonne*. In France, he was one of the main promoters of contemporary composers (like Wagner and Schumann) but also the classics (Mozart, Beethoven).

Angelo Mariani (1821-1873)

Italian composer, violinist and conductor specialising in opera. He was particularly appreciated by composers like Wagner, Rossini and Verdi. He was linked with Verdi by a bond of great friendship, which lapsed in Mariani's final years. Over the course of his career he conducted two premières (Verdi's *Aroldo* in Rimini and Faccio's *Amleto in* Genoa) and, in 1871, the Italian première of Wagner's *Lohengrin* in Bologna: this was the first time a work by the great German composer had been presented in Italy.

Giovanni Bottesini (1821-1889)

An Italian composer and conductor, also a virtuoso of the double bass, an instrument that he mastered with such skill that he was dubbed the "Paganini of the double bass". Renowned for being an outstanding instrumentalist, he was also much appreciated as conductor, of both his own works and those of others: Giuseppe Verdi chose him to direct the première of *Aida* in Cairo in 1872. When he directed in an opera house, he had the habit of playing double bass compositions inspired by the opera being performed between one act and another.

Anton Grigoryevich Rubinstein (1829-1894)

Russian pianist, composer and conductor. Virtuoso of the piano (Hans von Bülow called him "the Michelangelo of music") and prolific composer, Rubinstein was one of the leading players of the Russian and international music scene of the nineteenth century. In 1862, he founded the Conservatoire of St Petersburg (four years later his brother Nikolai id the same with the Conservatoire of Moscow) and he was one of the leading lights of the Russian Musical Society, where he conducted from 1859 to 1867. Known for this fiery temperament, both at the piano and on the podium, he was not always the most appreciated of men.

Hans von Bülow (1830-1894)

Pupil of Liszt, consummate pianist and intransigent conductor, his performances revealed the true spirit of the German classics, helping to establish the success of Wagner's operas. His orchestral performances are recalled as as being of rare technical and stylistic perfection. For this reason, Bülow is to be considered the conducting virtuoso who, by his example had enormous influence on all conductors who followed him (for better or for worse, as Felix Weingartner was to claim at a later date).

Johannes Brahms (1833-1897)

Regarded as one of the greatest composers of the nineteenth century, Brahms was also a virtuoso pianist and much appreciated conductor. His contemporaries viewed him as being too tied up with the classics, too academic, too rooted in tradition and tending towards an intimism that was alien to other composers of the time, like Berlioz e Wagner. This tendency was also reflected in the music he was wont to direct, a repertoire that ranged from Bach up to his time, excluding, however, exponents of the so-called "New German School".

Charles Lamoureux (1834-1899)

French violinist and conductor. Launching his career at an early age, he combined his activity as musician and conductor with that of concert organiser, often at his own expense, as in the case of the *Société Française de l'Harmonie Sacrée*, with which he performed for the first time in Paris some compositions by Handel and Bach. Economic problems forced him to seek new positions: from 1881 to 1897, he conducted the concerts of the *Société des Nouveaux-Concerts* (which would subsequently take his name), in which he proved to be an unflagging promoter of the music of Wagner.

Édouard Colonne (1838-1910)

French violinist and conductor. First violin with the Paris *Opéra* from 1858 to 1867, he received his first conducting commissions in 1871. Together with Georges Hartmann, he founded the association of *Concert National*, subsequently renamed *Association Artistique du Châtelet* and known up to the first half of the twentieth century as the *Concerts Colonne*. He was one of the chief promoters of the music of Berlioz, Wagner and Mahler, as well as being one of the first conductors to have his performances recorded.

Franco Faccio (1840-1891)

Italian conductor and composer of two operas, *I profughi fiamminghi*, with libretto by Emilio Praga and *Amleto*, with libretto by Arrigo Boito. He took to the podium in 1867. Four years later he was appointed musical director at La Scala, where, in 1872, he conducted the first Italian performance of Verdi's *Aida*. He was a great friend of Verdi's and in 1887 he gave the world première of his *Otello*. Renowned for his performances on the podium among his contemporaries, Faccio was also one of the main promoters of the renewal of interest in symphonic music in Italy.

Ettore Pinelli (1843-1915)

Italian violinist, composer and conductor. He began his violin studies as a child and his playing was much appreciated by Liszt. Pinelli's fame derives mainly for his commitment to the promotion of musical arts and the foundation of two institutes: the *Liceo Musicale*, which would subsequently become the Music Conservatoire of *Santa Cecilia*, in Rome (1869), and the *Società Orchestrale Romana*, of which he was director for twenty five years (1874). As conductor he often collaborated with the Royal Roman Philharmonic Academy.

Luigi Mancinelli (1848-1921)

An excellent Italian composer, cellist and conductor. Both as composer and conductor, Mancinelli exploited his in-depth knowledge of the orchestra. He composed some operas and incidental music for the theatre as well as some film scores. His conducting career unfolded both in Italy and abroad, where he became famous as a performer of Wagner, Puccini and Verdi. He conducted Verdi's *Falstaff* and *Otello* for their premières in the United States.

Arthur Nikisch (1855-1922)

Hungarian conductor. His musical career took off when he was engaged as violinist the Vienna Philharmonic, but he achieved his greatest success as conductor. In the 1890s he collaborated with the Boston Symphony Orchestra and the Budapest Opera, and was then appointed as conductor with both the *Gewandhaus* of Leipzig and the Berlin Philharmonic (1895), positions he was to hold for the rest of his life. He is considered one of the finest interpreters of the music of Bruckner, Beethoven, Liszt, Tchaikovsky and Brahms.

Giuseppe Martucci (1856-1909)

Italian pianist, composer and conductor. Son of a trumpeter, he was something of a child prodigy, and he gave piano concerts at the age of only eight, enjoying his first successes as a musician. His debut on the podium was in 1881. Martucci was one of the first admirers of Wagner's music in Italy: indeed, it was he who, in 1888, conducted the Italian première of *Tristan und Isolde*. With his teaching and composing activities, he did much to promote symphonic music in Italy: his compositions would find a faithful performer in Arturo Toscanini.

Gustav Mahler (1860-1911)

Mahler was a late romantic Austrian composer, whose music spans the great divide between late nineteenth-century tradition and the modernist innovations of the twentieth century. This meant that his compositions were not fully appreciated until after the Second World war. However, his conducting career brought him universal recognition as one of the finest conductors of his age, noted for the power of his performance and the careful attention paid to the orchestration and the mise-en-scène.

Cleofonte Campanini (1860-1919)

Italian conductor, brother of the tenor Italo Campanini and husband of the soprano Eva Tetrazzini (whom he married in 1889). After his debut in 1880 he was appointed to numerous positions in Italy and, especially, abroad. He was chief conductor ta La Scala for three years (1903-1906), during which he conducted the première of Puccini's *Madama Butterfly*. In 1906, he moved to the United States and in 1901 he became the first conductor of the Chicago Grand Opera Company, a position he would hold until his death.

Claude Debussy (1862-1918)

French composer profoundly influenced by literary symbolism and for this reason deemed to be an exponent of musical impressionism, a label Debussy was not particularly fond of. His music is distinguished by its originality of scales and chromaticism, which he used in a far from traditional way. During his long career, he also did some conducting, especially of his own works.

Paul Felix Weingartner (1863-1942)

An Austrian pianist, composer and conductor, Weingartner was one of the last pupils of Liszt. He carried out his conducting activities in Berlin, Munich, Vienna and Hamburg, distinguishing himself for his quite outstanding performances. In 1907, he replaced Mahler as chief of the *Wiener Hofoper* and conducted with the Vienna philharmonic until 1927. He was the first conductor ever to record Beethoven's nine symphonies for commercial purposes. He also published several essays, including a treatise on orchestral conducting, intended to complement that of Wagner from 1869.

Richard Strauss (1864-1949)

A brilliant German composer and conductor, Strauss is considered is considered to be one of the last exponents of musical romanticism. Chiefly famous for his operas and symphonic poems, Strauss was also a well-regarded conductor, whose performances were full of daring and fantasy. Throughout his career he was involved in numerous gramophone recordings. In 1944, on the occasion of his eightieth birthday, he conducting the Vienna Philharmonic in his most important orchestral works.

Arturo Toscanini (1867-1957)

An extraordinary Italian conductor, among the greats of all time. Gifted with a perfect ear, Toscanini was able to induce his orchestras to produce an amazing intensity of sound. He was always meticulous about detail, had a photographic memory and could conduct without a score. He attained international fame through his television and radio broadcasts, in particular, with the NBC Symphony Orchestra of New York, created specially for him. Considered one of the finest performers of Verdi, Beethoven, Brahms and Wagner.

Henry Wood (1869-1944)

British conductor. He began by studying the organ, then branched out to conducting in 1887: in 1891he became director of the *Carl Rosa Opera Company* and in 1892 he was chosen for the British première Tchaikovsky's *Eugene Onegin*. Wood's name is mainly associated with his Promenade concerts "the Proms", classical music concerts aimed at a large audience, which he organised for nearly fifty years, declining even highly prestigious positions to focus on them (with the New York Philharmonic and Boston Symphony Orchestra).

Joseph Willem Mengelberg (1871-1951)

Excellent Dutch conductor and composer who at the tender age of twenty four became chief conductor with the Amsterdam Royal *Concertgebouw* Orchestra, a position he held for half a century (from 1895 to 1945). he was friend to some of the most significant composers of the time, including Strauss and Bartok, a privilege that allowed him to conduct some extremely important premières. Undoubtedly his most important association was with Gustav Mahler: the *Concertgebouw* Orchestra is still renowned today for its Mahlerian tradition.

Serge Alexandrovich Koussevitsky (1874-1951)

Russian composer, conductor and double bass player (naturalised US citizen from 1941). He became quite famous with his double bass playing, and took to the podium in 1908. The next year, having returned to Moscow, he founded a musical publishing house (*Editions Russes de Musique*) and an orchestra. After three years leading the Petrograd State Philharmonic Orchestra, he moved to the United States, where he directed the Boston Symphony Orchestra for twenty five years. He was a lively personality and his performances of Russian and French pieces were outstanding.

Pierre Monteux (1875-1964)

Legendary French conductor. He became famous between 1911 and 1914 by conducting some premières for the travelling *Ballets Russes* Company, including Stravinsky's *Rite of Spring*. From 1917, he collaborated with the New York Opera, and conducted the orchestras of Boston, of the *Concertgebouw* of Amsterdam, of Paris and of San Francisco (this was when he acquired US citizenship); finally, three years before his death (1961), he was appointed conductor of the London Symphony Orchestra. He was also involved in teaching, and founded a conducting school in Hancock (Maine).

Bruno Walter (1876-1962)

German pianist, composer and conductor, principally operating in Germany and the United States. He had very precise ideas about the conductor's duties: he considered himself a mere "postman" of music who had to ensure that the musical letters reached their destination. During his extraordinary conducting career he worked substantially alongside Gustav Mahler, conducting the premières of his Ninth symphony and *Das Lied von der Erde*.

Tullio Serafin (1878-1968)

Considered to be one of the greatest opera conductors of his time. Apart from promoting a wholesale reassessment of the operas of Bellini, Rossini and Donizetti – which thanks to him would become standards in twentieth century repertoires – Serafin was also a good talent scout: he had an eye and an ear for the brightest promises in opera: Maria Callas was one such find. He worked both in Italy (Rome, Milan) and abroad, especially for the New York Metropolitan Opera, where he stayed for ten years.

Thomas Beecham (1879-1961)

Probably the first British conductor to achieve international acclaim. Very comfortably off financially, Beecham combined his conducting activities (starting in 1899) with those of impresario, exploiting his family's wealth to fund various projects, including the foundation of the London Philharmonic Orchestra (1932) and the Royal Philharmonic (1946). In this way, he helped to spread the music and composers that had never been successful in Britain, above all, Berlioz.

Antonio Guarnieri (1880-1952)

An Italian composer and cellist who distinguished himself as one of the finest Italian conductors of the first half of the twentieth century. Worked in Italy and abroad, including Vienna (where he was involved in a scandal from which he was saved by the outbreak of the Great War) and Buenos Aires. He was seen as the great rival of Arturo Toscanini, with whom he vied for the crown of the best conductor at La Scala of Milan, where he first performed in 1922. *Belfagor* by Ottorino Respighi featured among his premières.

Leopold Stokowski (1882-1977)

A British conductor, considered one of the greats of the twentieth century, particularly in the United States, where he made his debut in1909. He conducted the orchestras of Cincinnati, Houston and New York, as well as the NBC Symphony Orchestra, but the highlight of his career was with the Philadelphia Symphony Orchestra. Stokowski conducted with his hands, without a baton. He was involved in radio, television and cinema and is famous for his participation (and appearance) in Walt Disney's *Fantasia* (1940).

Lazare Saminsky (1882-1959)

Ukrainian composer and conductor. After years of study in his native land, he moved to France and then Britain; in the latter he held various positions, until he relocated to the United States in 1920. Here, in his capacity as composer, essayist and conductor, he continued to promote the dissemination of Jewish music. Among his publications stands out *Music of our Day: Essentials and Prophecies* (1932), which contains a chapter on conducting, later republished separately under the title *Essentials of Conducting* in 1958.

Václav Talich (1883-1961)

Czech conductor, violinist and teacher. He began with violin studies, but his admiration for Arthur Nikisch –with who he was subsequently to study – persuaded him to take up a conducting career. His debut on the podium was in 1906, but he found international fame with his long collaboration with the Czech Philharmonic Orchestra, which under his leadership (from 1919 to 1941) attained quite extraordinary levels of excellence. He promoted the compositions of great Czech composers like Antonin Dvořak, Bedřich Smetana and Josef Suk, as well as the operas of Leoš Janáček.

Otto Klemperer (1885-1973)

A German composer universally acknowledged as one of the greatest conductors of the twentieth century. In 1905 he met Mahler: the friendship between the two led Klemperer to the direction of the Prague Opera. In the following years he held various conducting positions, including an important spell with the *Kroll Opera* of Berlin, before moving to the United States. After the Second World War, his activities became somewhat itinerant. At that time he worked substantially with the London Philharmonia, with which he made numerous recordings.

Vittorio Gui (1885-1975)

An Italian composer and conductor who studied at the *Accademia Nazionale di Santa Cecilia* in Rome. His debut on the podium was in 1907, after which he was inundated with invitations and appointments from all over Italy. In 1928 he moved to Florence, where he founded the *Stabile Orchestrale Fiorentina*, which five years later would become the *Maggio Musicale Fiorentino*, directed by him until 1936. His career progressed with important projects in Italy and abroad, various recordings and even compositions for the silent cinema.

Wilhelm Furtwängler (1886-1954)

German pianist and composer, considered one of the major conductors of the twentieth century. He held the position of principal conductor of the Berlin Philharmonic for over twenty years (from 1922 to 1945) and collaborated frequently with the *Gewandhaus* Orchestra and Philharmonic of Vienna. His conducting technique was unique. He viewed symphonic music as a creation of nature: on the basis of this principle his favourite works were those of Beethoven, Brahms, Bruckner and Wagner.

Fritz Reiner (1888-1963)

Hungarian conductor who moved to the USA in 1922, where he became a naturalised citizen. He was active mainly in North America and is most famous for the decade spent in charge of the Chicago Symphony Orchestra: Stravinsky asserted that under Reiner's baton, it was "the most versatile and precise orchestra in the world". His conducting style was expressive, but extremely contained – it was said that the movements of the tip of his baton were limited to the space of a postage stamp.

Hermann Scherchen (1891-1966)

A German violinist and conductor, he made his debut on the podium in 1912. He was principal conductor at Riga, Leipzig, Frankfurt, Konigsberg and particularly Winterthur, where he stayed from 1922 to 1950. He had a lifelong commitment to promoting the composers of his time, also through the foundation of a magazine (*Melos*) and a publishing house (*Ars Viva Verlag*). Moreover, he produced a number of important essays, particularly his treatise on conducting, *Lehrbuch des Dirigierens*, first published in 1929. He died on the podium while conducting at the *Maggio Fiorentino* in Florence.

Victor de Sabata (1892-1967)

Italian conductor and composer. His command over the orchestra was astonishing thanks to his ability to play every instrument. At the age of only twenty six, he was appointed musical director of the Opéra de Monte-Carlo, where he conducted at the première of Ravel's *L'enfant et le sortileges*. He remained there until 1927 and from 1929 to 1957 he was musical director at La Scala, Milan. Considered one of the great opera conductors of the twentieth century, Wagner, Verdi and the French impressionists featured particularly in his repertoire.

Dimitri Mitropoulos (1896-1960)

Greek conductor, pianist and composer. In 1930, at the beginning of his career, he conducted the Berlin Philharmonic and played Prokofiev's Third symphony as soloist. He debuted in the United States, where he became a naturalised citizen, in 1936. In 1949 he began to collaborate with the New York Philharmonic, becoming its main conductor in 1951; he was to remain there until 1958. he also distinguished himself in opera performances: he was principal conductor with the Metropolitan Opera from 1954 until his death in 1960.

George Szell (1897-1970)

Hungarian composer and conductor, who subsequently became a US citizen. The most important tenure he held in his career – from 1946 until his death – was as conductor with the Cleveland Orchestra (Ohio), which under his baton reached an amazingly high level, so much so that it was included among the top five US orchestras (the "Big Five"). He exhibited almost manic precision at rehearsals, to the extent that he was criticised for his coldness and lack of passion: "As far as I'm concerned," he responded to his critics, "artistic ability does not mean disorder".

Lovro von Matačić (1899-1985)

A Croatian-born conductor, he was one of the leading figures in the Yugoslavian musical scene. After his early engagements in his native land and abroad he was appointed conductor with the Belgrade Philharmonic and the Belgrade Opera. After the Second World War, he began to assert himself at an international level, both as conductor and production director. Resounding successes and acknowledgements followed – including his appointment as chief conductor with the Frankfurt Municipal Opera (1961) and subsequently, with the Opéra de Monte-Carlo (1974) – and continued for the rest of his life.

Eugene Ormandy (1899-1985)

Hungarian conductor and violinist, later naturalised US citizen. His most important position was as chief conductor with the Philadelphia Orchestra, which he held for an amazing forty four years. He conducted from memory, often without baton. His repertoire featured especially the romantics (including Bruckner, Debussy, Strauss and Tchaikovsky) and the great composers of the early twentieth century, above all the music of Rachmaninov, which Ormandy helped to promote and spread.

Eduard van Beinum (1901-1959)

A Dutch conductor, whose family had a passion for music (his grandfather conducted a military band, his father played the double bass with the Arnhem Orkest, while his brother was a violinist). In 1931 he was appointed second conductor with the Royal *Concertgebouw* Orchestra, where he worked under the guidance of Mengelberg, whom he replaced after the Second World War. His conducting was meticulous and impassioned. In 1959, he suffered a fatal heart attack during rehearsals with the *Concertgebouw*.

Yevgeny Alexandrovich Mravinsky (1903-1988)

A Russian conductor famous for his long tenure with the Leningrad Philharmonic (from 1938 to 1988, the year of his death). He was one of the greatest interpreters of the music of Shostakovich and conducted several premières, including that of Prokofiev's Sixth Symphony (1947). Mravinsky, a conductor who was impetuous and composed at the same time, had an uncanny command over the orchestra and sometimes conducted without baton. Even today, on the anniversary of his death, surviving orchestra players lay flowers at his grave.

Herbert von Karajan (1908-1989)

Austrian conductor, considered one of the all-time greats in music history. Capable of adapting a sound for all seasons, a sound that was refined, moulded and of calculated voluptuousness, Karajan holds the record for the number of recordings he made, especially with the *Berliner Philharmoniker*, with whom he worked for thirty five years. A sublime performer of the romantic repertoire, his reading of the Wagnerian tetralogy, distilled of the heaviness of earlier German conductors, is outstanding.

Karel Ančerl (1908-1973)

A Czech conductor who studied under Hermann Scherchen and Václav Talich. His career was dramatically interrupted by the Second World War and internment in Auschwitz, which Ančerl survived, losing, however, his wife and son. After the war, he conducted for Radio Prague and became artistic director of the Czech Philharmonic Orchestra, a position he held for eighteen years. To escape the political turmoil in his homeland, at the end of the 1970s he emigrated to Canada, where he conducted the Toronto Symphony Orchestra until his death.

Gianandrea Gavazzeni (1909-1996)

Italian composer, music critic, essayist and conductor. He studied firstly at the Conservatoire of *Santa Cecilia*, Rome, and then the Conservatoire of Milan. He made his debut on the podium in 1933; he held numerous positions both in Italy and abroad. His association with La Scala began in 1948, and, after various engagements with the opera house, he became musical director in 1965 and artistic director in 1966. Shunning the "star system", Gavazzeni was famous for his controversial opinions, particularly his criticism of proponents of a philological approach to music as an end in itself.

Franco Ferrara (1911-1985)

Italian composer and violinist. He trained at the Bologna Conservatoire and embarked on his musical career as violinist; he only took up his conducting activities at a later stage. He debuted on the podium in 1938 and established himself definitively with the Orchestra of the *Accademia Nazionale di Santa Cecilia* (from 1939 to 1945) in Rome. After that he devoted himself to teaching and giving conducting masterclasses, which would take him to many of the most important institutes in Italy (such as the *Accademia Musicale Chigiana* of Siena) and Europe.

Sergiu Celibidache (1912-1996)

Renowned Rumanian conductor, composer and teacher. He was particularly celebrated for his profound interpretations of the symphonies of Bruckner, Brahms and the refined works of French composers. Celibidache was extremely interested in musical phenomenology. Influenced by certain aspects of Zen Buddhism, he maintained that every performance should be a transcendental experience. He had a long-standing association with the Munich and Berlin Philharmonics, as well as the *Orchestra Sinfonica Siciliana*.

276

Igor Markevitch (1912-1983)

Ukrainian composer and conductor who became a naturalised Italian (1947) and subsequently French (1982) citizen. He began to enjoy his first successes from 1929, particularly as composer. In 1930 he made his debut on the podium with the Royal *Concertgebouw* Orchestra of Amsterdam. He was especially acclaimed for his interpretations of Russian, French and German composers of the twentieth century. Later, in the 1960s, he often conducted his own work, contributing to the reassessment of his compositions on the musical scene.

Georg Solti (1912-1997)

A Hungarian pianist and conductor, who became a naturalised British citizen in 1972. Among the most important positions he held were as chief conductor of the Frankfurt Opera (between 1952 and 1961), of the Covent Garden Opera Company (1961 to 1971), which under his leadership gained the title of the Royal Opera, and finally the Chicago Symphony Orchestra, a tenure he held for twenty two years. On account of his outstanding knowledge of the theatrical medium, Solti was renowned above all as opera director.

Carlo Maria Giulini (1914-2005)

An Italian conductor who trained at the *Accademia Nazionale di Santa Cecilia* in Rome. His conducting career was interrupted by the Second World War, but resumed immediately afterwards. At the beginning of the 1950s, he attracted the attention of Toscanini and de Sabata. In the following half century, he worked with orchestras and opera houses all over the world. With his sober, authoritative style, he was a much appreciated conductor of Beethoven, Schubert, Brahms and Ravel.

Leonard Bernstein (1918-1990)

An fascinating American composer, excellent pianist and flamboyant composer, he is considered one of the all-time conducting greats. He worked with the Israel Philharmonic, the London Symphony Orchestra and he was the first musical director of the New

York Philharmonic to be born in the USA – a position he held for ten years. He was an impetuous conductor and sometimes directed seated at the piano. He gained international fame as a composer, particularly with the musical *West Side Story*, which is still incredibly popular today.

Guido Cantelli (1920-1956)

An Italian conductor who studied music from a very young age (his father conducted the military band of Novara) and entered the Milan Conservatoire in 1939. He debuted on the podium in 1943 but was called up for military service; at the end of the Second World War he resumed his activities, achieving resounding success, establishing himself as one of the potential successors of Toscanini and de Sabata. In November 1956, however, after being appointed as chief conductor at La Scala, Milan, he died in a plane crash.

Pierre Boulez (1925-2016)

French composer and conductor. Self-taught, under the guidance of various important figures (especially George Szell), Boulez is considered one of the major conductors of the twentieth century. In the course of his career, he worked with, among others, the Philharmonics of New York, Berlin and Vienna as well as with the symphony orchestras of Chicago, London and of the BBC. Gifted with a magnificent ear, he conducted without baton, favouring especially modernist and contemporary composers.

Karl Richter (1926-1981)

A German conductor, who trained in Dresden and Leipzig, organ and clavichord virtuoso. His repertoire embraced a wide range of symphonic music, but Richter was celebrated above all for his performances of the sacred music of Handel and Bach. As far as the latter was concerned, he insisted on the need to steer clear of romantic principles and to be faithful to more impromptu baroque ones – for this reason, every performance sounded different from previous ones. As he tended towards a more rigid conceptualisation of music philology, his approach was increasingly met with scepticism.

Lorin Maazel (1930-2014)

US conductor, composer and violinist. Considered one of the child prodigies in the conducting art (he took to the podium at the tender age of eight), he began to establish himself in his career from 1953. In 1960, he became the first American director of the Bayreuth Festival and in the following years his fame also began to spread in his native land, where he held numerous positions, including with the Cleveland Orchestra (from 1972 to 1982) and the Pittsburgh Symphony Orchestra (from 1988 to 1996). Gifted with a prodigious memory, he was particularly fêted for his conducting techniques and use of the baton.

Carlos Kleiber (1930-2004)

Austrian conductor (German-born, with music in the family veins), considered one of the greats of the twentieth century. At the beginning of the 1950s, he abandoned his chemistry studies to devote himself to music. From 1958 to 1973 he held the position of *Kapellmeister* in various German cities (Düsseldorf, Duisburg, Stuttgart) and had various engagements in Zurich and Munich, after which he worked mainly as a freelance conductor. Elusive, reserved and extraneous to the "star system", Kleiber's performances were characterised by an obsessive perfectionism which never, however, lacked passion or inspiration.

Claudio Abbado (1933-2014)

Italian pianist and conductor, considered one of the greats of the twentieth century. He trained at the Milan Conservatoire and debuted on the podium in 1958 and at La Scala in 1960. Nine years later, he was appointed chief conductor at the prestigious Milan opera house, with which he continued to collaborate until 1986. Among his most important international positions as conductor we might mention those with the symphony orchestras of London and Chicago, with the Vienna Opera and the Berlin Philharmonic. He founded and directed the Lucerne festival and committed himself to the promotion of young artists.

Riccardo Muti (1941)

Italian conductor. After studying piano, composition and conducting, he made his debut on the podium in 1967. A year later he was appointed musical director of the Florentine *Maggio Musicale*, a tenure he held until 1980. His most important positions include conducting at La Scala (from 1986 to 2005) and with the Chicago Symphony Orchestra (starting in 2010 and expected to continue until al 2020). Muti is considered one of the finest conductors of Giuseppe Verdi's operas.

John Eliot Gardiner (1943)

British conductor. While still at university, he debuted on the podium in 1964 in Cambridge and in London in 1966. His enthusiasm for baroque music crystallised into the foundation of the Monteverdi Choir and Orchestra, the latter being renamed the English Baroque Soloists in 1978, when the musicians adopted period instruments. In addition to these interests, his repertoire also extends to the romantics, with one exception: "I really loathe Wagner – everything he stands for – and I don't even like his music very much".

James Levine (1943)

American violinist, pianist and conductor. He studied at the new York Juilliard School of Music and was assistant to George Szell in Cleveland, debuting on the podium in 1965. His most important positions include conducting with the Chicago Symphony Orchestra, at the Ravinia Festival (1973-1993) and, especially, with the Metropolitan Opera, a tenure he was to hold (with various interruptions) for forty years (1976-2016). Leading the Chicago symphony Orchestra, he appeared in Disney's *Fantasia 2000* , as Stokowsky had done seventy years before.

Riccardo Chailly (1953)

Italian conductor. After training at the Conservatoire and studying conducting at the *Accademia Musicale Chigiana* of Siena under Franco Ferrara, he became assistant to Claudio Abbado in 1973. His debut dates from the next year (1974), while his debut on the podium at La Scala took place in 1978. After distinguished positions and collaborations all over the world (in particular, with the *Concertgebouw* Orchestra of Amsterdam and the *Gewandhaus* of Leipzig), he was appointed musical director of the prestigious Milan Opera House in 2017.

Simon Rattle (1955)

British conductor. He established his reputation in his long tenure with the City of Birmingham Symphony Orchestra (a position he held from 1980 to 1998). In 1999 he was appointed chief conductor of the *Berliner Philharmoniker*, succeeding Claudio Abbado. More recently (September 2017) he took up the position of musical director of the London Symphony Orchestra, which he had already conducted in 2012 on the occasion of the London Olympics. His repertoire embraces mainly composers of the nineteenth and early twentieth centuries, with a predilection for the music of Mahler.

Antonio Pappano (1959)

British pianist and conductor of Italian origin, later naturalised as US citizen. He is one of the few living conductors who never obtained any formal qualification in musical studies. After an early experience with the New York City Opera (1981), he became assistant to Daniel Barenboim at the Bayreuth Festival. After holding various positions (including with the Belgian Royal Opera House from 1992 to 2002), he was appointed musical director at the Royal Opera House, London (from 2002 to 2017) and the Orchestra of the *Accademia Nazionale di Santa Cecilia* (Rome) (from 2005).

Kirill Petrenko (1972)

Austrian conductor of Russian origin, son of a violinist and a musicologist. After his studies, he debuted on the podium at Vorarlberg (Austria) in 1995. Other important positions included with the *Vienna Volksoper* (1997-1999) and the *Meininger Staatstheater* (1999-2002). In 2010 he was appointed *Generalmusikdirektor* of the Bavarian State Opera (a tenure he holds until 2021) and in 2015, he also became the new musical director of the Berlin Philharmonic, starting from summer 2019.

MUSICAL SKETCHES

by Victor de Sabata Jr. (1923-1997)
Doctor, writer, designer, violinist, quartet player.

On hearing an old recording that featured Arturo Toscanini yelling: "No! No! No! Rubbish! CRAP!!!", at his poor orchestra for a slight imperfection, I wondered what even more vituperative comments the Venerable Old Maestro might have to make today when, for labour union reasons, only half an hour is allowed for a rehearsal of a symphony by Gustav Mahler, which lasts an hour and a half. (1984)

There was a memorable performance of *Die Walküre* at La Scala, conducted by Wilhelm Furtwängler: during the first act, he suddenly stopped conducting and rested for some time, leaning on the railing of the podium, as if absorbed in contemplation; during the interval someone asked him the reason for this "absence". Was he not feeling well? "Oh no", the maestro replied with a blissful smile, "it was just that they were playing so well I didn't want to disturb them!". (1986)

Stravinsky allowed himself to be "duped" into recording an LP of music conducted by himself with the Columbia Symphony Orchestra. But he was furious about it. He kept complaining: "I cannot conduct Stravinsky, it's too goddamn difficult!". And to anyone who tried to reason with him that he had composed the music, who better than he could conduct it, he replied: "Balls. Go find that Japanese chap... what's his name, Seiji Ozawa or something like that. HE can conduct Stravinsky a hell of a lot better than I". (1986)

On returning from his first tour in the United States, my uncle, the esteemed maestro told me that for the first time in his life he had been whistled at, so that at the end of the concert at the Carnegie Hall he wanted to break his contract and come home, mortally offended. Fortunately, the impresario, seeing his woebegone face and learning the reason for his despair, cleared up the misunderstanding, explaining that unlike in Europe, it was the custom for American audiences to applaud and whistle and hoot simultaneously, as a sign of overwhelming enthusiasm. A habit that has been adopted by us in recent years, in evident imitation of the Americans. (1986)

Anton Bruckner was crazy about the tremolo effects of the strings and indulgently inserted them for minutes at a time in his symphonies, while perhaps a theme with the horns or trumpets developed. One day I was at La Scala for a rehearsal of his Third Symphony, directed by a young conductor who happened to be my cousin-by-marriage, Aldo Ceccato. When the inexorable moment of the tremolos came, apart from themselves lasting long enough to make all the twenty four violinist cataleptic, the passage had to be repeated because the horns were out of tune. In the end, one of the older violinists could contain himself no longer and burst out: "But Maestro, with all this sawing going on we're going to end up building a wooden hut!".

You tell me if there exists anything in the world more intellectual, more abstract, sophisticated and therefore unnatural than a fugue by Bach; or anything catchier than a Mazurka by Chopin. (1985)

If one goes to listen to a concert, or sees one on television, one cannot but admire the bravura with which each performer plays his instrument. But let's imagine what would happen if the instruments were assigned at the last moment by drawing lots, and the violinist got the horn, the flautist the double bass, the tympanist the clarinet and so on, with maybe a would-be second bassoon on the podium. The greatest orchestra in the world would be suddenly turned into a bedlam of hissing, banging, rattling and flatulence... my God, if you listen to Stockhausen, Luciano Berio, Sylvano Bussotti and John Cage, you can get an idea of what it would sound like! (1984)

On the subject of music, we have to clear up two cliches for once and for all. One, that music is a "universal language". Two, that its is the most "instinctive" and thus the closest to nature. A universal language should by definition be understood by everyone. So how is it that eastern music makes you want to throw up? And how is it that J. S. Bach's sonatas for solo violin made my Afghani nurse smile tenderly? The truth is that music is not a universal language, but a foreign language for everyone, which you have to learn before you can understand it. As far as instinct is concerned, nothing could be further from the truth: music makes use of an artificially constructed language (that of sound, to be precise) to express or convey ideas that are otherwise inexpressible; it is the most "intellectual" of all the arts and thus the furthest from nature, not the closest. (1948)

Herbert Weinstock recounted to me that Igor Stravinsky, discharged from a clinic pretty well recovered from his first cerebral thrombosis episode, managed to walk out on his own two feet, surrounded by solicitous nurses, relatives and friends. And he stepped down the short staircase leading to the street under his own steam – where just at that moment a hearse was passing, to which Stravinsky snapped his fingers as if hailing a taxi and called to the driver: "Excuse me... are you free?". (1986)

Aphorisms and other "Musicalia"

Music is a strange thing – *Lord Byron*

Only music has the power to make us enter ourselves; the other arts only offer us a strange external pleasure – *Honoré De Balzac*

Music is the refuge of souls ulcerated by happiness – *E.M. Cioran*

Music is the eye of the ear – *Thomas Draxe*

Composers shouldn't think too much - it interferes with their plagiarism – *Howard Dietz*

These days what's not worth saying gets set to music – *Beaumarchais*

A German prima donna! I should as soon expect to receive pleasure from the neighing of my horse – *Frederick II, King of Prussia*

Hell is full of musical amateurs: music is the brandy of the damned – *George Bernard Shaw*

The Emperor Joseph II: " Too many notes, my dear Mozart, too many notes!" "Exactly as many as are necessary, Your Majesty" – *W.A. Mozart*

Just after the Second World War, the great Greek conductor Dimitri Mitropoulos was preparing a summer festival of open-air concerts in the ancient theatre of Epidaurus. To test the acoustics, having assembled the orchestra and begun the rehearsal, he sent one of his assistants high up into a field where the audience would be. There was a shepherd with his sheep. When asked by the assistant what he thought, the shepherd replied: "I don't understand why there are so many people playing and only one dancing!"

Experts say that the English Broadwood was not Beethoven's favourite make of piano. Apparently, he preferred the Austrian Graf. Probably if he had played the Broadwood more, it would not have been in such a good condition after its recent restoration. Beethoven was well known as one who hammered on the piano, especially when he was in a bad mood. On one famous occasion, when he was performing his new concerto, he forgot that he was the soloist, so he jumped up and began to conduct in his own peculiar fashion. At the first *sforzando*, he threw out his arms so wide that he knocked over both the lamps from the music stand of the piano. He stopped the orchestra and started again, this time with two choirboys standing next to him holding the lamps. But when he reached the same *sforzando,* he slapped one of the boys so hard he dropped the lamp while the other boy had to duck down to avoid the blow. Beethoven was so furious at the audience's riotous laughter that when he struck the first chord of the solo, six of the piano strings broke.
– *Glasgow Herald*

When Donizetti heard that Rossini had completed his *Barbiere di Siviglia* in three weeks, he shook his head and exclaimed: "Yes, I quite believe it, Rossini has always been such a lazy fellow" – *Gaetano Donizetti*

Rossini composed the the first and last act of Guglielmo Tell. God composed the second act – *Gaetano Donizetti*

Rossini was sitting with a group of friends when the waiter announced that a famous tenor wished to see him. "Of course", replied Rossini "but please ask him to leave his highest pitched notes in the cloakroom along with his hat and cane. Naturally, he can pick them up when he leaves" – *Gioachino Rossini*

How wonderful opera would be if it weren't for the singers – *Gioachino Rossini*

You can't judge *Lohengrin* after one listening, and I certainly don't intend to listen to it a second time – *Gioachino Rossini*

On the occasion of Rossini's seventieth birthday, his friends collected 20,000 francs to erect a monument to him. "What a waste of money", the composer complained. "Just give me the money and I'll stand on the pedestal myself" – *Victor Borge*

Rossini was never dogmatic; his approach to music was instinctive rather than intellectual. This is shown in his famous comment: "There are only two kinds of music, the good or the bad"; or again in a less well-known pontification: "All genres of music are good, except the boring ones" – *Francis Toye*

I could never have composed operas like *Don Giovanni* and *Figaro*. I find them disgusting. They are too frivolous for me – *Ludwig van Beethoven*

It will be generally admitted that Beethoven's Fifth Symphony is the most sublime noise that has ever penetrated into the ear of man – *E. M. Foster*

A young composer approached Brahms and asked him if he could play a funeral march he had written in memory of Beethoven. Permission was duly granted and the young man began playing. When he had finished, he asked Brahms for his opinion. "Put it this way", said the great man frankly, "I'd happier if you were dead and Beethoven had written the march" – *Andre Previn*

Opinions are much divided concerning the merits of the Pastoral Symphony of Beethoven, though very few venture to deny that it is much too long – *William Ayrton*

Of course there are splendid things in Wagner. But he goes on and on – he needed a good sub-editor – *Constant Lambert*

Wagner has lovely moments, but awful quarters of an hour – *Gioachino Rossini*

The old poisoner – *Claude Debussy referring to Wagner*

Richard Wagner was a musician who wrote music which was better than it sounds – *Mark Twain*

I like Wagner's music better than anybody's. It is so loud that one can talk the whole time without other people hearing what one says – *Oscar Wilde*

Is Wagner a human being at all? Is he not rather a disease? – *Friedrich Nietzsche*

A man visited Cherubini with a score attributed to Méhul. After examining it, Cherubini said: "It's not by Méhul, it's not good enough to be his". "Would you believe me if I told you that it's mine?" said the visitor. "No, it's too good to be yours" – *F.J. Crowest*

Napoleon Bonaparte : " "My dear Cherubini, you are certainly an excellent musician; but really, your music is so noisy and complicated, that I can make nothing of it." Luigi Cherubini: "My dear general, you are certainly an excellent soldier; but, in regard to music, you must excuse me if I don't think it necessary to adapt my compositions to your comprehension" – *Bellais*

Berlioz was a freak, without a spark of talent – *Felix Mendelssohn*

Once dead, he will live for a long time – *Stephen Heller on Berlioz*

What you say of Berlioz' Overture I thoroughly agree with. It is a chaotic, prosaic piece, and yet more humanly conceived than some of his others. His orchestration is such a frightful muddle, such an incongruous mess, that one ought to wash one's hands after handling one of his scores – *Felix Mendelssohn*

Mendelssohn has an enormous, extraordinary, superb and prodigious talent. I cannot be accused of uduly flattering him in telling you this because he told me frankly that he did not understand my music at all – *Hector Berlioz*

Franz Liszt had a repertoire of response for young women who asked for undeserved praise for their singing. "Maestro", one young songstress asked, "Do you think I have a good voice?". Liszt allegedly replied: "Good is not the word" – *Herbert Prochnow*

I have composed too much – *Antonin Dvořak*

You really compose a bit too hurriedly – *Johannes Brahms to Dvořak*

Bruckner? That's a swindle that will be forgotten a year or two after my death – *Johannes Brahms apropos Bruckner*

The Bach Choir gave a concert […]. I was not present. There are some experiences which should not be demanded twice from any man," he remarked, "and one of them is listening to Brahms's Requiem – *George Bernard Shaw*

Once I sent the sheet music to one of my songs to Brahms, with a request that he put a cross where he found a fault. Brahms returned it untouched, remarking: "I don't want to make a cemetery of your composition" – *Hugo Wolf*

Brahms is a proficient musician who knows his counterpoint, to whom occur ideas now and then good, occasionally excellent, now and then bad, here and there familiar, and frequently no ideas at all – *Hugo Wolf*

"Hats off, gentlemen, a genius!" Reviewing Variations on Mozart's *Là ci darem la mano* for Piano and Orchestra by Chopin in the *Allgemeine Musikalische Zeitung* – *Robert Schumann*

Play Mozart in memory of me – *Frédéric Chopin*

Critics hew down timber, turning the lofty oak into sawdust – *Robert Schumann*

One has in the mouth the bizarre and delightful taste of a pink bonbon stuffed with snow – *Claude Debussy on the music of Grieg*

When Verdi was asked by a journalist if he, like Wagner, had a theory about the theatre, Verdi replied, "Yes. The theatre should be full" – *Anonymous*

I am sure my music has a taste of codfish in it – *Edvard Grieg*

ow wonderful it would be if operas didn't have singers – *Giuseppe Verdi*

Never let the horns and woodwinds out of your sight; if you can hear them at all, they are too loud – *Richard Strauss*

What I would like most: to be able to devote myself to music from time to time – *Richard Strauss*

Too many pieces of music finish too long after their end – *Igor Stravinsky*

At a concert which featured a piece by Debussy, I asked Rimsky-Korsakov what he thought of it. He replied: "Better not listen to it," he said, "otherwise you run the risk of getting accustomed to it, and you'll end by liking it" – *Igor Stravinsky*

I thought nightingales sang in tune until I discovered Stravinsky – *Graffito in the Royal Academy of Music*

In Geneva I was unable to hold a rehearsal in the hall on the day of my concert since there was a ballet performance going on. During my concert in the evening, the piano sounded muffled. As I continued to play I saw something sticking out the part where the strings are contained – it was a ballerina's bodice!
Rudolf Serkin

Please don't shoot the piano player, He's doing the best he can – *Oscar Wilde*

Why do we in England engage at our concerts so many third-rate continental conductors when we have so many second-rate ones of our own? – *Sir Thomas Beecham*

Beecham was rehearsing the triumph scene of Verdi's *Aida*. He was making the choir repeat a particular part several times when one of the horses defecated on stage. Sir Thomas stopped the rehearsal and, looking at the offending creature reproachfully, exclaimed: "A distressing spectacle, to be sure, but, Gad, what a critic!" – *Sir Thomas Beecham*

Asked if he had ever conducted any Stockhausen, he said, "No, but I once trod in some." – *Sir Thomas Beecham*

A musicologist is a man who can read music but can't hear it – *Sir Thomas Beecham*

At a concert in Carlisle, the pianist Peter Katin, having played a Rachmaninov concerto, was relaxing in the Green Room, while the orchestra continued the concert with Dvořak's New world Symphony. The union representative, bored by the music, walked into the Green Room. "Why are you not playing with the others?" he demanded. "There's no piano part in the New World Symphony" replied Katin. After reflecting for a moment the man said: "In that case you'll get paid less than the others" – *Peter Katin*

I don't know how, with no vibrato, Bach could have so many sons – *Paul Hindemith*

Bach is a Colossus of Rhodes, beneath whom all musicians pass and will continue to pass. Mozart is the most beautiful, Rossini the most brilliant, but Bach is the most comprehensive: he has said all there is to say – *Charles Gounod*

A tenor is not a man, but a disease – *Hans von Bülow*

At the beginning of a rehearsal, Jacques Offenbach, addressing the orchestra, said: "My dear friends, before we begin, I should like to apologise in advance for all the unpleasant things I am surely going to be saying to you in a moment" – *Jacques Offenbach*

Tchaikovsky's Violin Concerto gives us for the first time the hideous notion that there can be music that stinks to the ear – *Eduard Hanslick*

Alas for the music of Mahler! What a fuss about nothing! What a to-do about a few commonplace musical thoughts, hardly worthy of being called ideas – *L. A. Sloper*

Reger might be epitomized as a composer whose name is the same either forward or backward, and whose music, curiously, often displays the same characteristic – *Irving Kolodin*

It is said to be difficult to translate a noise into musical score form. In his Five Orchestral Pieces Schoenberg certainly succeeded. There were passages that suggested a bomb in a poultry yards, cracks, yells, meows and then a crash – *Luis Elson*

One day I'll be able to relax a bit, and try and become a good composer – *Benjamin Britten*

I react very positively to certain birds, especially eagles; and now, from my experience in my dreams, I know that in my past life I was a bird of this particular species, because I know exactly the the sensation of flying and being in the body of that bird – *Karlheinz Stockhausen*

Most composers bore me, because most composers are boring – *Samuel Barber*

When I'm with composers I say I'm a conductor. When I'm with conductors I say I'm a composer – *Leonard Bernstein*

I never use a score when I conduct my orchestra... Does a lion tamer enter the cage with a book on how to tame lions? – *Dimitri Mitropoulos*

A conductor in German is *Dirigent*, *Chef d'Orchestre* in French and *Direttore d'Orchestra* in Italian. The first time I went to the United States, having got off the plane, I had to pass through the customs and the official asked me, among other things, what my job was, to which I replied "Conductor". He then asked "Tram or train conductor?" – *Aldo Ceccato*

If I had the power I would insist on all oratorios being sung in the costume of the period –with a possible exception in the case of The Creation – *Sir Ernest Newman*

Acting is very important in opera. Of course it can also be useful to have a voice – *Tito Gobbi*

In Vienna, everyone was too busy waltzing to worry about anything else. The balls usually went on from ten in the evening until seven in the morning... it got to the stage that some ball-rooms had special rooms where pregnant women could give birth without having to give up the pleasure of dancing. And other ballrooms had special rooms where young women could have the pleasure of becoming future mothers – *Victor Borge*

Don't worry about what the critics say. No statue has ever been erected to a critic – *Jean Sibelius*

Critics love mediocrity – *Giacomo Puccini*

If there is to be a chair for critics, I think it had better be an electric chair – *Sir Thomas Beecham*

Bibliography

Letters of Franz Liszt (1894), collected by "La Mara", translated by Constance Backe, published by Grevel & Co, London [accessed on archive.org]

The Orchestral Conductor, Theory of his Art (1902), by Hector Berlioz, published by Carl Fischer, New York [accessed on gutenberg.org]

Advice to Young Musicians (1860), by Robert Schumann, translated by H. H. Pierson, published by J. Schuberth & Co, Leipzig and New York [accessed on violinist.com]

On Conducting (1869), by Richard Wagner, translated by Edward Dannreuther, published by W. Reeves, London [accessed on fulltextarchive.com]

Mozart's Don Giovanni, a Commentary (1890), by Charles Gounod, translated by W. Clark and J. T. Hutchison, published by Robert Cocks & Co, London [accessed on imslp.org]

On Conducting (1895), by Felix Weingartner, translated by Ernest Newman, published by Breitkopf & Hartel, London [accessed on archive.org]

Translator's Note: in some cases I have slightly adapted the texts and updated some spellings and archaisms. Occasionally I have borrowed from different editions. I am extremely grateful to the providers of the above-mentioned online resources. Unless otherwise specified, the translations from Italian are my own. GHR

Printed in Bologna (Italy) by NW on January 2020